Praise for Anna Castle's *Moriarty Meets His Match*

"Sherlock Holmes fans will find *Moriarty Meets His Match* exquisitely well-done: true to the nature and characters of both men, but adding extra dimensions to Professor Moriarty's character that greatly enhance the entire Holmes scenario. Very highly recommended as a 'must' for Sherlock enthusiasts and anyone who relishes a good whodunit mystery." — D. Donovan, Senior Reviewer, Midwest Book Review

"Fans of both Sherlock Holmes and the man he dubbed the 'Napoleon of Crime' will absolutely love Castle's fidelity to the details and atmosphere of the canon, and newcomers who have never read Arthur Conan Doyle (or, for that matter, John Gardner's great Moriarty novels) will also find themselves eagerly reading along, thanks to Castle's great skill as a storyteller. Enthusiastically recommended." — Steve Donoghue, Historical Novel Society Reviews

Praise for *Moriarty Takes His Medicine*

"A captured wife, a clever and devious doctor, and women in disguise ... all the trappings of a Holmes case are embellished and enhanced throughout, contributing to a mystery whose tension is well-drawn and whose plot is satisfyingly unpredictable and complex... Especially recommended for fans of Sherlock Holmes, this addition to a growing series continues to add nuances and details that grow characters and present plots that are engaging, fun, and complex." — D. Donovan, Senior Reviewer, Midwest Book Review.

Praise for *Murder by Misrule*

Murder by Misrule was selected as one of Kirkus Review's Best Indie Books of 2014.

"Castle's characters brim with zest and real feeling... Though the plot keeps the pages turning, the characters, major and minor, and the well-wrought historical details will make readers want to linger in the 16th century. A laugh-out loud mystery that will delight fans of the genre." — Kirkus, starred review

"*Murder by Misrule* is a delightful debut with characters that leap off the page, especially the brilliant if unwilling detective Francis Bacon and his street smart man Tom Clarady. Elizabeth Tudor rules, but Anna Castle triumphs." — Karen Harper, NY Times best-selling author of *The Queen's Governess*

"Well-researched... *Murder by Misrule* is also enormously entertaining; a mystery shot through with a series of misadventures, misunderstandings, and mendacity worthy of a Shakespearian comedy." — M. Louisa Locke, author of the Victorian San Francisco Mystery Series

"Castle's period research is thorough but unobtrusive, and her delight in the clashing personalities of her crime-fighting duo is palpable: this is the winning fictional odd couple of the year, with Bacon's near-omniscience being effectively grounded by Clarady's street smarts. An extremely promising debut." — Steve Donoghue, Historical Novel Society

Praise for *Death by Disputation*

Death by Disputation won the 2015 Chaucer Awards First In Category Award for the Elizabethan/Tudor period.

"Accurate historical details, page turning plot, bodacious, lovable and believable characters, gorgeous depictions and bewitching use of language will transfer you through time and space back to Elizabethan England." — Edi's Book Lighthouse

"This second book in the Francis Bacon mystery series is as strong as the first. At times bawdy and rowdy, at times thought-provoking

… Castle weaves religious-political intrigue, murder mystery, and Tom's colorful friendships and love life into a tightly-paced plot."
— Amber Foxx, Indies Who Publish Everywhere

Praise for *The Widows Guild*

The Widows Guild was longlisted for the 2017 Historical Novel Society's Indie Award.

"As in Castle's earlier book, *Murder by Misrule*, she brings the Elizabethan world wonderfully to life, and if Francis Bacon himself seems a bit overshadowed at times, it's because the great, fun creation of the Widow's Guild itself easily steals the spotlight. Strongly Recommended." — Editor's Choice, Historical Novel Society.

Also by Anna Castle

The Francis Bacon Mystery Series

Murder by Misrule
Death by Disputation
The Widow's Guild
Publish and Perish
Let Slip the Dogs
The Spymaster's Brother

The Professor & Mrs. Moriarty Mystery Series

Moriarty Meets His Match
Moriarty Takes His Medicine
Moriarty Brings Down the House
Moriarty Lifts the Veil

The Lost Hat, Texas Mystery Series

Black & White & Dead All Over
Flash Memory

Moriarty Lifts the Veil

A Professor & Mrs. Moriarty Mystery — Book 4

ANNA CASTLE

Moriarty Lifts the Veil
A Professor & Mrs. Moriarty Mystery — Book 4

Print Edition | March 2020
Discover more works by Anna Castle at www.annacastle.com

Copyright © 2020 by Anna Castle
Cover design by Jennifer Quinlan
Editorial services by Jennifer Quinlan, Historical Editorial
Chapter ornaments created by Alvaro_cabrera at Freepik.com.

All rights reserved. No parts of this book may be used or reproduced in any manner whatsoever, including Internet usage, without written permission from the author, except in the case of brief quotations embodied in critical articles and reviews.

This is a work of fiction. Characters, places, and events are the product of the author's imagination or are used fictitiously and are not to be construed as real. Any resemblance to events, locales, organizations, or persons, living or dead, is entirely coincidental.

ISBN-10: 1-945382-27-7
ISBN-13: 978-1-945382-27-7
Library of Congress Control Number: 2020900112
Produced in the United States of America

ONE

London, 8 August 1888

"She has a certain appeal, I suppose. But is she really your type?" James Moriarty peered over his friend's shoulder at a poster on the wall beside the Empire Theatre of Varieties on Shoreditch High Street.

The yard-high poster displayed a young woman garbed in layers of filmy gauze colored red, gold, and white. She raised her arms and lifted one foot in the *Dance of the Seven Veils*, according to the billing. Her costume spoke of the Orient, but her peaches-and-cream complexion betrayed her English origins.

Gabriel Sandy shot him a wry grin. "She might be, if she were the real thing. But she's a former farm girl from Yorkshire."

"Evidently." Moriarty chuckled. "That's why I asked. You seemed especially interested."

Sandy's grin faded as he shook his head. "No, not really. She just reminds me of something." He turned away before adding under his breath, "Something that doesn't matter anymore."

Moriarty let it go, though one didn't need the interpretive skill of a confidence trickster to see that whatever it was mattered a great deal. He wouldn't pry, though he did wish his friend had someone to come home to after a long night of work — someone other than the Cockney urchin he'd informally adopted.

The Moriartys had celebrated their third anniversary in May. They'd had their ups and downs, but he wouldn't trade the conjugal life for anything. Sandy was thirty-four and had a thriving trade driving a hansom cab in the theater district. He wasn't precisely handsome, but his wide smile, ginger hair, and abundant freckles gave him a friendly look. He had a sound intellect, an even temper, and a warm heart. He'd make some lucky woman an excellent husband.

However, no bachelor liked to be nagged on that tender subject. "Where is this flat you've found?"

"One more street, then we turn to the right. It isn't far."

All the streets looked the same to Moriarty — stark gray facades fronting dirty gray pavements. Even the music hall presented a bare stone front, unlike the ornate Roman stylings of the West End theaters. The people in the East End looked grayer too. No fashionable peacocks here, strutting and strolling in the latest styles. These people hunched their shoulders into shabby overcoats and hurried along their way.

Moriarty had seldom set foot in this half of the city, though his wife had grown up here. Her father had moved her and her twin siblings from one cheap hotel to another, evading creditors while sticking close to the variety halls where the children earned their living. Angelina had shown no interest in sharing her past with her husband beyond the bare facts. He respected her choice but couldn't help being a little curious.

Sandy knew the district well enough to drive it in his sleep by this time, at least the major arteries and larger side streets. He and his assistant, Zeke, lived above the stable where he kept his horses and cab. The current desire to move had been prompted by a rise in rent, despite the landlord's refusal to repair a leaky roof and a broken window sash. Enough was enough.

They reached the target street and turned onto it, steering around a puddle left by yesterday's torrential downpour. Today the sun was out, lifting wisps of steam from the wet streets. Moriarty was glad he'd left his coat at home. It was already warm enough to dampen the brow under his short topper.

"Ah, there's a sad sight!" Sandy pointed his chin at a man in a tattered red army jacket sitting cross-legged on a patch of newspapers. He slumped against the wall in a dejected posture that spoke of hard years and bad luck. A shapeless hat lay upturned before him. This side street seemed a poor choice for begging, but perhaps the police had driven him off the high street.

Sandy reached into his pocket for a few coins. Moriarty did the same. They each bent down to drop them into the hat. "Where'd you serve, Soldier?" Sandy asked.

The man looked up at him with a queer gleam in his brown eyes. Then two other men in red jackets appeared in a rush of movement. One grabbed Moriarty, turning him around and gripping his arms behind his back.

"Give me your money," the man growled. "You've more than a few pence in those fine pockets, I'll wager."

Sandy dodged his assailant with a quick twist. He aimed a square fist at the man's bearded jaw, then froze as his mouth dropped open. "Danny Digby? Is that you?"

The soldier gaped at his would-be victim. "What's this? You're the spit of my dear old Captain Sandy, apart from that beard."

Sandy lowered his fist. "Your own chin has grown bushy since we parted, old friend."

Digby was a wiry little man, all nerves and muscles. He had a ragged black beard and bright blue eyes under thick black eyebrows. The two men shook their heads at one other, grinning like loons. Then they gathered each other in a hug, laughing, with great manly claps about the shoulders.

Moriarty and his attacker traded doubtful looks. "You may as well turn me loose," Moriarty said. "We appear to be in the midst of a reunion."

"It's Captain Sandy," his assailant said, shaking his head in wonder. "As large as life." He released Moriarty's arms, patting his shoulders in a rough apology. Then he stepped right in front of him. "Remember me, Captain? I'm Nate Fowler."

"Corporal Fowler? Well, I'll be dashed!" Sandy cried. "Of course I remember you."

"I made sergeant before I left." Fowler puffed out his broad chest. He lifted his square chin, which sported a stiff blond beard.

"I'm not the least surprised." Sandy grinned. He wagged his finger at the fake beggar. "Then this rascal must be Private Webb. Luther, isn't it?"

"Calvin." The soldier unpacked his long limbs and got to his feet. "We thought you was dead, Captain."

"Dead? Me?" Sandy scoffed. "Nonsense. If those Afghan ghazis couldn't kill me in the Maiwand Pass, nothing can."

The three former soldiers guffawed and punched each other's arms.

Moriarty had no personal experience of war, thank goodness, but he read *The Times* and *The Daily Telegraph* every day. He'd followed the last Afghan war with interest. These men must be possessed of extraordinary courage and fortitude to have survived the infamous Battle of Maiwand, where nearly a thousand British soldiers had been cut down.

"But you three," Sandy said, giving them a stern look. "What's happened to you? Last I knew you were soldiers in good standing. Now here you are, luring innocent passersby into a mugging."

Sergeant Fowler's broad face darkened. "That's a long story, Captain. And not a pretty one."

"I'd like to hear it." Sandy caught Moriarty's eyes. "That flat can wait. But you must have other plans this morning . . ."

"None whatsoever. I've been banished from the theater until the electrification is completed. I'm told I get in the way of the workmen with all my questions." He spoke to the men who had almost taken his wallet. "I'd be honored to buy you men a drink, and perhaps a spot of lunch. Is there a decent place nearby?"

"The Two Bells is as good as any." Fowler jerked a thumb toward the Shoreditch High Street. The others nodded eagerly. Moriarty wondered how often these veterans sat down to a hot meal. He'd had no idea that soldiers could face such desperate poverty when they left the army.

They trooped along the pavement in rank order, with Moriarty off to Sandy's side. The Two Bells spanned the corner down the street from the Empire, its black columns and tall windows advertising its qualities from a distance. The public room wasn't crowded at half past ten, but it was by no means empty either. An assortment of men in work clothes or cheap suits stood at the bar or sat at the nearest tables. The tapster raised his eyebrows when they entered — not at the soldiers' scruffy clothes, but at Moriarty's well-cut gray linen lounge suit. Sandy's neat checked suit and rounded hat got a long look as well.

Sergeant Fowler led them through the main room to a quiet alcove. Here, under the low-beamed ceiling, well away from the sun-streaked front windows, all was dimness and beer-scented cool. It felt good to get out of the sultry morning.

The plain furniture had been polished by the backsides and elbows of the men who used it. The three soldiers sat facing the two gentlemen — although Sandy was technically no longer a gentleman, having descended to the cabman's trade. But he'd been born the third son of a Devonshire viscount and attended Eton and Oxford before joining the cavalry. He still possessed the patrician accent and the ramrod back, but he was far more at home in this working man's establishment than Moriarty.

Then again, Moriarty had lived a sheltered life until he'd met Angelina, though he hadn't known it. He'd gone straight from his father's vicarage to Rugby and from there to Cambridge. After earning his doctorate, he'd taken a post at the University of Durham, whose senior common room had formed the center of his limited social life. He'd barely seen the inside of a pub until he moved to London.

They ordered pints of lager all around. Moriarty asked for plates of bread and cheese with pickles and sausages. The men gave the provisions their full attention. Their unwashed condition made itself more apparent in this close environment, but Moriarty stuck his nose in his mug and soon got used to it. The sour smell doubtless meant they were sleeping rough.

Sandy jerked a thumb toward him. "This is my good friend James Moriarty. He used to be a professor of mathematics, and now he owns the Galaxy Theater on Leicester Square."

The three men's faces reflected precisely the same mixture of bafflement and wonder that Moriarty felt whenever he reflected on how much his life had changed in the past three years. They chorused variations on "Glad to make your acquaintance."

Then Sandy winked at Digby and turned toward Moriarty. "This odd duck was my batman, right from the beginning. From England to Afghanistan, through the nightmare at Maiwand, and on to the Fifth Bombay in Jaipur, where he had nothing to do but polish my boots and fatten up my horse."

"Never." Digby pretended to be affronted. "That animal was in perfect trim."

"Horses love this man," Sandy said, shaking a finger at him.

"Can't say as much for women," Webb added. They all snorted at the comfortable insult.

Digby's smile disappeared. "You left without a word, Captain. I had to find out what happened to you through the bush telegraph."

"I couldn't face you, Digby. Not any of you. After Oxwich cashiered me for a crime I'd never even heard of, I traded my uniform for street clothes and walked right out the gate. I caught the first train leaving the station and ended up in Calcutta. I kicked around for a while — Burma, South Africa — scratching a living any way I could. Finally ended up back here with enough to buy my own hansom cab."

Fowler grunted, impressed. "That must have taken a fair bit of brass, if you don't mind my saying it."

Sandy's hazel eyes twinkled. "One pair of pearl earrings, to be precise. Payment for services of a personal nature." He winked, and the three men burst into howls of laughter, slapping their hands on the table so hard their mugs jumped.

"That sounds like our captain," Fowler said. "You wouldn't think it to look at him, Professor, especially not with that hedge growing around his chin, but women flocked to him. He had to beat them off with a fly whisk."

"You astonish me." Moriarty had learned more about his closest friend in the past ten minutes than he had in two years. Services of a *personal* nature?

Sandy grinned at Digby with the pleasure of a man rediscovering a very dear friend. "You'll have to come along and meet my pair one day. They're working girls, mind you. None of your cavalry prima donnas. They pull a cab every day, taking turns."

"I'd love to see them." Digby's thin face shone with longing. "Don't get to spend much time with horses anymore."

"How's that?" Sandy set his folded arms on the table. "What happened to you men? You've been discharged, I assume. You're not deserters — not you three."

That was received with a round of scowls.

Moriarty Lifts the Veil

Sergeant Fowler took a draught of his ale and set the mug down with a thump. "You told your story short and sweet, Captain. I'll do the same. We was cheated by Her Majesty's Royal Army, that's what happened. I was done out of most of my due, dashing my hopes of starting a trade. These two were cast into the street without a penny of their discharge pay, with stains upon their characters to boot."

"What!" Sandy gaped at them, aghast. "I've never met three more honorable men. And I should know. I commanded your company during the toughest battle of our lives."

"See for yourself." Digby pulled out a grimy square of paper and handed it across the table.

Sandy opened it, smoothing the folds with his thumb. "This one says 'with ignominy.'" He shook his head. "Right there, under *Character*. I see the words, but I can't believe them."

He handed the paper to Moriarty. The top of the sheet was adorned with the crest of the British Army. The bottom third was taken up with a pair of signatures. In between were a few rows of standard data — age, weight, and height. The years of service were given, along with the regiment in which Digby had served. The field labeled *Character* held the damning words.

"I had to ask another officer what that meant." Digby's eyes glittered with tears. "Never been put to such shame. I never done no ignominy, Captain, not in all my life."

"I know it," Sandy said. "You're as honest as the day is long."

"They made me out to be incorrigible," Webb said. "They say that means a drunkard, which I ain't now, nor never was."

"Nobody will hire them with those characters." Fowler's square jaw jutted forward. "This paper's the first thing they ask you for once they see you're a soldier."

"Those are bald-faced lies," Sandy said. "There must be some way to appeal them. The captain who wrote that must've been drunk, or he confused you with someone else."

Fowler said, "Our captain at that time was a fellow named Avery Walker."

"I remember Walker," Sandy said. "He was a lieutenant in my day. I thought he was a decent man."

"And so he was. And is," Fowler said. "But he's not the one who wrote it. That'd be Captain Greenway, the colonel's adjutant. He does all the paperwork. He come in from the other regiment. They put us together three years ago, when we rotated out of India to Odstone Barracks. They merged a bunch of regiments here and there around the country, for efficiency, they said."

Sandy nodded, explaining it to Moriarty. "There've been a whole series of reforms over the past ten to twenty years. Each time they rearrange some of the units. It can be dashed confusing."

Confusion of that kind — the bookkeeping kind — made a fertile ground for fraud. Moriarty's moustache tingled. Something smelled wrong here. "I presume these negative characters are what allowed the army to retain your . . . What did you call it? Your discharge pay? Is that some sort of bonus?"

"Bonus!" Webb practically spat the word. "We earned that money fair and square." He looked at Sandy for confirmation.

The cabman frowned. "I'm afraid I never paid much attention to that sort of thing. I left money matters to the regiment office. That's why I made such an easy scapegoat when funds were found missing from the officers' mess."

Moriarty had heard that part of Sandy's story. Officers had to pay into a common fund to supply their mess with meals of a quality befitting their social class, among other amenities. They took turns managing this fund. When monies went missing during Sandy's term, he was accused of embezzlement. The real culprits, he believed, were Major Samuel Oxwich, as he was then. He was the commanding officer, working through his corrupt batman. But Sandy had no proof, or even any idea what might constitute proof, so he simply ran.

"It's called deferred pay, Professor." Fowler set an elbow on the table so he could wag his index finger to underscore his words. "The army says they'll pay you a shilling a day when you first sign up. Which they do, minus fees for everything from boots to medicine. They give us our bed and board, so it's not a bad deal. That's our straight-up pay, which most of us spend as quick as we get it. They know that, those generals up at the top. But they want us to have a bit of savings when we leave, to help us find a useful trade. They know we won't save it ourselves, so they do it for us. They add a penny a day to our pay, but they keep hold of it. In the Bank of

England, I always reckoned. They pay it out to us when we're discharged in one fat lump."

Sandy said, "I remember the lump sum. It's meant to discourage desertion. It also encourages good behavior, they say, because they withhold payment if you're discharged with a bad character."

"That was all I had in the world," Digby said, his eyes bleak. "Fourteen years of my life and nothing to show for it."

"A penny a day for fourteen years?" Moriarty pulled out his notebook and pencil and scribbled some numbers. "That's twenty-one pounds, five shillings, and ten pence."

The soldiers looked at him as astonished as if he'd pulled a live rabbit out of his hat.

"Twenty-one pounds," Digby said. "A man could live a long time on that."

Sandy nodded. "It'd keep body and soul together long enough to find a job at least."

Fowler regarded Moriarty with a crafty gleam in his brown eyes. "I see you're handy with figures, Professor. Here's a harder puzzle for you. I joined the army as a tender lad of eighteen, having neither parents nor prospects. I signed up for the standard seven years at the standard shilling a day with that penny a day deferred. I found the life suited me, so when my time came, I took on another ten. By then, I'd learned a thing or two and started climbing up the ranks. First, I made lance corporal. That's another halfpence a day added to my savings. Two years later, I rose to corporal. That brings me up to tuppence a day. Three years after that, I made sergeant, as which I served Her Majesty for five good years. That's three pennies a day, tucked up neat and proper for me when I left."

He folded his arms and sat back, meeting Moriarty's gaze with a challenge in his eyes. "Reckon that if you can."

Many mathematicians were hopeless at arithmetic. They could barely add two and two for a consistent result of four. Happily, Moriarty was not one of that kind. He enjoyed exercising his wits in such puzzles. He lined up the varying years of service in rows and calculated the sums. "By my calculations, they owed you forty-seven pounds, two shillings, and eleven pence." He exhibited the page to show his work, but no one looked at it.

Fowler crowed, "That's right! I kept my own tally, you see. I put a mark inside the lid of my trunk every single day. 'Cept when we was in the heat of battle, but then I caught up my marks as soon as I could. I drew a line whenever I rose in rank. When I came near my time, I asked Corporal Turner to do the sums for me. He keeps the books for the whole regiment, and he's a decent sort. He worked out the same sum as you. I stored it up here." He pointed at his temple. "So I'd be ready to count what they gave me."

Forty-seven pounds was a considerable sum for a man of Fowler's station. A skilled carpenter might make that much in a year building sets at the Galaxy and find it enough to support a wife and three children in comfort.

"You said you were shorted," Moriarty said. "How much did you get?"

"They got the shillings and pence right. But they only gave me seventeen pounds." Fowler's mouth tightened in anger. "For seventeen years of honorable service. Does that sound fair to you?"

"No," Moriarty said. "You were cheated." But had it been deliberate or accidental? An act of fraud or a simple mistake?

He wrote the number seventeen under the forty-seven scrawled in his notebook. He cocked his head and squinted at it. If the four had been poorly written with a nearly empty quill, it might have been construed as a one by whoever copied the data onto that form. There must be an original file or logbook somewhere with more complete records.

The conversation had moved on without him. Sandy asked Fowler, "What were you planning to do with your pay?"

"I meant to buy a place in the carter's trade. I'm handy with wagons and horses. Thought I might enjoy traveling hither and yon with my load of goods, meeting the folk and seeing the countryside. But I had to spend that seventeen quid keeping a roof over our heads. Now we don't even have that anymore."

Webb said, "That's why we've stooped to thieving. It's that or starve."

"Not while I'm alive," Sandy said. "You can sleep at my place or in the stables below. It's not fancy, but I can scrounge a few blankets. And it's dry."

"I'd love to sleep in a stable again," Digby said with longing in his voice. "I miss the smells and the soft whickers at night."

The other men hummed their agreement.

"What happens to that deferred pay if you don't get it?" Moriarty asked.

The soldiers shrugged. "I suppose the bank keeps it," Webb said.

Fowler said, "I kicked up a row when Captain Greenway counted those seventeen pounds into my hand. He had two corporals escort me off the base, and they were none too gentle. They slammed the gate behind my back, and that was that."

Silence fell as the four veterans contemplated their respective abuses. Mugs were emptied as the cheese and sausages disappeared. When Moriarty signaled the barmaid to bring them another round of drinks, Sandy turned to him with a measuring look.

"This appears to be a case of flagrant injustice, possibly involving some kind of financial chicanery. I should think it would be right up your street."

Moriarty had to agree. These men had been deprived of substantial sums of money by the standards of the laboring class. How many soldiers were discharged every year? If you falsified the characters or fiddled the years of service for even a fraction of them, you could squirrel away a small fortune.

But surely the army had layers of checks and balances. This would doubtless turn out to be a case of one careless officer mixing up the names of men he hardly knew. The money would still be out there, earning interest in one of the army's infinite accounts. It couldn't be easy to get money out of the Bank of England under false pretenses.

He realized all four men were watching him with expectant smiles.

"I can't make any promises now. In all honesty, I don't even know where to start." Their evident disappointment made him add, "But I can poke around a bit in the public records, see if there's anything to be seen."

"Just believing us makes a difference," Fowler said.

The hurt and hardship on the man's face stung Moriarty's conscience. He determined to give it a try. They were only asking him to sort out the financial mechanisms of the British Army. How hard could that be?

TWO

"It seems to be warming up." Angelina stood by the front window in her drawing room, surveying the limited view. "Look at those patches of blue sky." She turned toward Peg, her old friend and theater dresser, and set her hands on her hips. "I am going to open this window."

"If you must, you must." Peg, like Angelina, had grown up in cheap lodgings in the East End, where windows were only opened in case of fire or threat of suffocation. But here in South Kensington, a mere stroll from the vast green acres of Hyde Park, the air had a more wholesome quality. One might risk allowing it inside the house on a fine summer day.

Angelina turned the latch and pressed the lower sash up. It moved as smoothly as if the channel had been waxed. She pushed it all the way to the top and leaned out, inhaling a lungful of air. It smelled marvelously fresh. Yesterday's downpour had washed away the city soot, leaving the streets sparkling clean. The breeze emerging from the tiny park across the street felt cool, but the sill beneath her hands had already been warmed by the sun.

"It's going to be a fine day. We should do something out of doors, don't you think? A ride in the park?"

"Me? Ride?" Peg barked a laugh. "I'm meeting Tweedy at the local for a mug this afternoon. We'll sit on a bench in the garden. That counts as out of doors, don't it?"

"You're incorrigible," Angelina scolded, but she couldn't help smiling. Peg and Timothy Tweedy, a comic actor, had been in love many years ago. Peg had left him behind to flee the country with Angelina, escaping her father's tyranny. She'd never once mentioned him in all the years spent traveling the Continent and America. Angelina had thought the affair long forgotten. But a seed still lurked deep underneath, and the romance had blossomed again when they were reunited at the Galaxy. By the time the Christmas pantomime left to tour the provinces, Tweedy and Peg had moved into the three-room flat above the mews at Bellenden Crescent.

It was the perfect solution. James never really liked having Peg in the house, but Angelina couldn't bear to part with her.

Angelina gazed down into the empty street and sighed. She'd grown restless after three months of idleness. It would be glorious to act on a stage lighted by electric bulbs, or so she'd been told, but in the meantime, she had nothing to do. She might dress like a lady and talk like a lady, but she hadn't been bred like one. She wanted work.

A black four-wheeler pulled by two high-stepping grays turned onto the crescent street below. Angelina crossed her fingers. *Let that be for us.*

Sure enough, it stopped before the door of Number Twenty-Eight. Stopped and did nothing. The persons inside, if there were any, did not so much as twitch the curtain to peek out. A full minute ticked past on the clock on the mantel. Then the driver clucked his tongue, the sharp sound echoing on the white stucco facade of the terrace, and the horses took a neat step forward.

Angelina clucked her own tongue in disappointment.

Then the coach stopped again, scarcely one foot farther up the street. Another long pause; another false start. Then an abrupt halt upon which the door flew open. A barefoot boy in a yellow turban leapt down to lower the step. Out came a woman dressed in yellow striped silk cascading from a beribboned bustle. She wore a darling little straw boater perched on a heap of glossy black hair. She carried a black reticule dripping with fringe over one arm and swung a yellow-and-white-striped parasol in the other hand.

She mounted the steps and lifted the knocker. Three booms sounded through the house.

Angelina clapped her hands. "Company," she sang. She skipped to the mirror over the mantel to smooth her hair and pinch some color into her cheeks. "Could be an actress come to wheedle for a part, but given the dithering, I'm betting on a client."

"Don't get too excited, ducky," Peg said. "She'll only have to come back when the professor's here."

"I can listen to her," Angelina retorted. "I'm very good at listening. I can at least find out if it's something James would be interested in." She plopped into her armchair and snatched up *Weldon's Ladies' Journal*, posing as a lady of leisure at home on a Wednesday morning.

Rolly, their young footman, appeared at the door. "Missus Julia Reynolds to see Miz Lina Lovington." He winked broadly, then stepped back to allow the visitor to enter the room.

But she didn't. She stopped on the threshold, clasping her lace-gloved hands under her chin with rapture written on her pretty face. "Oh, Miss Lovington! Here you *are*! I am one of your most *devoted* admirers. I've seen everything you've done since your return to the London stage. Absolutely everything!"

Angelina repressed a sigh of disappointment as she set down her magazine and rose. Now she'd have to make polite conversation while working the creature back out the door. They really must establish some sort of rule. If a stranger arrived with no advance warning asking for Lina Lovington, they should be firmly, but courteously, turned away.

She shot Peg a wide-eyed look and got a short nod in return. Her ally would create some urgent excuse in a few minutes.

"How kind you are," Angelina said. "Do come in." She gestured at the most uncomfortable chair, a stylish, yet somewhat rickety, Louis Quinze. Its seat was covered with a slippery lime-green brocade. James loathed it, but bad chairs had their uses.

Mrs. Reynolds gave a squeal of delight and crossed the room to take the seat. The fine lines around her eyes and a certain hardness around her mouth put her closer to forty than thirty — older than her jaunty costume and girlish manner led one to expect. Still, she'd kept herself well. Her skin was smooth and her throat uncreased, as much of it as showed above the lacy frill of her high collar. She sat with her hands in her lap, gazing at Angelina with naked adoration.

Angelina gestured toward Peg. "This is my companion, Miss Margaret Barwick." Lady's maids did not normally lounge about the drawing room with their mistresses, but Peg was not a normal lady's maid. She was a theatrical costumier, a co-conspirator, and a confidante. The term 'companion' simplified things.

Mrs. Reynolds batted her eyes. "*So* pleased to make your acquaintance."

Peg hummed a response. No amount of travel or cultured living could drive the Cockney from her voice, so in situations like this, she contrived to say nothing.

Angelina resumed her seat. "What brings you out on this fine morning?" She decided not to offer refreshment. It would only prolong the agony. "I poked my head out the window just now to sample the air. I believe it's going to be quite hot this afternoon."

"Oh, nothing is hot in England, not compared to India. I didn't know what the word *meant* before Major Reynolds was posted to Delhi."

"Your husband is a military man?"

"Cavalry. Which makes me a military wife." Mrs. Reynolds giggled. "Tiresome shifting from one place to another, mostly, though I have met some important people."

"India must be utterly fascinating."

"There are some marvelous birds and flowers. And of course an endless *sea* of servants."

That seemed a lukewarm endorsement for the jewel in Her Majesty's crown. But Angelina could be equally dismissive of the wonders of the American West in certain moods.

Two short minutes and they'd exhausted both the weather and India. She could ask the woman what she'd liked best about *Hamlet Travestie*, the Galaxy's spring burlesque, but she hated to sound needy.

Before she could conjure a fresh topic, Mrs. Reynolds leaned forward and threaded her fingers together. "It is *so* wonderful to meet you in person and to see your *charming* home, but I must confess that isn't the reason I'm here. I've been worrying about a problem for more than a fortnight, and I finally decided to ask for help."

"What sort of problem?" This was more like it. Theatergoers didn't barge into your house on a weekday morning. They came to your dressing room after the show or wangled an invitation to a party.

"The sort that Linda Bell — do you know her?"

"Linda?" Angelina rolled her eyes. "Longer than I care to admit. She's at the Royal Trocadero now, isn't she?"

Mrs. Reynolds nodded. "She's part of our set — we officers' wives, I mean. Our husbands serve with the Middlesex regiment at Odstone Barracks. Near Staines-upon-Thames?" She lifted her eyebrows inquiringly at Angelina, who merely shook her head. None of that meant anything to her.

"Well," Mrs. Reynolds went on, "Miss Bell. She fits in so well with our little group. She adds a bit of sparkle and keeps us from going too stale. We love fun, and she's such a lively person." She lowered her voice to a throaty whisper, raising a hand to shield her lips. "She's been seeing one of our captains lately. But don't tell anyone!" This revelation was followed by a broad wink.

"Mum's the word." Angelina returned the wink. Linda fit in everywhere. She was that rare successful actress who truly had no enemies. She loved to dance and sing and was very good at both. She loved a good time and made friends easily, with no scheming or elbowing other actresses off the stage. She conducted her love affairs with same easy come, easy go attitude.

"One evening," Mrs. Reynolds said, "when we were chatting on the veranda, I asked her if she knew you. She said she did! Well, *that* was exciting, but then she told me that you and your husband, who is some sort of *professor*, if I heard her correctly, have a curious sort of consulting practice. You solve little puzzles for people. Trouble with an employer or an employee. Lost things. Lost *persons*."

"Who have you lost?" Angelina asked, hoping it wasn't a pet.

"My ayah, Ganesa."

Angelina cocked her head. "What's an ayah ganesa?"

Mrs. Reynolds emitted a high-pitched staccato laugh that pierced Angelina's ears like a steel spike. "An ayah is an Indian maidservant. They take care of children mostly, but they also look after the memsahib." Her face wrinkled up in what she probably considered a droll expression. "That's me."

"I know that word," Angelina said drily. "I didn't recognize the second part. Is Ganesa the woman's name?"

Mrs. Reynolds nodded. "She's my favorite, a perfect marvel. She always knows what I want before I even know it myself. Am I tired? Look, here are my slippers. Am I thirsty? Here is a drink, hot or cool, according to the season. I hired her to take care of the children in

Delhi and on the passage home, but now they're at school, she has only me to tend to."

"I see."

It sounded like the poor *ayah* was expected to wait upon her mistress hand and foot. The Moriartys' servants were kindhearted people, grateful for having been rescued from one dire fate or another. The housemaids, Dolly and Molly, had been threatened with the worst sort of abuse from their former master. The cook, Antoine LeClerq, had committed forgery to help out a friend who had then thrown him into the path of the French Sûreté. He'd fled to England and found his way to the Moriartys' home. He'd only recently begun to venture out to do a bit of shopping or visit a neighboring cook. Rolly had been one of London's myriad street urchins, living on his wits and the contents of careless people's pockets. He'd dubbed himself 'Wellington' for want of any other surname and had flourished in this unconventional household.

They'd grown fond of their master and mistress — an affection which was returned — and took excellent care of them. But Angelina couldn't imagine any of them paying her such close attention. She wouldn't allow it. Poor James would have to lock himself in his study to avoid them.

This Ganesa had probably just run away. If so, she might be in trouble. "You say she's been gone a fortnight. That's a long time for a woman to be on her own, especially one who doesn't know her way around. Does she have any friends in London? Anywhere she might go?"

"She's never been in London." Mrs. Reynolds whisked that away with a flick of her gloved hand. "We came straight from Portsmouth to Ripley Park — that's our country house, not far from Odstone. She speaks a fair bit of English, but she doesn't have any friends, apart from the other Indian servants. Where would she meet them?" That idea seemed to amuse her.

"The other wives' servants, perhaps? Do you take her with you when you spend a weekend somewhere?"

"Oh yes. She's quite the expert lady's maid. *Hopeless* about current fashions, of course, but I can supply that side of things." Mrs. Reynolds licked her lips and glanced first toward the door and then at Peg. She leaned forward again and lowered her voice. "Just between you and me and Miss Barwick, I suspect she may have been *poached*. It's been much longer than a fortnight, actually. I've been expecting her to come back."

"Ah." Angelina sat back in her chair. "Is poaching common among your set?"

"It's not unheard of. But it's usually cooks, isn't it?"

"Don't even hint at such a thing! We'd starve if Antoine left us." Angelina shuddered at the mere thought. "I assume you've asked your other servants. Don't any of them know anything?"

"No. At least nothing they're willing to tell. They can be inscrutable when they want."

"Have you inquired among your friends?" Angelina asked. "They can't all be guilty."

"It isn't that simple." Mrs. Reynolds's eyes cut down and to the side. She licked her lips before giving Angelina a knowing look. "Miss Bell told me that you were especially clever at winkling your way into places — with the people, I mean. She was a bit drunk, mind you. So was I. But she said you masqueraded as an American heiress some years ago and fooled the whole of London society for months!"

"Oh, that." Angelina shrugged as if it had been nothing. She shot a glance at Peg, who was shaking her head with a wry smile. Try as you might, you could never put some escapades behind you.

"That's the sort of thing I'm hoping for," Mrs. Reynolds said. "If you poke around the other houses and somebody notices, they won't mind as much as they would if it were me." Her eyes dropped to her lap.

Angelina got a whiff of something unsaid, something held back. This woman knew more about her disappearing ayah than she let on. "I believe I understand. You want me to work my way into your circle of friends and get invited to their houses so I can spy about and try to tease out a confidence or two."

Mrs. Reynolds nodded rapidly. "It could be great fun, you know. We have a polo match at Aldershot this Saturday. The Prince of Wales will be there. That would be the ideal place to start."

"Polo?" Angelina had heard of the game, but just barely. Something horsey and rather upper crust.

"It's very exciting. The men are *so* dashing in their tight trousers, galloping up and down, swinging their mallets." Mrs. Reynolds's eyes sparkled, especially around the words 'tight trousers.' It would appear polo provided an opportunity for a bit of discreet ogling.

Angelina considered her own husband to have the finest of masculine physiques, but she didn't mind observing other samples. And it would get her out of the house. "That does sound like fun."

"We have picnics by the river too, under lovely big shade trees. And we play whist on Tuesdays. Once a month we have a weekend party at Lord Chetwood's house. *Those* are quite something. We play charades, among other games." Mrs. Reynolds's brown eyes took on an excited gleam.

"Well now, that *does* sound tempting."

What were the other games, she wondered? Charades could range from stuffy historical tableaux to erotic dances in risqué costumes. It sounded like this set would tend toward the more daring end of the spectrum. James would not approve. But Angelina had been dreadfully bored these past few weeks. This case would allow her to mix business and pleasure, and she doubted it would take long to solve.

"It won't be easy," Mrs. Reynolds said, contradicting her thought. "Ganesa might've been bundled up with some of the other Indian girls by mistake. They look so much alike, you know. Brown hair, brown skin, brown eyes. But Ganesa is taller than most, and she has two gold teeth — one up and one down." She pointed to her upper and lower right jaw. "I put my people in different colors to help tell them apart, though I seldom need to."

Angelina pasted a smile on her face to hide her shock at the breezy indifference. Her housemaids, Dolly and Molly, were practically twins, but no one had any trouble telling them apart. They were two distinct people with different personalities.

Mrs. Reynolds chattered on, unaware that her stock had sunk. "They're inside most of the time. They have their work, of course. There's always another fireplace to black, isn't there? And they don't speak English or really know where they are. But some of the wives are terribly strict. They barely let the girls out for a breath of fresh air on alternate Wednesdays."

She underscored that awkward joke with a burst of staccato laughter.

Angelina smiled through her teeth. She'd find that missing ayah, by heaven. And then she'd find the poor woman a better job at twice the pay.

She managed to hold the smile through a meandering reminiscence about life in India. The dominant themes were heat and boredom, slightly alleviated by an army of servants turning fans, washing feet, and waving off the flying insects that got in everywhere. After about five minutes, Angelina signaled Peg by wiggling her fingers down by her side.

Peg put down her sewing and ostentatiously gaped at the clock. She made a little cry of shock, clapping her hands to her cheeks and leaping from her chair. That interrupted the flow of Mrs. Reynolds's narrative and allowed Angelina to stare at the clock in turn.

"Oh my!" She clapped a hand to her breast. "We've lost *all* track of time. I fear we have another engagement in a few minutes."

"Do forgive me." Mrs. Reynolds stood up. "I've imposed on you far too long."

They issued the usual pleasantries while edging toward the door. At last, the beastly woman left.

"What do you think?" Angelina asked after the front door closed with a thud.

"I ain't going to no polo match," Peg said. "Sounds dusty, and you know how I hate the sun."

"It sounds like fun to me. But I meant the missing servant. What do you bet she's simply run away?"

"You forgot to ask if she was pretty. I don't suppose that cow ever noticed. I'd start with the local tradesmen. Any of them gone missing too?"

"That's a good thought. I'll ask James to find Ripley Park on a map and note the nearby towns. Staines is one, I think she said."

James would go straight down on the train and start asking questions, putting the poacher on her guard. He could never comprehend the way gossip traveled. She would do a better job of it on her own.

And wasn't *that* an intriguing thought? Taking on a case without James. She'd never done it. But why shouldn't she? She'd contributed her share to their other puzzles.

Angelina and Peg had lunch around noon, during which they bickered about the pros and cons of working on a stage lit by electric lamps instead of gas flames. After lunch, Peg went off to the local to meet Tweedy while Angelina stretched out on the sofa for a nap. She was awakened by Rolly clearing his throat at the door.

"Telegram, Missus. It's from the perfessor."

"From James?" Angelina sat up and took the folded sheet. She read it swiftly and exhaled a sigh of relief. "All is well. He's bringing Sandy and Zeke home for tea. We're to ask Antoine to fix something heartier than lemon cake since tea is the main meal of the day for a working man. As if *we* needed reminding."

"Sausage and mash," Rolly said, licking his lips. "Or kippers on toast."

"Can you imagine Antoine frying up a mess of sausage and beans?" They both laughed.

She underestimated the Frenchman. Humble food, prepared by a gifted chef, could please the fussiest gourmand. When the men arrived and had a chance to freshen up, they entered the dining room to find a feast laid upon the board. There was the usual assortment of light sandwiches, along with the usual tempting cake — ginger today, with an orange glaze. That would normally suffice for James and Angelina.

Today, Antoine had added a large cottage pie with a gravy so rich they each paused to inhale its meaty aroma before taking their seats. Another stoneware casserole held baked beans dotted with chunks of bacon. The basket in the center held loaves of crusty brown bread to soak it all up.

Angelina poured the tea and passed the cups while the men loaded their plates. After the first hunger was satisfied, James told her about their adventures in the East End, meeting the three soldiers and hearing their sad story.

"Cheated by the British Army, if you can credit it," James said. "At least that's what they think. I'm more inclined to put it down to plain old incompetence. Errors in accounting are endemic in large public institutions. But you'd think the army would treat its heroes better."

"Are they heroes?" Angelina asked.

Sandy said, "In my book, every man who served at the Battle of Maiwand counts as a hero."

"You've mentioned that twice now," Angelina said. "What is the Battle of Maiwand?" The men blinked at her as if she'd asked who was queen that year. She shrugged. "You know I don't read political news."

James recovered first. "You were probably still abroad at that time, my dear. I doubt it got much play in the foreign press."

"It was the twenty-seventh of July 1880," Sandy added.

Angelina paused, a cress sandwich in her hand, as she counted back. "I believe I was in Vienna around that time. And since I don't read German, I wouldn't have bothered with any newspapers. But you must be a hero too, Sandy, by your own rule. What was the battle about?"

Sandy shook his head. "Nothing, in the end. Our general mission was to keep Afghanistan from falling into the hands of the Russians. We don't want the bear peering over the threshold of India."

"Indeed not," James said. Angelina had to agree that didn't sound very nice.

Sandy went on, "What that meant in practice was constant skirmishing with bands of Afghan tribesman. Fierce warriors fighting for spoils and the love of battle more than loyalty to their amir. We were frightfully overconfident, so we kept underestimating them. That particular campaign was a mess from start to finish. They caught us with our knickers down and made us pay for our arrogance. A thousand men died that day, officers and enlisted, British and Indian. Almost half our number."

"Good Lord," Angelina breathed. "I'm so grateful you weren't one of them."

"I'll always know I'm a lucky man, whatever else may happen." Sandy shot a sidelong glance at her, then addressed his next words to the rubber plant in the corner. "The noise is what I remember most. Booming guns and clashing sabers. We roared at each other like madmen, the enemy and us, pumping up our courage. My throat hurt for weeks afterward. Worst was the screaming, both men and horses. Dust swirled everywhere, mixing with the smoke of the guns, blinding you, getting up your nose. We were all so desperately thirsty." He shook his head as if waking from a dream. "It's not a fit story for the dining table. I apologize."

"Not at all, darling. You're family, you know that. You can say anything you like in this house. We are always, *always* ready to listen and to offer you our love and support."

She stretched a hand toward him, but he evaded it by handing her his teacup. She filled it, adding the large splash of cream and two lumps of sugar he always took. She ignored the shimmer of tears in his eyes as she handed it back.

James said, "It burns my heart to think of those veterans we met risking their lives in defense of the empire and then being cast out on the street like so much rubbish."

"I hope you didn't leave them there," Angelina said. "Please tell me you did more than listen."

Sandy nodded. "We gave them what money we had in our pockets, though they didn't like taking it. We had to call it a loan. Then we brought them back to my flat, or rather the stables, and handed them over to Zeke. They're old hands with horses. Digby's half-horse himself." He chuckled. "They allowed me to offer them room and board in exchange for taking care of the horses."

"What did Zeke have to say about that?" Angelina asked.

"He grumbled a bit until he realized that meant someone else would do the mucking out. They'll get along, and it's only temporary."

"You should write letters for them, James."

"Letters? What, references?"

"Yes, references. You said those papers gave them bad characters. Well, you can give them good ones. The sort of thing one writes for servants. Be as pompous as you can be and sign it with all your degrees and titles." Angelina smiled pertly at him. James could be monumentally pompous when he chose.

He frowned and nodded. "It can't be far different from recommending a student to a teaching post. We'll do it this evening. Sandy can give me a hand."

"Is there any chance of getting their money back?" Sandy asked.

"Well," James said, scratching his bearded cheek, "I have thought of one thing."

"I knew it!" Sandy crowed.

"Don't get too excited." James hated fuss, as he called any form of compliment. "I just remembered we know a man who served in Afghanistan as a doctor. He was wounded at Maiwand, as a matter of fact. His name's John Watson."

"Doesn't ring a bell," Sandy said, "but it's been years. And doctors got moved around more than most. There were never enough of them."

"I'll send him a note asking for a visit," James said. "He might know something about those discharge forms. He'd have had more to do with paperwork than you, I should think. He must've discharged plenty of men for medical reasons."

"Does this mean you're taking the case?" Sandy asked.

"I wouldn't put it that way. But it wouldn't hurt to hear what Watson has to say. Afterward, I could pop over to the War Office and see if anyone cares to answer a few questions from an interested citizen. We do pay their salaries, after all."

"Sounds like you'll be busy for the next few days. But don't worry about little old me." Angelina batted her lashes. "I have a case of my own to pursue."

"You do?" James sounded a shade too surprised to be flattering.

She gave him a haughty look. "I do meet people on my own from time to time, you know. I had a rather interesting visitor this morning, as it happens." She told them about Mrs. Reynolds and her missing servant.

"I hope you find her in someone else's house," Sandy said, "though I fear the worst. The major's wife might have left the poor woman in the train station or some such place and forgotten all about it. As I recall, the memsahibs treated their servants like furniture that could be ordered to move itself. Many of them never even learned their names."

"That was my impression," Angelina said. "But this ayah was a favorite of the children, apparently. I'm hoping she's simply been locked in someone else's nursery." She pulled over the glass plate with the ginger cake and began to cut slices. "Although how I'll get a peek into any of these nurseries is a mystery to me."

James accepted his slice with a knowing smile. "You'll find a way. And you get to attend a polo match — with royalty, no less. I imagine that will require a new hat."

Angelina shot him a dark look.

Before she could frame a stinging retort, Sandy said, "English matches aren't much like the Indian ones. I've seen a couple, sitting well away from the officer set, of course. Lots of dramatic galloping up and down, but nothing like the skill and daring of Indian horsemen. We had some bloody great matches back in Jaipur, I can tell you." The echo of his words caught up with him. "Pardon my language."

Angelina waved that off. "It's an ideal way to gain entrée into the circle. It should be a fairly informal setting, with lots going on to divert their attention."

"How will you make your approach?" James asked. He seemed a touch chagrined, as well he should be.

"My first step, like yours, will be to consult an old acquaintance. Mrs. Reynolds heard of our 'consulting practice' from Linda Bell. I've known her for simply ages. I'll pay her a call and get the inside view of these wives. She can help me plan my angle of attack."

"I can tell you a little," Sandy said. "I don't suppose things have changed so much in the seven years since I left the service. Army wives are faster, more restless, and more eager for fun than the civil service wives. Your quiet, steady girls don't choose cavalry officers for helpmates." He chuckled roundly at that idea. "They marry for excitement, and then spend their lives moving from one remote outpost to another. It might seem romantic at the start, but before they know it, they're saddled with a potbellied curmudgeon in the habit of barking commands and three fussy children. I enjoyed dancing with the daughters, but the wives were too tough for me."

Angelina pointed at him with her cake fork. "That is a very useful insight, Sandy. Thank you."

James pushed his empty plate aside. "Who would like a splash of port? We can toast our new projects. I'll play footman. I'm sure the boys are still stuffing themselves with cottage pie downstairs in the servants' hall." He went to the sideboard, poured three small glasses, and passed them around.

"You'll be working on different cases for a change," Sandy said. "That's new." He took a sip of the tawny port and hummed a note of pleasure.

"A refreshing change of pace," Angelina said. She gave her husband a speculative look. "What would you say to a little wager, darling? Who finishes first with the best solution?"

"That's a subjective term," James objected. "What would we wager? My money is yours, and vice versa."

"Hmm." Angelina sipped her port while she thought about it. "I've got it. If you win, I'll spend two weeks in Switzerland with you, including one full day walking up and down those beastly mountains. I will *ooh* at the snow-capped peaks and *aah* at the waterfalls without complaint."

"Ho, ho, ho!" James winked broadly at Sandy. "Now there's a prize worth winning. All right, then. Let's see." He sipped some port and cast his gaze toward the window. "Ha! I've got it. If you win, I'll spend two whole evenings at the opera or operetta of your choice, *and* I will not fall asleep, not even for a minute."

"Oh, will you!" Angelina crossed her arms. "I don't believe you could do it. You'd make some excuse and cry off."

"Never. I'll have a large cup of coffee before the opening curtain and another at the interval."

"Done." Angelina held out her hand, and they shook. "Sandy, you're our witness. And you'll be the judge of the quality of our solutions."

"I accept," Sandy said, laughing. "I have sympathies with both cases, so I can be impartial."

James raised his glass, and the others followed suit. "Let the games begin! And may the best sleuth win."

THREE

Moriarty sent a letter to John Watson that evening, begging a half hour of his time at his earliest convenience. The doctor responded by the next post that he would be pleased to offer the professor and his friend a cup of tea on Thursday afternoon, if that would suit.

Sandy collected Moriarty shortly before three o'clock to drive through the dense traffic between Bellenden Crescent and Baker Street. Leaving Zeke to mind the horse, they knocked on the front door. A boy of about thirteen years opened it. He cocked his head toward the stairs to signal their admittance, and up they went.

Watson opened the door before they could knock. He must have been watching from the window. "Welcome, gentlemen. Do come in. It's good to see you again, Professor." His gaze turned toward Sandy.

"Allow me to introduce my friend, Mr. Gabriel Sandy." Gesturing toward their host, Moriarty completed the formula. "Sandy, this is Dr. John Watson."

The visitors removed their hats, dropping them on the red sofa near the door. Moriarty noticed that the plush fabric was free of ashes, as was the well-worn Turkey carpet. Indeed, the crowded flat displayed an unusual degree of tidiness. No knife impaled the wooden mantelpiece, and no acrid odor of chemical experiments lingered in the air.

"I perceive that Holmes is no longer in residence," he remarked.

Watson chuckled. "I won't ask how you made that deduction. He's been gone a few months, on a case that's taken him far afield. But I've just had a letter informing me he'll be home in a few days. Your timing is impeccable."

He spoke to Moriarty, but his eyes kept returning to Sandy, studying his face with a sort of wonder. "Forgive me for asking, Mr. Sandy, but have you always worn that beard?"

"No," Sandy said, giving it a light scratch. His closely cut beard was a splendid mix of ginger shades, from a light tawny to a rusty red. "They don't allow beards in the cavalry, where I used to serve. Fortunately, the cabman's trade has more lenient rules."

"Cavalry." Watson snapped his fingers. "I knew it. You're the man who saved my life on the twenty-seventh of July in 1880."

"Maiwand?" Sandy looked taken aback. "Did I?"

"Indeed, you did!" Watson clutched Sandy by both shoulders, staring into his face as if seeing a brother long given up for dead. "I never learned your name, old chap, but I owe you my very existence!"

"Glad to be of service." Sandy seemed discommoded by the attention. Like Moriarty, he hated fuss.

Watson stepped away. "Forgive my enthusiasm. I searched for you for weeks — at least I asked everyone in the hospital at Delhi. I'm afraid they thought I was raving. My, my. This is a very special day for me. But where's my hospitality! Please sit down, gentlemen." He guided Sandy to Holmes's favorite chair, leaving Moriarty the armless chair typically reserved for clients.

The doctor bustled about, folding up his newspaper and hovering over the drinks table. "Mrs. Hudson will be up with tea in a minute, but surely we need more than that for this august occasion. Holmes has a very fine amontillado. May I offer you a glass?"

Sandy accepted one and took a sip. "Mmph. Delicious. Your friend has excellent taste in spirits."

"Oh, Holmes will drink anything." Watson passed Moriarty a glass without ceremony. "Luckily for me, some of his clients are quite sophisticated." He took his own chair, leaving his glass untouched. "Gabriel Sandy." He spoke the words like an invocation. "At last, I know your name."

Moriarty gave them both a look of mock impatience. "That's quite enough hinting, gentlemen. Won't one of you please tell me the story?"

"I don't know it," Sandy said. "That day was a mad, chaotic blur. I remember galloping like fury and roaring like a beast. I chopped down a dozen ghazis — more, perhaps. I really don't know. Then after that endless, harrowing retreat, I was too tired to remember much of anything."

"I'll tell it," Watson said. "I'll start a bit farther back, if you'll indulge me. You may not know, Professor, that I received my medical degree from the University of London. From there, I went on to Netley to train as an army surgeon. Seemed like a sound choice. I'd always wanted to see a bit of the world. I ended up in the Sixty-Sixth Regiment of Foot."

"Aha," Sandy said. "That explains why I didn't know you."

"We only came together for that disastrous action in the pass. We were overwhelmed so quickly by the Afghan troops, which were vastly larger than we'd been led to believe. I had my hands full rushing from one wounded man to another. I was so intent on my work, I grew careless. I caught a bullet in the leg that took me right down."

"We call that courage," Sandy informed Moriarty. "Not carelessness."

Watson made a dismissive sound. "Well, there I was in agony, wondering if I could muster up the strength to crawl off the field, when a huge ghazi rode straight toward me, his lance raised to strike. I said what I thought would be my last prayer. Then this man" — he gestured with an open hand at Sandy — "came galloping up out of nowhere, dodging through a hail of bullets. He hung himself down the side of his horse, holding on who knows how, and grabbed me by the armpits. He hauled me up by main force, flinging me over the back of his steed. Then he wheeled around and sped to the rear, where the retreat had already begun, and tossed me onto an ammunition wagon with a heap of other wounded men. And then he galloped into the dust before I could even ask his name."

Watson sighed, shaking his head, gazing at Sandy as if he could never his get his fill. "You've never seen anything like it, Professor. Utterly fearless. And what a horseman!"

"Bah," Sandy said. "I was young and reckless."

"I've always known him for an honorable man," Moriarty said. Both the story and the response to it suited his friend to a tee. "As for the fearlessness, I've seen him drive through London during the peak of traffic."

That made them all laugh, relieving Sandy's embarrassment. "Though they seldom shoot at me here," he said, "at least not in the West End." He raised his glass to Watson. "Seems I did a better deed that day than I knew. Well met, John Watson."

"What happened to you after the battle?" Watson asked. "If you don't mind my asking. One doesn't commonly find a war hero driving a hansom cab."

"I'm no hero. Once Major Blackwood called the retreat, I decided to start saving Englishmen in favor of killing more Afghans. I hit a bit of a snag about a year later." He gave Watson the brief summary of his promotion, secondment, the short period of enjoyable Indian pursuits, and his final humiliation.

"That's an outrage." Watson's brushy moustache bristled. "An absolute crime. There must be something you can do to dispute it."

"Not at this late date. Besides, I truly believe I've landed on my feet. I love this city, especially from the back of my cab. I'd be bored to tears running training exercises at the Middlesex barracks. No, London is the place for me."

"My wife says the same thing," Moriarty said.

"So does Holmes." Watson gave a short laugh. "I sometimes talk about moving my practice to a small town or a county seat. Good clean air, take your patients from cradle to grave. Yet here I remain, year after year."

The boy opened the door, and Mrs. Hudson entered with a large tea tray. Moriarty held it while she and Watson set up the table. Watson reminded her that she'd met the professor before and then clapped a hand on Sandy's shoulder. "This, you may be pleased to learn, is Gabriel Sandy, the man who saved my life in Afghanistan."

She clapped her hands in delight. Sandy stoically endured another spate of praise. And then she left them to serve themselves.

Soon they each had a large cup of Ceylon tea and sandwiches cut to please a man's palate — ham and sharp cheese rather than cucumber or watercress. They chatted about the variable weather they'd been experiencing that summer while they satisfied their appetites.

Then Watson refilled the cups, offered the sherry around again, and set an ashtray on the table. He presented cigars but got no takers. Moriarty only liked cigars with brandy, and it was too early for that.

His duties as a host fulfilled, Watson resumed his seat. "This is a red-letter day for me, but you gentlemen didn't come here to give me the surprise of my life. You wanted to consult me about something, Professor."

"It relates to your time in the army, as it happens." Moriarty told Watson about the encounter with the three soldiers yesterday. "All veterans of the — what was it?"

"B Battery of the Royal Horse Artillery," Sandy said. "But they were shifted to the Sixty-Sixth, which has now been consolidated into the 141st."

"I'm a mathematician, and that has my head spinning," Moriarty said.

"Just call it the Middlesex Regiment," Sandy suggested.

"Ah, the good old Sixty-Sixth," Watson said. "What are their names? I might have known them."

Sandy answered. "Sergeant Nate Fowler is the leader. He was a corporal back in 1880. Calvin Webb is still a private. So is my old batman, Daniel Digby."

"Your batman? What a chance meeting that was!" Watson thought for a moment. "I vaguely remember Fowler. Curious as a cat — always asking questions. Don't believe I ever met your batman. And Webb must've been the healthy sort."

"They've fallen on hard times," Moriarty said, "and from the same cause. They claim their discharge papers were falsified. Digby and Webb were given bad characters. Webb was labeled 'incorrigible,' and Digby was discharged 'with ignominy.' They lost their deferred pay, and now they can't get a job."

"That's hard," Watson said. "But are you certain they didn't earn those characters? There are some awful scoundrels in the enlisted ranks. The army's always been the employer of last resort for the lower classes."

Sandy shook his head. "Not these three. I could see Webb going sour if he fell in with a bad crowd, but Fowler kept him on the square. And Digby is as honest as the day is long. I'd have given them exemplary characters if they'd been discharged under my watch."

"It can't be a simple mistake," Moriarty said. "You can't write 'incorrigible' when you mean to write 'good.' Someone chose those terms deliberately."

"Not necessarily." Watson seemed to enjoy playing devil's advocate. "He might have mixed up the names. Perhaps he came from that other regiment — the one that was merged with theirs — and didn't know these men. How many are there in a company?"

"A hundred, more or less," Sandy said. "But I knew every man jack in mine, and half of them had tongue-twisting Indian names."

Watson smiled at him. "You were a good officer, I'll wager."

"I don't know how good I was," Sandy said, "but I did spend a great deal of time with my men. Training in the morning and polo in the afternoon, as often as not. But when the regiment's in England, you find your entertainment elsewhere, so I suppose you have less chance to get to know your men."

"That sounds plausible," Moriarty said, "but that character has serious consequences for the departing soldier. You'd think the captain would take greater care."

"Sadly," Watson said, "there are plenty of rascals and timeservers in the British Army, even among the officer ranks. Some of them are pressured into enlisting by their families and resent every minute of their term."

"Or their fathers force them to sign up as punishment for a scrape." Sandy grinned. That was how he had found himself in the cavalry. "The discipline straightens some of us up, but others are just further bent."

Moriarty grunted. "It appears that our most likely causes are carelessness, ignorance, vindictiveness, or vice."

"I'm afraid none of those are remediable," Watson said. "You won't find a British officer willing to say, 'By gad, I must have been drunk. Let me fix that at once.'"

The others laughed, although it reflected poorly on the moral character of the officer class.

"We still have Fowler's problem," Moriarty said. "He claims he was shorted, and I suspect he's right." He pulled his notebook from his pocket and walked Watson through his calculations. "He claims to have made a mark inside the lid of his trunk every day of every year to keep track and had a subaltern help him to do the sums when he neared the end. Unfortunately, the army kept the trunk, so he no longer has any proof."

"Ah, the penny a day," Watson said. "I remember that. Seemed like a good idea to me. Help the men save up for their future."

"It's an excellent idea," Moriarty said, "but given the difficulty of the sums and the low level of education among the ranks, it's also an opportunity for some subtle theft. Fowler expected forty-seven pounds and only got seventeen. Someone could easily have altered that number. I don't know how or who, but it's worth looking into."

"Did he lodge a complaint?" Watson asked.

"He says he went back to the barracks to demand an explanation. They sneered and told him to take it up with the War Office."

Sandy frowned. "But he could never do that, could he? Walk into that palace on Pall Mall with his hat in his hand, jabbering about marks in an old trunk. He'd look a fool."

"No doubt they knew that," Watson said, his face grim. "Who did the sneering?"

"I failed to ask," Moriarty said. "But the other two men came out worse. They received none of their deferred pay, thanks to those bad characters."

Watson nodded. "If you give a drunkard a ten-pound note, it will only end up in the nearest gin palace."

"Those men are not drunkards." Sandy pounded the arm of his chair with a clenched fist. "They were honest soldiers. If they say they've been cheated, I believe them."

"I know you'll think I'm only showing my bias." Moriarty offered Watson a self-deprecating smile. "When you have a hammer, everything looks like a nail. But I see ample opportunity for fraud here. Change one number — the years of service — and you cut a man's discharge pay by a significant amount."

"But how does your fraudster get the money into his own pocket?" Watson asked. "I should think it would simply sink back into the general fund."

Moriarty nodded. "That's one of the questions I'd like answered. But I'm not sure where to start. That discharge form Fowler showed us was light on detail."

"You want the service pension books," Watson said. "I filled out many an entry in my time. The *Character* field is where I listed the reasons for a medical discharge. Chronic fever, weak heart, that sort of thing." He stroked his droopy moustache while he thought for a moment. Then he pantomimed holding a large book with his hands about a foot apart. "Big volumes, as I recall. One row per man. Each row spans both pages, so there's a good deal of information. Basic physical data like date of birth, height, and weight, along with years of service and places served. India, Burma, etcetera. The character, of course, and a place for notes."

"Where can I find these books?" Moriarty rubbed his hands together. Government archives were his chief hunting grounds.

"At the barracks, I should think," Watson said. "Although there must be copies at the War Office."

"Can I just walk in and ask to see them?"

"I don't know. Medical information ought to be confidential, but perhaps you surrender that consideration when you join the army."

"There's no harm in trying, is there?" Sandy asked. "I'll go with you, if you like."

"I think this would be better done on my own," Moriarty said. "But I should come up with some excuse."

Watson barked a laugh. "Holmes would disguise himself as a janitor and spend a month mopping floors to get free rein with those books."

"I doubt my wife would appreciate my taking a job during evening hours." Moriarty smiled. He could see Sherlock Holmes in a custodian's coverall, dusting his way toward the targeted volumes. "But I have my own strengths. I am a member of the Royal Statistical Society. I can say I'm studying something like . . ." He smoothed his own trim moustache with thumb and forefinger for a moment. "Ah! I'll say I'm studying the correlation between character given at discharge and later employment of soldiers. I'll assure them that names and other identifying information will be redacted from any publications."

"That should do it," Watson said. "The army lends itself to all sorts of research projects, thanks to the vast number of subjects and the extensive records."

"That seems fitting," Sandy said, "since it's the vastness of those records that makes this wicked little bit of fraud possible."

FOUR

"I love fainting couches." Angelina eyed the ornate piece of furniture with something almost like lust. The swooping curves of its mahogany frame and the plushness of its velvet upholstery tugged at her love of drama. These things were made to display to advantage a shapely woman in a lacy tea gown, like her friend Linda Bell, who presently occupied the object of desire.

"Don't you have one?"

"No." Angelina sighed. "It was that or the piano, and I can't live without a piano."

"That is the disadvantage of living in hotels. The furniture is lovely and their staff takes care of it, but you never get your own piano. There is one in the lobby, though, and no one seems to mind if I slip down and play on it now and then."

"I'm sure they don't." Angelina beamed at her. Linda was adorable, for starters, with her blond curls, big brown eyes, and vivacious manner. She sang, danced, and did comedy sketches on the stage, but she was also a competent pianist. She favored crowd-pleasing ballads and cheery music hall favorites and could read a crowd the way James read a mathematical journal.

"The Langham seems quite nice," Angelina said. "I've never stayed here, though I lived in hotels for years." This room had been furnished some twenty years ago. Everything had that heavy middle-of-the-century look, with lots of deep reds and dark woods. Thick carpets muffled sound and red drapes shrouded the windows, which looked onto the hustle and bustle of Regent Street.

"Do you ever miss it?" Linda asked.

"Sometimes. I love the view of a city from ten stories up, especially at night. All those yellow lights twinkling down below. And it's very free, isn't it? When you get tired of one place, you just pack up and go somewhere else." She heard a touch of wistfulness in her tone and hastened to add, "But I love my house and my husband and our life together. We travel in the summer, so I still get to be pampered in fine hotels. Although James would rather see a great looming mountain outside the window, preferably capped with snow and looking horribly inhospitable."

Linda trilled a laugh. "Why do men love those horrid mountains? Give me London or Paris — or Berlin, in a pinch — any day."

"Me too." Angelina sipped her gin-and-lemon and contemplated the slate-gray sky, which was all she could see from this angle. "I think they like to imagine themselves pitted against the elements, fighting to survive with only their keen wits and a sharp knife."

They laughed, comfortable together. They had no need for the fine art of social fencing. They'd known each other for more years than either would admit, but they had never been rivals. They had different looks, different styles, and different voices. Linda seemed to have no particular ambition — or perhaps she just possessed the gift of contentment. She got all the attention a girl could want with her looks and her gaiety.

Linda popped a sugared almond into her mouth and crunched on it. "Cavalry officers don't dream about mountains. They dream about vast plains they can gallop across, in pursuit of . . . well, anything, really. They'd chase rabbits if there were nothing else, though they do love to slash their sabers about."

"They could cut grass," Angelina suggested. "Or harvest wheat."

Linda giggled. "Only if the wheat were somehow terrifying."

"You seem to know quite a bit about cavalry officers. One in particular?" Angelina gave her a *tell-me-all* look.

"You mean Roger." She hummed a note of pleasure and rolled her eyes. "*Such* a beautiful man! Blond hair and blue eyes, like a Nordic god, and with the shoulders of a god to boot. He's *irresistible* in his uniform, with the red sash and the bright brass buttons. And he's such great fun too, racing in Regent Park in total defiance of the police. Or dancing all night at a party. He's an absolutely exquisite dancer."

"Oh, exquisite, is he? Could this be love?" Angelina teased.

"No." Linda grinned at her surprise. "He's handsome, brave, and a fabulous kisser. But I'm starting to think those thoughts, you know? The ones about chubby little baby cheeks and pudgy little baby feet?"

"Oh, *those* thoughts," Angelina said. "I've heard of them, though they seldom cross my mind. My sister has two of the little darlings now. I can coo at them and bounce them on my knee whenever I like and then go home to a place without diapers or warming bottles. Or those earsplitting howls."

"Let them howl, I say. I don't mind noise or messes. I want three of them, at a minimum, and I don't think I can wait much longer." She dropped her voice to a whisper, though they were quite alone. "I'm almost twenty-nine."

Angelina mimed locking her lips. Age was a state secret in the theater world. "But don't you want dashing Nordic children? Or is Roger not the marrying kind?"

"The army doesn't approve of captains marrying. Majors may, but they're pushing forty by the time they reach that rank. I don't want an old man. And I don't want to live in India or South Africa or anywhere but England."

"I see your problem," Angelina said. "So are you giving Roger his marching orders?"

Linda gave her an impish look. "Not *quite* yet. But I have been seeing another sort of officer lately — a captain of industry. Something to do with rubber and bicycle tires. He's nothing like as delectable as Roger, but he's very rich and very sweet." She chose a square of ginger cake from the small table at her elbow and ate it in tiny bites. Then she took a sip of her gin-and-lemon and leveled her gaze at Angelina. "But you didn't come here to talk about my yearning for babies."

"No, although I wish you luck with your rubber king. An acquaintance of yours came to visit me yesterday — a Mrs. Julia Reynolds."

"At last! Are you going to find that missing servant for her? Because if you do, she'll owe me a favor."

"A small one," Angelina said. "I don't think it will be difficult, to be honest. All I have to do is sneak a peek inside her friends' nurseries, and you've just told me how. I'll pretend I'm thinking about babies and wondering what a good nursery requires. I imagine the ayah will be standing there airing nappies or whatever they do."

"How will you know it's the right one? They all look alike."

"I don't see how that's possible," Angelina said, with a touch of snap in her tone. "They have faces and figures. They must be as different as we are."

Linda shook her head. "But they're not. They all have brown hair, for one thing, and brown eyes. You'd be surprised what a difference that makes. And they wear those drapey costumes with the loose veils hanging down their backs, which hides their figures. Think about the fairy chorus in a pantomime. How different do they look, one from the other?"

"Not very, especially from the audience." Angelina gave a growl of frustration. "And here I've been enjoying myself, despising your Mrs. Reynolds for being unfeeling."

"Oh, they're unfeeling, all right. This ayah must be a perfect jewel to go to so much fuss. I only meant that it's harder to tell the Indian servants apart than you might think."

"Hmm. Well, if I can find my way into the nursery, I'll just say, 'Ganesa,' and see which one turns her head."

"That should do it." Linda rang a small silver bell. "Would you like another drink?"

"Why not?" This was Angelina's principal task for the day. James and Sandy had gone off to ask Dr. Watson about army records. They would undoubtedly have a drink or two. She could treat herself to two cocktails this afternoon, especially when the lemonade was so cool. They must have had ice sent up from the kitchens — another advantage of hotel life.

Priscilla, Linda's maid, delivered fresh drinks and an assortment of petits fours. Angelina loved the little treats. She could eat half a dozen of them without feeling like she was stuffing herself with cake. Thus refreshed, the two women snuggled more deeply into their well-upholstered seats. Time to get down to the serious gossip.

Linda started the ball rolling. "Apart from the servant issue, how did you like Mrs. Reynolds?"

"She has the most appalling laugh."

"Doesn't she?" Linda waved her hands in mock horror. "If she lived in London, I'd recommend a music teacher to take it down a notch of two. But she lives out there in the wilderness."

Moriarty Lifts the Veil

"When you say 'wilderness,' what exactly do you mean?" Angelina loathed the countryside, with its brambles and soggy fields.

"Oh, you know. The country — trees, grass, ponds, and so forth. You take a train to Staines, which is as far as you can get from London without leaving Middlesex County. You're met by a man in a turban with a dog cart, who drives you along a winding lane — very picturesque, with cows and whatnot — to a big box of red brick with a sort of Greek triangle over the front door. That's her house, Ripley Park."

"Is it very big?" Not everyone who lived in a country house was rich. People inherited the things from uncles or aunts, without necessarily getting any money along with it.

"Big enough for a troop of servants. And a large stable, of course. Cavalry men can't get enough of horses. They love fast coaches too — the newer, the better."

"I understand that. James never tires of mathematical puzzles; the more impossible, the better. But in fairness, we sing whether anyone's listening or not, don't we? And love nothing better than a new song."

"True, true!" Linda laughed gaily.

"So the men have the army and their horses. What do the women do?"

"They entertain themselves — picnics, races, theater, shopping. They don't sing or play instruments, so they play cards and gossip at parties instead of taking turns at the piano. But they're willing to try almost anything, and they can be quite gay. We went roller-skating at the Olympia once. Too droll!"

"That does sound like fun." Angelina had never skated on ice or rollers. She'd spent her childhood working on the stage and her twenties touring Europe pretending to be a decayed baroness reduced to singing opera for her living. Perhaps she could take Viola's children skating when they got a bit older. Being an auntie would let her catch up on some of the things she'd missed. "But if they have ayahs, they must have children. Don't they care for them?"

Linda pursed her perfect lips while she consulted her memory. "I believe most of the kids are grown, or at school. Of the women I mix with, only Mrs. Payne still has two at home."

"Then she must be the one who poached Ganesa." Could it really be this easy? All she had to do was make a pitch at La Payne, get invited to her house, and find a way to do some snooping. She'd be nudging James awake at *La Traviata* in no time. What penalty should she charge when he fell asleep?

But Linda was shaking her head, her bright curls bobbing. "She just returned from several months in India. Her husband's still there. She couldn't have been the actual poacher, though the girl might be there now. They seem to shift them around from time to time. From what I've heard, Mrs. Reynolds's ayah has a special talent for hair tonics and skin potions and a keen eye for color. She's more of a lady's maid now and something of an object of envy."

Angelina clucked her tongue. "I think she mentioned that. I forgot." That would teach her to count her chickens before she'd even found the eggs. Angelina sipped her drink, thinking. "Well, it shouldn't be so hard to find lady's maids. If I can get invited to a weekend, I can pop in when people are changing. Ask to borrow a comb or something. Or let Peg pretend to be sick and borrow a maid to do my hair."

Linda clapped her hands with delight. "You are *so* clever! I wouldn't have the least idea how to go about it. That's why you're so good at solving these odd little problems."

"Once you start doing it, your mind naturally turns in that direction. But tell me more about these women. Mrs. Payne must be younger than the rest. Is she nice?"

"They're all nice, in the sense of pleasant to spend the day with. They'll be delighted to bring you into their circle. Boredom seems to be their greatest enemy. Let's see . . ." She tilted her head, placing a finger on her round cheek. "I believe there are nine or ten married officers. Maybe that many again who are unmarried, like Roger. More, if you count lieutenants, but they're really only good for dancing. Some of them aren't particularly social. I don't know those people. Julia Reynolds is the best of the bunch, I think. Her husband is older and a little free with his hands, but not a bad sort, really. And she has a passion for the theater, which we can hardly complain about, can we?"

Angelina shook her head. "We encourage that sort of thing. Perhaps in time she'll be a little less gushing."

"She was like that with me at first. Then there's Mrs. Payne. She plays cards and comes to the parties, but there's something a little unhappy about her. I think there's trouble about money. That's usually what makes people unhappy, isn't it?"

"Often enough. Who else?"

"Well, the leader of the pack is Lady Chetwood. Lord Chetwood is a lieutenant colonel, so they have both rank and title." She wagged a finger at Angelina. "Rank is *everything* with military people, even among the wives."

"What's she like?" Angelina asked. "Is she very haughty?"

"Not in the least. She's quite jolly. They're older than the rest, though. Their children are long gone. They seem determined to have as much fun as possible until they wear themselves out. You *must* get invited to one of their weekends. But don't expect to get any sleep!"

"Sounds exciting."

"Oh, it is. Things can get pretty wild after the charades, which we always do after dinner on Saturday night." Linda gave her an appraising look. "But you can always slip away up to your room if it gets too much for you."

"Now you're just teasing me!" Angelina wondered if wild meant shooting at champagne bottles on the lawn or sneaking off to the summer house with someone else's husband. The latter, probably, given a major who was "a little free with his hands."

That fit with what Sandy had said, that army wives tended to be faster than their civilian sisters. That should work to her advantage. Fast sets bent on fun drank a lot, which meant people wandering around at all hours, with no one remembering much about what happened the night before. She could probably search the house room by room, if she wanted.

"How do you think I should start?" she asked. "Mrs. Reynolds mentioned a polo match, but she hasn't invited me yet." She finished her drink. She should head home in a minute. "But you know, it would be more convincing if I went to the match without her. Then I could stroll past her group and let myself be drawn in as if by accident."

Linda gave a little shriek. "You're like a detective in a novel! You really should write melodramas. But you can't go to a polo match alone. It isn't done. I'll go with you."

"You wouldn't mind?"

"Not in the least. Roger is playing." She gave a deep, dreamy sigh. "Those polo trousers are absolutely skintight. They're worth an hour on the train, believe me."

Handsome cavalry officers showing off before the Prince of Wales on a sunny afternoon? Angelina could think of worse ways to start an investigation — burying her nose in a stack of dusty books in some archive, for example. James had the sorry end of this bargain.

He had been right about one thing, though. This match would be the perfect opportunity to wear a smashing new hat.

FIVE

The War Office was housed in one of the least impressive buildings on Pall Mall; or rather, several undistinguished buildings since the office kept expanding. Three stories tall and built of the ubiquitous red brick, it had a plain facade with a minimum of white stone facings. But style wasn't everything. The immense size and thorough lack of ostentation suited the war department of a nation whose military forces spanned the globe.

Moriarty hoped someone inside would help him find the right clerk. There must be over a hundred pen-pushers scribbling away inside. He entered the marble-floored lobby and strode toward a semicircular desk at the center. A man in a red uniform watched him approach.

"Good morning. I'm James Moriarty. I'm a member of the Royal Statistical Society." He drew a card from his wallet that his cook, an expert forger, had drawn for him last night. It held his name followed by the initials DSc, indicating a doctorate in the sciences, over an encircled shock of wheat, the symbol of the Statistical Society. It wasn't quite proper to use the seal in this fashion, but he thought he'd get farther with something to show.

The desk officer nodded at it, waiting for the rest before troubling himself to speak.

Moriarty obliged him. "I'm planning a study based on army records. I'm interested in the correlation between years served and rate of employment after discharge. My uncle served in what is now the Middlesex Regiment of Foot, so I thought I'd use that as a starting point. I'm told the records I need are here. I'd like to speak with the clerk responsible for maintaining them. More recent ones will be of greater interest since the soldiers in question will be easier to locate."

"You want to see the discharge books for Middlesex." The officer gave him a penetrating look, as if expecting to catch him in a lie.

"I believe I just said that." Moriarty was impervious to such officious ploys.

The officer grunted. He opened a wide book on the ledge beneath his counter and leafed through it, running his index finger down the rows. "Ah, here it is. Middlesex. That would be Sergeant Brant, Army Pay Corps. Third floor, Schomberg House."

Moriarty glanced back toward the large glass doors. "Should I go back out and walk around?"

"No need." The officer turned sideways to point toward the open staircase at the rear of the lobby. "Up these stairs to the third floor, then left, right, right, and left again."

"Third floor, then left, right, right, and left," Moriarty echoed.

The officer gave him a dry look. "I believe I just said that."

Moriarty climbed the stairs, chanting the directions under his breath. He followed the trail of corridors, barely noticing when the carpet ended and the window frames changed from polished oak to painted pine. The last turn put him at one end of a long gallery with tall windows on one side. Each one illuminated a short length of desks with space for two or three men. Each station was equipped with a gas lamp and a set of cubbyholes. Men in suits or uniforms passed along the walkway, sometimes stopping to consult a clerk, sometimes simply walking straight through to some other section.

All the clerks were wearing red uniform jackets. Moriarty paused at the first row and asked, "Sergeant Brant?"

The man barely glanced up from his work. "Three down, outer desk."

Moriarty thanked the top of man's head and counted rows to find a slim young man with three gold stripes on the sleeve of his jacket. "Sergeant Brant?"

"Yes. How may I help you?" He still held his pen poised to write.

Moriarty introduced himself, displaying his card. He explained his proposed study. "The officer at the desk said you were the man for Middlesex, and so here I am."

"The Man for Middlesex? I like that!" Brant's light brown eyes shone with good humor. "Well, pull up a stool, Mr. Moriarty. You've come to the right place. I'll just finish this last paragraph, if you don't mind."

Moriarty found a stool and drew it forward. He politely turned his gaze to the windows so as not to seem to be reading over the man's shoulder. The sergeant focused on his work, writing quickly with a fountain pen. He was clean-shaven, with short brown hair and brushy side whiskers. He wore a pair of gold-rimmed spectacles. His neat features were a shade too close together, giving him a slightly pinched look.

He capped the pen and set it aside, then laid the paper on top of a short stack beyond his left elbow. He swiveled in his chair to face his visitor. "Years served and rate of employment after discharge, eh? That sounds intriguing. Should be achievable if you're willing to track down a significant sample."

"That's another advantage of focusing on the Middlesex Regiment," Moriarty said. "I'm likely to find a sufficient number within easy reach."

"A sound plan." Brant smiled again. He seemed pleased at the interruption and perhaps at the opportunity to display his expertise in this narrow domain. "Have you had a chance to examine a discharge book?"

"Not yet. I've seen my uncle's discharge papers. That supplied enough data to get me thinking about possible projects."

"There's a world of studies lurking in our records. I often wonder why we're not besieged by statisticians." Brant chuckled. "Let's have a look at a book, shall we?"

He pulled a thick ledger down from the top of his cubbyholes and opened it on the desk. He angled it toward Moriarty so they could look at it together. Each record spanned both left and right pages. The columns were labeled in block print, while the rows were written by hand.

Moriarty said, "This is easier to read than I anticipated. That handwriting is very regular. Very clear."

"Thank you. It's my job to copy out the book from the regiment office. I'm always conscious that I'm making a record meant to last forever. Who knows who might want to study this book a hundred years from now?"

"That's a commendable attitude for a clerk. I take it the original is kept in the regiment office? My uncle's form was signed by his captain. Are the original records written by regimental officers?"

"They can be quite untidy sometimes." Brant shook his head. "Captains don't put much stock in penmanship. The company clerk is more conscientious. He fills in most of the information obtained at enlistment, like age and height." He pointed at the column headings as he spoke. "Also the recruit's former trade, if there is one. The clerk records tours of duty abroad, usually in a batch when they're deployed. Finally, he enters the expected place of residence after discharge. You'll need that one, I should think."

Moriarty was impressed and let it show. "I'm astonished by the amount of information contained in these records. It's a miniature biography of each man." He read a few entries in silence, fascinated by the detail. "I may have to expand the scope of my study. I should at least consider trade before enlistment as well as years of service and add trade after discharge as a factor in rate of employment."

"That would be a richer study," Brant said. "I often wonder about these prior trades, though. Most of our recruits are too young to have done much. I suspect that sometimes they say, 'carpenter,' when all they did was sweep up at the end of the day."

"An interview might tease out some of that." Moriarty caught himself designing the study in detail and gave himself a mental shake. That was not his current mission. "It sounds like most of this information is entered by the clerk. Which fields are supplied by the captains?"

"The character, which is one of the most important. You'll want to add that your study. It won't matter if the man was a skilled carpenter before enlistment if he's discharged with a bad character. The army improves most men — service builds character, as we like to say — but not all. Some fall into vice and bad habits, I'm sorry to say, in spite of our best efforts."

"I suppose that's inevitable with any population." Moriarty scanned another entry, considering the source of each datum. "It appears that only two of these many fields contain a subjective value. A man's height is a simple fact, as are his years of service. But you suggest that a recruit might lie about his prior trade. And this character designation depends wholly on the judgment of the captain."

"That's an astute observation. I hadn't thought about it that way. At one end, we have the soldier's description of himself, and at the other, his commanding officer's summary opinion." Brant tapped the *Character* column with his index finger. "There is some difference between the two values, however. The man can say what he likes about his prior trade, but the captain's judgment is subject to oversight. If his commanding officer feels it's out of line, he can dictate a correction. The captain might also consult his sergeant about a man he doesn't know well. But a good captain knows his men pretty well, as a rule."

"I should think so." Moriarty reminded himself to ask Sandy about relations among officers and enlisted men. He knew precious little about the army when he came down to it.

Brant sat back in his slatted chair and grinned. "I must thank you, Mr. Moriarty. I sit here every day copying out these endless records. It's not terribly demanding of the intellect, though of course accuracy is paramount. But my mind has time to ponder the facts streaming beneath my pen and the multitude of uses to which these data could be put."

Moriarty smiled at his enthusiasm. "It must be a fascinating window on the qualities of the British working class. I'd be grateful if you would read the first draft of my paper once it's written."

"I'd be honored."

"How long have you worked here?"

"Ah, let's see. I transferred to the APO — that's the Army Pay Office — about five years ago. My eyesight isn't what it was" — he tapped the side of his spectacles — "but I like the army. It's steady work, and you always know where you stand. The move offered a chance of promotion as well, and you know a soldier never turns that down." He chuckled.

"Five years. That's a lot of records."

"A drop in the bucket." Brant pushed back his chair and got to his feet. "Let me show you the rest of the ocean. Give you a better sense of what you're getting yourself into."

He led the way through the far door and around a few corners to a door marked 'Records.' Brant drew a key from his pocket, unlocked the door, and opened it. He gestured for Moriarty to precede him, then closed the door behind them.

Moriarty's nose was assaulted by the powerful odor of books: ink, leather, and that ineffable smell of old paper. He blinked at the row upon row of shelves, eight feet high, filled with leather-bound volumes. "It's a treasure trove!" His statistician's heart quickened. Perhaps he really should conduct this study. He could contribute something substantial to the nation's knowledge of itself and exercise some mental muscles in danger of growing atrophied.

Brant mirrored his delight. "I see you are a kindred spirit, Mr. Moriarty."

Moriarty rubbed his hands together. "I can hardly wait to get started. But I see different sets of records, or at least different-colored volumes." Some were bound in green, some in brown, and others in red.

"That's right. The discharge books are brown. They go back a few years, as you can see. And of course they encompass every division in the army. Over thirteen thousand soldiers are discharged every year nationwide."

"Great Scott!" Moriarty cried. "Good thing I'm limiting myself to a single regiment. I'm thinking ten years should be the maximum depth of my researches."

"That sounds reasonable," Brant said. "I could guide you to the right volumes. Of course, these books never leave this building."

"Of course not." Moriarty's thoughts returned to the present time and place. "How do you manage the transfer from the original, if I may ask?"

"I carry the regimental record book back and forth. It's a great responsibility, of which I am always conscious. I travel directly from point to point — no stopping off for a quick pint at the local."

"I should say not!" They chuckled together, the two kindred spirits. Neither was the sort for quick pints in any event.

Brant gestured toward the door, and they left. He locked up and then paused. "We'll have to find you a desk, preferably in my section. I'll ask my superior if that could be allowed. Would five hours a week sometime between Monday and Friday, ten to four, suit you?"

"Admirably." Five hours with the most recent books ought to supply a list of men given bad characters, along with their present

Moriarty Lifts the Veil

addresses. He'd take down the years of service as well. Then he and Sandy could go visit a few and see how well their memories, and their discharge papers, accorded with the documentation.

Although these neat copies gave him no information about who had entered — or altered — a given record. He'd rather study the originals if he could find a way into that regimental office.

He followed Brant back to the APO section, where they resumed their seats. Brant leaned back in his chair again and offered his bright smile. "My CO will appreciate a bit more information about you. Might I ask about your educational background? Your card indicates a doctorate in the sciences. Did your studies include mathematics?"

Moriarty nodded. "I studied mathematics at Cambridge, Trinity College." His years of teaching at the University of Durham had ended badly, so he decided not to mention them. "Later, I worked in the Patent Office, specializing in engine designs, until I came into some money" — through gambling, though he wouldn't mention that either — "and retired. Now my time is my own, but it does want filling. Can't let the old noggin go entirely to pot, can we?"

"Indeed not. You've inspired me to raise my sights for my own retirement, when that happy day arrives." Brant leaned forward to smile confidentially. "Not anytime soon, of course."

Moriarty smiled and shifted his weight, ready to depart. But Brant raised an index finger to hold him for one more minute.

"I say, a man like you, with a fine education and time on his hands. I wonder if you might like doing a spot of teaching? We're always in need of coaches, you know. So many of our recruits come to us unable to read or write, much less do simple sums. We've a bit of a gap at Odstone Barracks — that's the Middlesex regiment — at the moment. Our maths coach moved to Scotland suddenly. Some family matter. We've hired another one, but he can't start for a few weeks." He gave Moriarty an encouraging look. "It'd give you a chance to talk to some of the men about your questions. Prior trade and future aspirations, that sort of thing."

Moriarty frowned, considering the offer. "Only a few weeks, you say? It does sound interesting. I'll have to talk it over with my wife. Five hours here and a few more at that barracks might be more than she's willing to bear."

"By all means, discuss it with her. I'll put in a word with the commanding officer. Then if you find time to pay a call, he'll know what it's about." Brant grabbed a sheet of notepaper and uncapped his pen to dash off directions to the barracks by train and cab. "You might send a telegram to the clerk — that's Corporal Nate Turner — before you go." He wrote out the name as he spoke and handed the sheet to Moriarty. Then he stood up to signal that the meeting was over.

Moriarty rose as well. They shook hands. "I can't thank you enough, Sergeant Brant. You've been exceedingly helpful and given me a lot to think about."

"Not at all, not at all." Brant smiled. "Can you find your way out?"

"I believe so." Moriarty touched the brim of his hat and walked away.

He paused outside the door to remember his original directions and repeat them backward. He had to chant them under his breath since his mind was overflowing with fresh ideas. He'd taken the soldiers' case partly from pity, but mainly because he truly did have time on his hands. Now he had an array of intriguing studies to pursue, which could result in a series of journal articles. To say nothing of a perfect excuse for getting into that barracks and nosing around.

SIX

On her way out of the Langham Hotel Thursday afternoon, Angelina had thought to ask the concierge how to get to Hounslow Heath for the polo match. He'd given her excellent directions all the way to the playing field. So today, she collected Linda in a hansom cab and drove south to Waterloo Station without a qualm.

She congratulated herself for learning something about trains without having to ask her husband. His joke about the hat still rankled. Unfairly, since she was in fact wearing an adorable new hat, but the remark betrayed a lack of respect for her abilities. And that made her doubly determined to succeed in her first independent investigation.

The concierge had warned her to go early because polo matches were frightfully popular. Who could have imagined it? She'd barely heard of them before this week. But if Prince Edward and Princess Alexandra were in the audience, people would go to see them. And after that never-ending rain in July, everyone was eager to get out of the city for a spot of sunshine.

The world and his sweetheart were heading out to Hounslow Heath that afternoon. Angelina and Linda had to queue for tickets, and even the first-class cars were crammed to the limit. They rocked along for an hour through increasingly lovely scenery to Hounslow, where they had to queue again for a cab. At least the crowd was cheerful and well dressed.

Eventually, they made it to the playing field, where they were greeted by cheers and shouts. Not for them, of course. Someone must have scored a goal or a strike or whatever it was they scored in this game.

They paused at the edge of the throng to be sure their bustles were straight and their skirts neatly draped. Angelina's coloring ruled out pastels, even in summer, but her blue-and-white-checked silk looked fresh and cool. She wore a straw hat with a wide brim liberally decked with flowers, tilted slightly downward, as if to hide her famous face. Linda wore dark pink with white stripes and a veritable flower garden of a hat, tied under the chin with a wide pink ribbon. The costume was much like those she wore on the stage. She would be recognized in an instant, which was exactly what they wanted.

Two grandstands had been set up on opposite sides of the field. One was draped in red-and-gold bunting, clearly intended for the royals and a hundred of their closest friends. The other had no decoration, apart from the colorful dresses of the ladies seated within. That group seemed to have divided itself loosely into a men's side and a women's. Many of the men wore military uniforms. They leaned forward, watching the game intently. The women kept their eyes on the field as well, but they chatted freely and whispered things behind their gloved hands that made them giggle.

The *hoi polloi* stood behind rail fences surrounding the oval field between the grandstands. These lesser sorts were also spiffily dressed. Avid sportsmen leaned over the railing and avid royal-watchers gazed at the bunting-clad stands, while those merely out for a day of leisure milled about nibbling on spice cakes or penny pies. The milliner's art was richly displayed — tall hats, short hats, straw hats, and silk; ribbons, chiffon, feathers, and an acre of silk flowers bobbed atop the heads of the ladies.

Angelina and Linda climbed the steps and made their way toward Mrs. Reynolds and her set. They pretended to be having trouble deciding where to sit. As they squeezed past the officers' wives, Angelina pretended to stumble. "Pardon me," she said, turning full-face toward them. Mrs. Reynold cried on cue, "Oh my lucky stars! It's Lina Lovington!"

Another woman gave a high-pitched gasp, then another one echoed, "Lina Lovington!" Yet another said, "She's come with Linda Bell. Linda, Linda — come sit with me!"

Linda said, "Look, Lina, here are the friends I told you about." She introduced Mrs. Julia Reynolds, Lady Cecily Chetwood, and Mrs. Rebecca Payne, each of whom stretched forth a hand to be lightly touched. They begged Angelina to join them.

"It would be *so* much fun," Mrs. Reynolds claimed.

Moriarty Lifts the Veil

And thus the deed was done. Mrs. Reynolds scooted over to make room for Angelina between her and Lady Chetwood. Linda said, "Forgive me, everyone, but you know I simply *must* have a better view of the game." She gave them a music hall wink and went down to sit near the railing.

Lady Chetwood beamed at Angelina. "We all *adored* your *Ali Baba*. I am simply in awe of your ability to race about dancing and sword-fighting. I don't know how you do it."

Angelina laughed. "Well, I sleep all day."

"So do I," Lady Chetwood confided. "I seldom rise before lunch."

Not for the same reason. She wore lime green, which might have been a good color for her younger self. She had blond hair and blue eyes, but the pink in her cheeks had been applied with a brush. Her eyelids were puffy and her eyes bloodshot. This woman stayed up late drinking, not dancing. She must not have an ayah with a talent for lotions and potions in her house either. Tight lines of dissatisfaction clustered at the corners of her rouged lips. She was handsomely dressed, well married, and free to spend her days — and nights — in perpetual leisure. Yet something kept her from being happy with her lot.

Angelina had learned the art of manipulation at her father's knee. The habit of cool assessment had stuck with her too. She could win this woman's trust easily enough by playing the fellow pleasure-seeker. A few nights of too much brandy and she'd have her in her palm. But toward what end?

"Tell me a bit about this game," Angelina said. "It looks like they're trying to keep that little ball away from each other with those long mallets. But how do they score? And which team is which?"

"The rules are fairly simple," Lady Chetwood said. "Each team tries to get the ball between those striped posts at the ends of the field. See?" She pointed. "They can't cross directly in front of each other, to avoid injuring their ponies, so they ride back and forth trying to get the advantage. The ones in blue are the Middlesex Cavalry. That's us. The red ones are from the Royal Horse."

"That explains His Royal Highness."

"Mm. And Windsor is only a few miles away."

"Are all the players officers?"

"Goodness, yes! Lieutenants and captains, for the most part. They're younger, with more to prove. And no home life to keep them from play." Lady Chetwood gave her a sly look. "On or off the field."

"They are awfully handsome," Angelina said. "What is it about a man on a horse?"

"Power over a big beast. And the way that posture shows off their legs and their tight little bottoms." Lady Chetwood clapped her lace-gloved hand to her lips, and both women laughed. "Have you picked a favorite yet?"

"Not yet," Angelina said. "Give me a chance to survey the field."

"I've got mine," Mrs. Reynolds murmured.

The words were spoken almost too softly to hear, but Angelina caught them. She followed Mrs. Reynolds's gaze. The major's wife seemed to be riveted on a long-limbed, dark-haired man who strained forward to reach his mallet toward the ball ahead of his rival. His back must have been made of India rubber. He controlled his mount so skillfully with his knees, man and beast seemed to move with one mind.

He and his rival pressed on, riding within a yard or two of the stands. Then he looked up, straight at Mrs. Reynolds, and shot her a saucy grin.

"Oh my!" Angelina made a droll face at her new friend, patting herself on the chest as if calming an overstimulated heart.

Mrs. Reynolds gave her an inscrutable look. *Hands off, he's mine.* Or perhaps, *You shouldn't have seen that.* Whichever, it told Angelina this was more than mere play. She remembered Linda saying that Mrs. Reynolds was some ten years younger than her husband. The children were grown, and Major Reynolds doubtless spent most of his time in the barracks. That left his wife on her own, still attractive, still yearning. Ripe for an affair.

Another useful bit of leverage. But Mrs. Reynolds couldn't be hiding her own servant, so her affairs were none of Angelina's business. Old habits were so hard to break.

She couldn't see much of Mrs. Payne, seated on Mrs. Reynolds's other side. Though she did notice that the woman kept stealing peeks at the silver watch she wore on a long chain around her neck. Counting the minutes — until what?

Angelina tilted her head toward the men's section of the stands. "Are those men in the Middlesex Regiment too?"

"Our husbands, among others. They sit apart from us because we gossip too much, or so they say." Lady Chetwood turned and gave the men a little wave.

One of them stared pointedly at Angelina, offering her a small salute.

"Who is that?" she asked.

"Major Reynolds." Lady Chetwood rolled her eyes. "He's always interested in fresh— ah, in a fresh face. We do get a bit bored with one another out in our little corner of the county." She returned her attention to the ongoing match. "I'll confess I pay more attention to the players' figures than their tactics. Sometimes I'm not even sure which side wins."

"They *are* dashing," Angelina said. "I'm glad my husband's not here. Is everyone in this stand in the army?" She laughed. "One way or another, I mean?"

"Apart from friends like you, I suppose so. Our commanding officer and his wife are on the other side." She pointed at the royal stands. "See the man in the blue uniform with the double row of brass buttons?"

"No," Angelina said. Then she remembered. "Silly me! I brought my opera glasses." She pulled the leather case from her reticule and took out the brass-and-mother-of-pearl instrument. Holding them to her eyes with the long handle in her left hand, she adjusted the sight with her right. "There he is! Oh yes. Very distinguished." She saw an older man with an elaborately waxed moustache and a weak chin. He must pine for the days when officers could wear full beards. "Is he a general?"

"Goodness, no. Regiments are commanded by colonels. That's Colonel Samuel Oxwich."

Oxwich! An icy shiver ran down Angelina's spine. She covered her shock with an obvious joke. "I've never heard of an ox-witch before. Does he enchant cows as well?"

Lady Chetwood granted that witticism a very small smile. "It's no use, Miss Lovington. Every possible joke has been made already. The enlisted men call him 'Old Ox-and-Pox' behind his back."

"Oh my!" Angelina laughed. She liked that nickname.

"The colonel commands the regiment, and his wife commands the wives. She's the woman in that ghastly brownish-purple next to him. The Honorable Flora Oxwich. Her father is Baron Tomley." Lady Chetwood leaned heavily against Angelina's shoulder to whisper, "The money comes from her mother's side."

"Good," Angelina said. "Women ought to hold the money. It makes for a better balance." She raised her glasses again to study the Honorable Flora.

It was only fair for her mother to leave her a pot of money because she hadn't given her much in the way of looks. The poor woman had a heavy jaw, thick black brows, and a faint shadow over her upper lip. She frowned deeply, whether at the crowds or her own thoughts, who could say? More likely that was her characteristic expression.

"How does she command you?" Angelina asked.

"Oh, she finds her ways," Lady Chetwood said. "She decides who's in and who's out, whatever the game is. She drops constant hints that she can influence our husbands' careers with a word if she wants. Not mine, of course. Now that Caspar has inherited the title and the estate, we're thinking of retiring. Besides, a lieutenant colonel can't be promoted until the colonel moves up, and those two are firmly planted. They rule the roost at Odstone Barracks."

Angelina knew three things about Colonel Oxwich, none of them good. First, he was the man who had embezzled funds from the officers' mess in India and pinned the blame on Gabriel Sandy. That was enough to condemn him in her book. Second, he'd once lent his name to the board of a corrupt company, duping innocent people into squandering their savings on unmarketable products. Third, and personally most damning, she happened to know the pearls he kept for his wife in the safe in his study were fake.

He was a crook, plain and simple. But he couldn't have anything to do with the missing servant, nor could his wife. They were too old to need an ayah, and no gifted lady's maid with a talent for colors would allow that woman to go out in that color. It made her look positively sallow.

But everyone knew corruption flowed from the top. Embezzling soldiers' pay came straight out of the old Oxwich playbook. If that was going on, the colonel surely knew about it and was most likely taking a cut. Angelina could hardly wait to get home and tell James about her discovery.

But wait! They had a bet riding on who finished first. She couldn't hand him such a monster clue, not before she managed to get inside a single house. Not after that crack about the hat.

She raised her glasses again to take another look at the old fraudster. He seemed bored — or sleepy. Well, he wasn't going anywhere anytime soon. She could wait a few days. Let James do his own investigating.

SEVEN

Moriarty stopped on the landing to check his pockets: notecase, notebook, pencil, spare pencil, handkerchief, magnifying glass. He wouldn't need an umbrella today. He thought of Angelina sitting in the stands at her polo match. He hoped they had a roof to supply a bit of shade because she'd forgotten her parasol. He could see the frilly object hanging on the umbrella stand by the front door.

He and Sandy were going in the opposite direction this afternoon, both geographically and socially. She'd traveled to the western edge of Middlesex, while they were venturing back into the heart of East London. Sergeant Fowler had told them about two other veterans of his regiment who had been given dubious discharges.

Satisfied that he was fully equipped for the afternoon, he jogged down the stairs. Rolly emerged from the dining room, where he'd been watching for Sandy's cab. "Will you be out late, Perfessor?"

"I shouldn't think so. Though Mrs. Moriarty won't be home much before dinner."

Rolly lifted Moriarty's hat from its peg and handed it to him. "Wish I could go wif you."

It must be hard for an active lad to spend his days cooped up in a house. He used to roam the streets at will from sunup to sundown. For want of a home, but still free. "Another time, perhaps."

The clop of a horse's hooves sounded on the macadam outside. Moriarty donned his hat and let Rolly open the door for him. "You see, not even Zeke is along today. I suspect he's grown too big to perch on the side of Sandy's seat."

"No bigger'n me." Rolly sighed and closed the door.

Moriarty jogged down the three steps to the pavement. He greeted Sandy and climbed inside the cab. They set off at a sprightly clip, turning south to travel along the Embankment before diving into the traffic on Fleet. So many things to be aware of driving through the great metropolis. Pedestrians, vendors with handcarts, nurses with prams. Omnibuses pulled by great plodding horses. Newsboys darting in and out with the fearlessness of youth. To say nothing of the other cabs and private coaches. Sandy's job required keen eyes and quick wits, as well as stamina.

They reached the Salvation Army shelter on Whitechapel Road, where the two veterans had found employment sweeping up and washing dishes. A woman in a dark suit with red epaulettes met them at the door, introducing herself as Captain Hughes. She led them to an empty dining hall and bade them wait. "I'm afraid there's no tea at this time of day."

"That's all right," Moriarty said. "We thought we'd take the men out for a light meal." He smiled, assuming she would approve the offer as a small act of kindness.

Instead, her narrow lips tightened. "If you give them beer or any other form of alcohol, they won't be allowed back in tonight."

"Understood." Moriarty and Sandy exchanged nods.

Two men in clean, if much-mended, street clothes appeared. The older one introduced himself as Corporal Tommy Hale and his mate as Private Charlie Appleton. Both wore the weary expressions of men living from day to day with little hope for the future.

The four men shook hands all around. Then Sandy said, "We spotted a pub on the corner called the Royal Oaks. We'd like to invite you for a bite to eat while we talk."

"We can't have beer," Corporal Hale snapped. "It's as much as our jobs are worth."

"We've been duly warned," Sandy said. "I'm sure they serve tea."

They left the cab where it was, with the reins tied to a post. Sandy tipped a man sitting on the stoop of the shelter to keep an eye on it. They walked down to the corner and found a table in the front room. The barmaid didn't raise an eyebrow when Moriarty ordered four pots of tea. She must be accustomed to the rules of the pub's largest neighbor.

After consulting his guests, he ordered sausage and mash all around. The sausage was gristly and the potatoes greasy, but the two soldiers eyed the dishes with such evident longing, Moriarty caught the barmaid's sleeve and asked for buns and a big plate of rashers.

Hale and Appleton told stories similar to those of the other soldiers. Appleton admitted to having trouble with drink most of his life. "They gave me ten pounds when I left, though Tommy says it should've been more. But I was lost in sinfulness and vice. I took what they gave me and spent it all in a gin palace. I might've died in that house of dereliction but for the good Christian soldiers who saved my life. I'm one of that number now, thanks to their prayers." He gave Moriarty and Sandy each a long look, doubtless meant to be persuasive. But the broken veins in his lumpy nose told their own story.

"How much do you think he should have received on discharge?" Moriarty asked the other man.

"He served for twenty-one years," Hale said. "I reckon it oughta been more like thirty pounds."

Twenty pounds stolen! Add that to the money taken from the other three and one approached the annual salary of a professional man, like a lawyer or a cavalry officer. Moriarty had no idea how many soldiers had been relieved of their pay in the last year. The total sum could be more — much more.

"Me, I got nothing," Hale said. "Captain Greenway gave me 'incorrigible' for my character. I'll show *him* incorrigible if I ever get the chance." He shook a clenched fist. Appleton covered the fist with a pacifying hand, which Hale shook off with a sour look.

"If it's any comfort to you now," Sandy said, "I would've given you both good characters. I won't say you were saints" — he gave Appleton a wry look — "but you were honest, hardworking soldiers. It seems the old company has changed since I left. Can you think of any reason Captain Greenway would mark you down? Some men can't tolerate the least bit of teasing. They consider it sauce, and they remember it."

"Never nuffink," Hale said, his dimpled chin jutting forward. "We was always 'Yes, sir, no sir,' as nice as you please. I've chewed on that character every night and come up with naught but spit. Now you're saying he done it for the money. I had fourteen years coming to me. That's twenty pounds and change. I could be building chairs in a fine shop. That's what I wanted to do. Always loved working with wood."

Moriarty Lifts the Veil

Five plausible victims in the past year alone. The rate of theft was breathtaking. If it hadn't been for a chance encounter, no one would suspect any wrongdoing — no one with the power to investigate it, that is. The meeting between Sandy and his old batman could never have been predicted. No self-respecting cavalry officer would wander around Shoreditch on foot, and it was only a matter of time before those men ended up in prison, destroying what little credibility they possessed.

Hale turned his bitter eyes on Moriarty. "Those do-gooders might've sold Charlie on their holy song and dance. Not me. I'm just biding my time till I can find something better. Fowler invited me in with his gang, but I said, 'No, thanks.' Risk jail for a few shillings? Not this old soldier. Captain Hughes here might be a right pain in my arse, but I'm clean and I'm fed and I've got a warm place to sleep. And now you say you might get my pay back for me. That's worth holding on for."

"I didn't say that." Moriarty held up a cautionary hand. "I said I was looking into the possibility of fraud. If that can be proved, there might be remedies down the road. But I caution you, it's a long road, and one that will likely lead nowhere."

Hale scowled at the table, where the plates now lay empty. "There oughta be some remedy, Mr. Moriarty. I didn't join the British Army to end up washing dishes for these play-actors."

Nothing could be said to that. They enjoyed pieces of surprisingly good blackberry pie with more cups of China tea. Moriarty's sense of futility was somewhat relieved by the men's pleasure in the treat. He couldn't restore their ruined lives, but he could give them one good meal.

They walked back to the shelter and found the man paid to guard the cab stroking Melisande's silky nose. "We're mates now, me and this beauty. Anytime you come this way again, you look for me first."

Sandy asked if he'd served in the Royal Horse Artillery, but he had not. "Me old dad was a stable hand."

Moriarty got inside while Sandy climbed up top. They kept the trap closed and their thoughts to themselves as they worked their way back down to the river. They crossed the Blackfriars Bridge and clattered onto the granite-surfaced Victoria Embankment. Moriarty spied a couple of rowers out on the Thames and wondered if he'd have time for a spot of exercise this evening.

They stopped just past the Waterloo Bridge. Moriarty craned his neck out the window and spotted the cause: a huge omnibus slowly turning onto Savoy Street. He sat back with a groan and glanced idly at the carriage trapped next to them.

Then he blinked and looked again. Peering through the window was the face of an Indian princess, or someone like it. Her bronzy face was a perfect oval, her almond-shaped eyes rimmed with lashes as thick as a young deer's.

The lovely face turned upward, her gaze fixed on Sandy. The shapely lips formed an O of astonishment. She cried out, "Gabriel!" Sandy, glancing down, shouted, "Zuri!" He followed that with a string of words in another language.

A hand — a man's hand — jerked the curtain closed. The carriage moved up, edging past the rear of the omnibus. Sandy clucked at his horse and the cab jolted forward, cutting in front of another cab and veering around the omnibus. The reins slapped down on the mare's back and she quickened her pace, trotting after the carriage.

"Clear the way!" Sandy shouted, nearly running over a couple foolishly crossing in the middle of the road. The carriage, being large and having two horses, bored through the traffic. Sandy followed in its wake as close as he could get.

Two hansom cabs drove up onto the pavement, scattering the shrieking pedestrians. Policemen blew whistles, but the carriage rattled on, with Sandy relentlessly on its tail. Moriarty held on to the straps for dear life, being tossed from side to side.

Now an enormous goods van pulled by two great draught horses lumbered toward the Embankment from the Charing Cross station. The driver of the four-wheeler shouted, "Hup! Hup!" The carriage lurched forward just as the mighty horses clopped onto the road. Sandy was forced to haul back on his reins, flinging Moriarty into the sloping front door.

The carriage was long gone by the time the furniture van made its turn and the flow of traffic was restored. Moriarty could hear Sandy cursing even with the trap closed. He decided to wait until they'd reached home before asking for an explanation.

Moriarty Lifts the Veil

They pulled up at the house on Bellenden Crescent. Sandy unlocked the cab door with his lever, remaining in his seat as if he meant to let his passenger out and drive on.

But Moriarty wasn't having it, not after the ride he'd just endured. He stepped out and looked up. "Who was she?"

"A dream from the past."

"I gathered that much." He eyed the set of Sandy's jaw. "A glass of whiskey for the tale? I promise not to tell Angelina if you don't want me to."

Sandy gave Moriarty a closed, angry look. Then he heaved a great sigh. "I could use a glass." He climbed down from his perch and tied the reins to the post. Then he followed Moriarty into the house.

Rolly took their hats. Moriarty went upstairs to empty his pockets and clean up at the washstand, leaving the bathroom on the second-floor landing for Sandy's use. They met again in the drawing room.

Moriarty went straight to the sideboard and poured two large glasses of his best scotch. When Rolly appeared, he said, "We won't be wanting anything to eat just now. And close the door, if you please." Rolly looked offended, but the boy couldn't expect to hear every conversation that took place in this house.

Moriarty handed a glass to Sandy and sat down. "Who is she?"

Sandy took a good-sized swallow and let out a sigh. "Zuri Padmani, the Star of the East. That was her stage name anyway. She was a dancer when I saw her last. She performed in a gentlemen's club, for lack of a better term, in Jaipur. It had a mixed audience — British officers, foreign merchants. Men who found themselves at loose ends in the evening and wanted refined entertainment. It was a highly respectable establishment. They didn't even serve drink, just mint tea or coffee. They had hookahs on every table, which you could have filled with tobacco or hashish. The air was thick enough to get a lungful whether you wanted it or not."

He stopped to down the rest of his whiskey. Moriarty rose to pour him another tot.

Sandy went on, speaking to the glass in his hand. "They had other entertainment, of course — jugglers, singers, that sort of thing. None of them mattered once I saw Zuri. She was magnificent. These classical Hindu dancers perform most of their dance with their eyes and their hands, kneeling on a cushion. She wore red silk crusted with gold threads that gleamed in the candlelight. She had thick, loose trousers under her skirts and her dress came up to her neck. Only her hands and her face — that beautiful face — were bare. And her feet, which were filthy. She had silver rings on her toes."

He smiled at the memory. "Her hands told a story about love at first sight that night, and that's what happened, for both of us. Those big dark eyes looked straight into my soul. It was kismet." He lifted his glass to his lips but didn't drink for a long moment. Then he tossed that ration back too.

"How did you manage to meet her?" Moriarty asked. "She must have had many admirers." Like the wishful swains lining up at Angelina's dressing room door, only to be met by a scowling husband.

"She did, but she didn't care about them. She danced for the joy of it. I don't know what she saw in me. She sent me a message that first night, inviting me to a private supper there at the club. Her escort, an older man, sat behind her the whole time. Her English was not bad, and my Hindi was serviceable by that time, so we managed well enough. We told each other our whole life stories right there, over lentils and chapatis. We met as often as we could after that, always with the chaperone. We were most dreadfully in love but didn't know what to do about it. Her parents had arranged a marriage for her with a wealthy kinsman years before. She'd only met him once. She didn't want to marry anyone anyway. She wanted to dance. She made me tell her everything I knew about the music halls in London."

"That would take some time," Moriarty said. Sandy was one of variety theater's greatest aficionados.

Sandy acknowledged the truth of that with a nod. "I intended to bring her home with me when we rotated out, one way or another. I wanted to marry her. Failing that, I'd hide her in a basket to get her on board the ship. I wasn't much for planning back then, living one day at a time."

He does that now, Moriarty thought. But his job was terribly dangerous. How could a man plan for the future when death waited for him around every hill?

Moriarty Lifts the Veil

"I left without saying good-bye." Sandy's eyes were bleak. "I was such a bloody idiot, letting Oxwich and his minion use me to cover themselves. I packed my bag and ran, like a coward. When I was held up in Calcutta waiting for passage to Burma, I wrote to her. I poured it all out, sitting in the bar in that roach-infested hotel. Everything I had — my love for her, my shame, my burning desire to disappear and leave the old Sandy behind. Thought I'd never see her again. I've no idea if she ever saw that letter. Of course she couldn't respond. I had no fixed address until I rented the flat in Shoreditch."

Moriarty poured another round. "Are you certain it was her today?" The chance of there being another Indian woman who might cry out to Sandy from a carriage was slim but had to be considered.

Sandy dismissed that with a snort. "I'd recognize an eyebrow or the curve of her lips from farther away than that. I know that face. I dream about it every night."

Moriarty understood. He could recognize Angelina from the curve of a shoulder across a crowded casino. "How do you suppose she found her way to London?"

Sandy shook his head. "Best I can figure is that she married that kinsman and came here with him. He was some sort of businessman, I think. I never asked." He looked Moriarty in the eye. "I have to find her. I have to know. If she's happy, well enough. I'll leave it there. But if she's not . . ."

"A man's hand closed the curtain," Moriarty said. "Whoever he was, he didn't want her to speak to you. Perhaps not to anyone."

"Indian husbands are very strict, as a rule." Sandy frowned. "I hope he didn't punish her for calling my name. He might not know anything about me, but now he's bound to wonder."

That was an evil thought. "That carriage is our best clue. Black, four-wheeler, good condition. Did you notice anything special about the horses?"

"Good stock, well tended. A perfectly matched pair. That means expensive. But there are plenty of those around town too."

Moriarty cast his mind back. "It seems to me the driver was wearing a dark blue coat. And there was something on the door, like a coat of arms. Blue and white, with a spot of gold in it. I can see a

71

horse's head atop a shield with crossed sabers — unless I'm making it up."

"Unlikely," Sandy said. "I didn't see it at all. Could you make a sketch, do you think? I'll ask around, keep my eyes peeled. It's a damned fine clue."

"I'll do my best. I have some colored pencils upstairs. You might try showing it to someone at the College of Arms. They're in the city, I think. Near the Guildhall."

"You're a genius." Sandy raised a thumb to him. "I never would have thought of that."

Moriarty waved off the praise. "I'm just an old scholar who knows how to look things up."

"A valuable skill. And no man could ask for a better friend." Sandy polished off the last of his drink and set the glass down with a thump. "Now I'd best be off. Melisande needs water and a good brushing after her exercise." And so he left.

Moriarty glanced at the clock and poured himself another short drink. He stared blankly out the window, pondering the coincidence of catching a glimpse of an Indian woman who was being kept in the shadows by someone for some reason within days of learning about another Indian woman gone missing.

Coincidences happened every day, especially in a bustling world capital. Moriarty accepted that; he'd be a fool not to. But he didn't trust coincidences, not without further examination.

"Bah." He savored the last swallow of the peaty liquor. There must be a hundred Indian women in and around London. Besides, the missing servant was none of his concern, and Angelina wouldn't welcome his interference. Let her find out if her search converged with Sandy's and decide what to do about it if and when that happened.

EIGHT

The Moriartys breakfasted late on Sunday mornings, not necessarily at the same time. Today, Angelina found her husband lingering over a last slice of toast and what was probably his third cup of tea. She filled a plate with scrambled eggs and ham, both lukewarm by now, but she didn't mind. She did want fresh toast, however, so she rang the bell and asked Rolly to bring some. "And another pot of tea, please."

She kissed her husband on the cheek and sat down to her meal. "I've been invited to a garden party this afternoon by my army wives. Would you like to come?"

"Wouldn't that violate our rules?"

"What rules?"

"I thought we agreed not to encroach on each other's investigations."

"Did we? Well, it does seem only fair, given the wager." Then she caught a hint of something in James's eyes. A dart, a flicker. "You're hiding something. You know something about my missing servant, don't you?"

"No." He gave her that stern professor look meant to quell all dispute. It might have worked on his undergraduates once upon a time.

"Hmph." She forked up a mouthful of fluffy eggs. He wouldn't lie to her face, so he must not have anything solid. But he certainly had some sort of inkling about something. Then again, so did she. She buttered a slice of toast with an air of virtuous unconcern.

James knew her almost as well as she knew him. "I did have the sense last night that you picked up something at your polo match relating to my soldiers. What was it, if I may ask?"

Angelina cocked her head and frowned as if she had no idea what he meant. "I saw and heard many things yesterday. Those officers' wives gossip like fiends. I couldn't begin to imagine what you would or wouldn't like to know."

James tucked his tongue in his cheek and gave her a wry look. Then he poured her a cup of tea from the fresh pot. He stirred in her two lumps of sugar and added just the right dash of milk. "Very well, my dear. Let's agree not to meddle in or interfere with one another's investigations. Unless danger should arise, which I consider unlikely."

"Danger for either one of us."

"Naturally."

They raised their cups and clicked them together to seal the agreement.

Angelina said, "Since our Breakfast Accord bars you from my garden party, I'll make your excuses. What will you do today?"

"Enjoy a day of leisure, I suppose. I can only pursue my case on weekdays. I thought I might take Rolly to the Museum of Natural History. He'll enjoy the dinosaurs, and he's been a bit restless lately. It's hard for a boy his age to be indoors all the time."

Angelina set down her fork, got up, and went around the table to kiss him soundly on the top of his bald head. "Have I told you how much I love you this morning, my darling man?"

* * *

Once again, she met Linda Bell at the Langham to travel on through Waterloo to Staines-upon-Thames. Their hostess had sent a pony trap to meet them. They had ample time to appreciate the scenery, which consisted of layer upon layer of green grass and leafy trees, bobbing and dappling in the summer sunshine. The effect was hypnotic and vaguely disturbing. What lurked behind all that serenity?

"Our hostess has good luck, it would seem," Angelina said. "Two sunny days in a row are nothing short of a miracle this summer."

"Perhaps she brought the sun with her from India," Linda said. "Mrs. Payne and her children have only been home for a few weeks."

"And Mr. Payne? Or no, it's Major Payne, isn't it?"

"He's still there."

Moriarty Lifts the Veil

"Brave of her to have a party so soon after a long journey."

Linda gave her a wry look. "When Mrs. Oxwich tells you it's your turn, you find a way."

"So I've heard. Will your captain be here?"

"Oh yes. I'm fond of you, Lina, but otherwise I'd probably stay home. I found the sweetest letter from my rubber king yesterday evening. I think it's time to give him my full attention. This afternoon will be a sweet farewell." She giggled. "So don't expect to see much of me!"

The trap pulled up before a large house with a plain white front and a slate roof. The architect might have been trying for something French, but the result was bare and dull, not stately and classical. The central house had two stories with gable windows poking out from the attic. Three-story towers stood on either side. Angelina would bet a fiver that the nursery was at the top of one of those towers. She'd try to get a look inside that afternoon.

A tall Indian man in a turban helped them down and led them straight through the house, which was sparsely furnished with threadbare carpets. Outside, the veranda showed spots of moss between the stones, which were not entirely level. The lawn was a brilliant green, however, and appeared to be freshly clipped. The servant led them to a cluster of linen-draped tables shaded by three magnificent oaks. The tables were far enough from the river for the ground to be dry but near enough to fall into a reverie by the glistening waters, if one so desired.

Two people in wicker armchairs seemed to be doing that very thing. Other men in summer suits and women in white dresses sat at the tables talking. Lady Chetwood waved her wine glass cheerily at them. The man sitting next to her, who looked old enough to be Lord Chetwood, raised his as well. Children in straw hats with streaming ribbons ran laughing across the grass. A group to the left was playing croquet.

All in all, a typical English garden party.

Except for one thing — the troupe of brown-skinned servants, dressed in their native garb, gliding among the guests. The men wore loose cotton trousers with high-collared cotton coats buttoned to the thigh, with turbans wound upon their heads. The women wore long, loose skirts with waist-length blouses and striped shawls draped over their heads. They went to and from the house carrying trays, shawls, and pillows. The guests seemed oblivious to them, receiving whatever was offered without a glance at the one offering it.

Mrs. Payne approached with hands outstretched to welcome them. She looked a little frazzled, a few brown hairs escaping their pins and a damp shadow of perspiration on the edges of the chiffon scarf pinned at the top of her strawberry-sprigged dress.

"I'm so sorry my husband couldn't come," Angelina said. "He has a bit of a headache today."

Mrs. Payne made the polite response. Then she cocked her head at Linda. "I believe Captain Maycott is skipping stones by the river. You'll find him beyond the croquet court."

"Toodles!" Linda waggled her fingers at them and skipped away.

Mrs. Payne smiled at Angelina. "I hope we can find something to amuse you, Mrs. Lovington."

Angelina didn't bother to correct her. Strictly speaking, her stage name was *Miss* Lina Lovington, but even James had come to accept the common mistake. "Your beautiful garden has already refreshed me, Mrs. Payne. It's *such* a treat to get out of the smoky old city and catch a breath of real country air." She placed a hand on her breast and demonstrated the simple pleasure. "And I *adore* croquet. Do you think they'd mind if I slid myself into the game?"

"Not in the least! Everyone is eager to meet you."

The players, both men and women, did make a small fuss when she joined them, though they returned their attention quickly to the game. These army folk were competitive. Angelina had played croquet at many a country house during her season pretending to be an American heiress. Those games had merely been something to do between meals and an excuse for mild flirtations. No one had much cared about the outcome.

But these people employed both skill and strategy. The women weren't bad, but the men played as if the Empire depended upon them. They left Angelina in the dust.

She stood behind her ball, studying the field. Her best option was beyond her scope and missing would only make things worse. Then she felt a pair of strong arms encircling hers and the warmth of a large man pressing against her bustle. She glanced over her shoulder to meet the brown eyes and ruddy face of Major Reynolds.

"Here, let me give you few pointers." His breath tickled her cheek. "You're looking at a long shot, so you want to grip the mallet right about here." He took her hands and shifted them up an inch. "Is that better?" He spoke in a mellow voice, clearly meant to be seductive.

She found him quite the opposite, and not only because he was a good ten years older. His face had that hard, ruddy cast of men who spent too much time in the sun, and his eyes had the hard, flat look of men who spent too much time in the bar.

"I am a married woman, Major," she murmured as she eased herself out of his unwanted embrace. She stood with her mallet planted firmly between them.

He grinned, undaunted. "Just thought you might enjoy a quick strike. But I'll leave you to your own devices, if you like."

She pretended he'd been talking about croquet. "I can't improve my game if I don't keep swacking at it." She gave the mallet a little kick in his direction.

He chuckled, touched his hat, and moved off. She took her shot, sending her ball flying into the shrubbery. "Oh blast!" she cried, playing the hapless female.

Everyone laughed, enjoying the show. She lost badly but made some friends, which was her goal at this stage. People liked you better when you lost. And Major Reynolds seemed to take her rejection in stride.

The players wandered toward the tea tables. "Sit with me, Miss Lovington," Mrs. Oxwich called from the best-positioned table. The tone was more command than invitation. Angelina readily obeyed. She wanted a chance to get to know the colonel's wife.

"I'm sorry we didn't get to meet yesterday at the match," she said. "It must have been thrilling to sit so near Their Royal Highnesses."

Mrs. Oxwich granted her a condescending smile. "One grows accustomed to such things over time."

Ouch! That's put me in my place! Angelina adopted a look of envious admiration. "Such a lovely party, isn't it?" She craned her neck to eye the dishes being offered by the legion of servants.

Mrs. Oxwich beckoned to the nearest ones. One of them bore a plate of lobster salad, which Angelina gladly accepted. Another added a slice of duck pâté and a crusty roll. A third hurried up with glasses of white and red wine. Angelina chose white.

"Look at these delicious treats," she said. "Our hostess seems to have thought of everything. And what a beautifully trained staff." She gazed openly at the Indian men and women bustling about. "They add quite an exotic touch, don't they?"

"A taste of India." Mrs. Oxwich sniffed suspiciously at a spoonful of salad, as if doubtful of its freshness.

"It's delightful. Didn't Mrs. Payne just come home? I don't think I could manage such a lovely party after a long journey."

"Everyone contributes to these little gatherings — servants, food, wine. We're forced to rely on ourselves for entertainment in India, you see, and we tend to continue those traditions at home as well."

"I can only imagine," Angelina said truthfully. The most exotic place she'd ever lived was Santa Fe in the Territory of New Mexico, where the Spanish were more conservative than the ones in Madrid. But the Americans were easy to get to know, and she hadn't been there long.

She proceeded to consume an enormous tea, moving from the lobster and pâté to cheesecake and fruit. She also switched from wine to ginger ale. A good investigator had to keep her wits about her.

Mrs. Oxwich ate little and drank less while conducting a thorough interview concerning her guest's personal and professional history. Angelina had no trouble fielding the questions. She'd crafted biographies for all occasions and never mixed them up. They got through her travels in Europe, her acting history, and her family's ownership of the Galaxy Theater. Finally, they came to the terrace house in South Kensington.

"I suppose you find it convenient to live near your place of employment," Mrs. Oxwich said. Her disdain for places of employment and those who required them had resounded throughout the conversation.

"Have you always lived in the country?" Angelina asked, knowing she hadn't.

"We had a house in Mayfair for a year or two." Mrs. Oxwich's lip curled. "But we were robbed, you know, one night when we took a few days holiday in Brighton. They spared our collection of Indian art, but they took every scrap of my silver."

"The beasts!" Angelina didn't recall there being much silver at the Oxwich home, though the houses they'd burgled that season had rather run together. "I suppose that is a hazard of life in the city."

"No, that won't do," Mrs. Oxwich said.

"Pardon?" Angelina had been dribbling raspberries over her chocolate puff pastry. She stopped in mid-dribble, uncertain how she had offended.

But the older woman's basilisk glare had turned toward one of the smaller servants. The girl sat on a banquette at the far end of the terrace, kicking her heels against the stones. Worked off her feet, no doubt, but she shouldn't take her break in full view of the guests. Mrs. Oxwich excused herself without a glance at Angelina and stalked off to correct the miscreant.

Angelina ate her chocolate-and-raspberry confection in grateful peace. She sank back in her chair and gazed at the scene around her with an air of a well-stuffed woman enjoying the summer afternoon. She didn't love nature the way James did, but she could appreciate the dappled light under a green tree and the sweetness of a breeze untarnished by horse dung or coal smoke — in small doses, at any rate.

After a while, she noticed that some of the servants seemed to be shadowing other ones. New arrivals being trained, perhaps. There seemed to be four of these trainees. Perhaps they'd just come over with Mrs. Payne. She couldn't possibly afford so many servants herself, judging by the condition of the house.

None of the pairs were men, curiously. She didn't think of it until a man began silently tidying her table, removing soiled plates and glasses to his tray. Angelina smiled at him and said, "Thank you. You're all doing a lovely job today."

He blinked at her. "Yes, lady."

"Have you been here long?"

"Yes, lady."

Hmm. That might be all the English he knew. On the other hand, an English footman wouldn't say much more than that either. She watched him work, wondering if he were the same man who had greeted them when they arrived. And then she scolded herself for being unable to tell one Indian from the other. That smooth brown skin seemed to wash out the differences among their features.

But they must look as different to one another as the English did. Angelina prided herself on her ability to read people's faces. How could she do that if she couldn't even tell them apart?

Shrill laughter rose from Lady Chetwood's table, where they had moved on from dessert to concentrated drinking. The servants now set opened bottles on the tables, not bothering to refill individual glasses. It looked like a good time to slip away and explore the house.

Angelina strolled to the terrace and through the French doors. No one spoke a word to her, though Mrs. Oxwich cast a glance in her direction. Angelina swiftly toured the rooms downstairs, backing out of a rear parlor where Linda and her captain lay entwined on a settee. She peeked into the dining room, which had been partially prepared to seat everyone in case of rain. Linens were laid upon the long table with flowers and candlesticks lined up along the center.

Angelina heard a snuffle. She whirled around to find an Indian girl sitting on a side chair weeping. She recognized the beautiful red-and-yellow-striped shawl. The child — she couldn't have been more than fourteen — had dark skin and black eyes with luscious lashes. The pudginess around her cheeks would disappear as she grew older. She might turn out to be quite a beauty.

Angelina knelt beside her. "What's wrong, dearie? Are you hurt?"

The girl frowned at her. Probably frightened at the attention, poor thing.

"I won't hurt you."

"Help you, Memsahib?" A stern man's voice spoke from the doorway. He strode toward them and took Angelina's elbow to raise her to her feet. He maintained the grip as he turned her firmly toward the door.

She gave an awkward laugh, ignoring the girl she clearly wasn't supposed to see. "Lavatory?"

"Up two, Memsahib." He pointed toward the stairs. "Go now."

She went. At least she had recognized the man — he was the one who had met the pony trap. He must be in charge of the house and thus also of the other servants. That poor girl should never have been set to work the garden party. She was obviously out of her depth. She'd probably only just arrived and was overwhelmed by the strangeness of it all.

The man's directions had been vague enough to allow her to poke her nose into every room on the second floor. Mrs. Payne lay on the bed in one, snoring softly with a cloth over her eyes. There were three other bedrooms, two closets for linens, and a bathing room, all empty. She found the water closet and took advantage of the opportunity.

Then she faced the steep attic stairs with a grim sense of determination. She had to hitch her skirts up to her knees and take each step on her tippy toes, but she made it. She found one long room with a steeply sloping ceiling. Two rows of mats lined the long walls, each with a folded blanket and a small pillow. A spare turban on a trunk told her this was where the male servants slept.

She went down the steps backward, grateful that no one saw her awkward performance. Time to broach the two towers. The top floor on the first one had a similar row of mats and blankets and a lingering scent of hair oil. The women's room. Angelina compared the bare mats with the comfortable beds her maids slept in — narrow, yes, but with proper mattresses, sheets, quilts, and good-sized pillows. They also had a chair, a chest of drawers with a mirror, and a small tiled fireplace. You wouldn't call it luxury; at least not until you saw this chilly, barren dormitory.

She could have predicted the nursery would be the last room she found. This was a pleasant, well-lit room spanning the top of the tower. Each window had a seat covered with cushions with a variety of toys perched among them. No children played here — they must still be running around outside — but two Indian women sat together sewing. They stared at her with wide eyes.

"Ganesa?" she asked.

One pressed her lips together and looked down at her lap. The other shot her partner a challenging glance and pointed at herself. "Jasmin." Then she pointed at the other one, who was now shaking her head, and said, "Sonika."

"Jasmin and Sonika," Angelina said. "Pleased to make your acquaintance." She pointed at herself. "Angelina."

They both frowned at her, shocked. One step too far.

But she had to push a little. "Do you know where Ganesa is? Which memsahib? Mrs. Oxwich? Lady Chetwood?"

Now they both shook their heads. They picked up their work and sewed as if their lives depended on it. Perhaps they did.

Angelina gave up and left. It was too frustrating not to know if they hadn't answered because they didn't understand her or because they didn't know — or because they didn't dare to speak. They seemed afraid of her or her presence, but so had the girl downstairs. Maybe they'd been trained not to speak to strangers, but whether by the memsahibs or their own mothers, who could say?

Angelina whisked downstairs and went out through the French doors. No one seemed to have missed her. She strolled over to a table where several of the croquet players sat, grabbing a glass of champagne from a passing servant. Another one brought a chair, and she joined the lively group.

She gave their banter half an ear, smiling and laughing in the right places, as she considered ways around the language obstacle. Really, it was *too* unfair! All of James's informants spoke English natively.

She needed an ally who spoke at least a bit of Hindi. Sandy must have picked up some of the lingo while he was training that Indian troop. Why should James have exclusive use of his talents? She'd met him first. Unfortunately, some of the officers would probably recognize him.

What about John Watson? He'd been out there too, and he was a doctor. He might have treated natives as well as British soldiers. He was a curious-minded man who liked to learn things. He might know enough Hindi to coax one of these girls into speech. The Indian servants knew each other and had a fair idea of each other's circumstances, as isolated as they were out there in darkest Middlesex. Crack one and find them all.

NINE

Rolly brought up the post on Monday morning as Moriarty was finishing his last cup of tea. There, among the usual advertisements for discounted furnishings and new grocers' shops that went straight into the fire, was a letter from Odstone Barracks.

"I'll bet I know what this about." Moriarty picked up the silver letter opener and slit the envelope. It was an invitation to present himself at the regimental office in regard to the position of mathematics coach. Sergeant Brant must have sent a letter on Friday. Not surprising; an efficient man took care of small chores right away to keep them from obstructing larger matters.

He started to read it aloud to his wife, but she held up a finger to stop him.

"If it relates to your case, you mustn't tell me. Shall I go upstairs so you can crow out loud?"

"That won't be necessary. But I will be out all morning. Best not to wait for me for lunch. I'll grab something somewhere."

"In that case, I'll have lunch with my sister. I'm off for another round of the Servants' Registries this morning." Angelina sighed wearily. "I can't put off a decision much longer. Dolly and Molly are panting to go north and start making cheese. If I don't find anyone suitable, I'll hire a daily. That will do us for a while, don't you think?"

Moriarty knew she wouldn't find anyone suitable on those lists of the eminently respectable. Their unconventional household required persons with a certain degree of flexibility with respect to the strict application of the law. "A daily sounds perfect for us at this juncture. But do whatever you think is best, my dear." He rose and kissed her on the cheek, ignoring the cross little crease between her eyebrows. He went upstairs to prepare for his excursion.

Moriarty filled his pockets with the usual tools, making sure he had fresh pencils. He couldn't bring teaching materials, assuming he would be hired, since he had no idea where these soldiers stood in terms of mathematical knowledge. Not very high, from what he'd seen.

The journey to Staines-upon-Thames, the nearest station to the barracks, was uneventful. Moriarty enjoyed observing the transition from city to country. It was curious how this corner of Middlesex had become the center of his and Angelina's lives in the past week. But such was the work of the consulting detective. One never knew where one's services would be required next.

Security was not a priority at Odstone Barracks. The guard at the front gate barely glanced at Moriarty's letter, being fully absorbed in the race results in today's issue of *Sporting Life*. When pressed, he managed to jerk a thumb toward the center of a low brick building. Bands of black and white stones created long horizontal lines and sections had been pushed out with slate-clad gable roofs. The effect was more aesthetically pleasing than one would expect for a military facility.

The interior, however, was as utilitarian as any government institution. The walls were painted a dull white, and the wood floors were bare. They both showed signs of much scrubbing and smelled faintly of carbolic. A sign over the first door on his right read "Regimental Office," so he went in.

This room contained two desks and several chairs. A young man stooped before a battered filing cabinet. He wore a red uniform like Sergeant Brant's, but with only two stripes on his sleeve. Moriarty cleared his throat, and the fellow jumped as if shocked by a wire.

"Good morning," he said. "How may I help you?"

"I'm James Moriarty. I'm here about the position teaching mathematics."

"Ah, excellent!" The man strode forward, thrusting out a hand for a vigorous shake. "I'm the one who wrote to you — Corporal Nate Turner."

"I believe the letter was signed 'Captain Greenway.'"

"The adjutant officer signs everything — and reads them, never fear — but I do most of the writing. I'm our regimental man-of-all-work." He sounded proud of that fact.

"Then you're the man I want to see." Moriarty took an instant liking to the fellow. He had an honest round face with thin brown hair that kept falling into his round eyes. He had the air of a man who had found his place in the world and liked it. "What can you tell me about this position?"

"Well, it's temporary. That's the first thing." Turner gestured to a seat and waited until Moriarty took it before plopping into the swivel chair beside a desk piled high with paper. "The last man left us in a bit of a fix. Some family matter arose, and off he went."

"That is unfortunate."

"He wasn't the best, to put it mildly, so we're not sorry to see him go. But the new man can't start until mid-September. We'd like to finish out the summer term, which means two more weeks. It's bad for morale to treat these classes lightly."

"That's very wise," Moriarty said. "What type of curriculum are you expecting?"

Turner grinned at the word. "We're looking for very basic instruction, Mr. Moriarty. The men you'll be teaching have no education whatsoever. Some of them can't read or write, but we have another coach for literacy."

"I'm glad to hear it." Two years ago, Moriarty would've been at a complete loss. He'd taught statistics to university students, not simple sums to the illiterate. But having plucked his footman from the streets at his wife's request, he'd gained some experience teaching a rank beginner. "Basic arithmetic, then — sums, subtraction, times tables — that sort of thing."

"That's the ticket! We ask for three classes a week — Monday, Wednesday, and Friday — at ten o'clock. That should give you time to get here from London on the train. An hour is as much learning as our boys can stand, so you'll be free to go at eleven."

"I can manage that easily."

Turner folded his hands over his stomach and smiled. "Now you'll want to know about your pay."

"That was my next question." Moriarty didn't care about the pay, but it would seem odd not to ask.

"You'll get seven shillings a week for the three hours." Turner quirked a wry smile. "It's not enough to live on, of course, being so few hours, but it is a very good rate. And we can offer you lunch in the soldiers' mess."

"I have other resources," Moriarty said. "That sounds fair to me, factoring in the train trip."

"Then do we have an agreement?" When Moriarty answered, "We do," Turner clapped his hands on his thighs with an air of finality and rose. "If you'll wait one moment, Mr. Moriarty, Captain Greenway would like to have a look at you."

"By all means."

Turner vanished through an inner door. Moriarty gazed idly at a map of the world pinned to a cork board while he thought about ways of teaching sums to men who couldn't read. He'd have to teach some of them their numbers first, but then how to keep the others from growing bored?

Turner returned, followed by a tall man in an officer's blue jacket with three gold diamonds on his epaulettes. Moriarty rose to greet him. "James Moriarty." He held out his hand.

"Alan Greenway." The officer's grip was firm but a little moist. His posture was erect and his figure trim, but his jawline had started to sag. He had dark circles under his eyes and the tense expression of a man with a throbbing hangover. "So you're our new maths coach, eh?"

"I hope to give satisfaction."

"Ha. Well. You could hardly be worse than the last chappie. He had the bright idea of teaching the men their numbers with playing cards. No idea how much of their pay they lost."

"Do you mean to tell me he took money from his students?" Moriarty was genuinely shocked.

"Ha. Well. Their lookout, wasn't it? No one told them to risk their coin." He turned his head to clear his throat. "Sorry. Not quite up to snuff today. Just popping over to the mess to see if the steward can sort me out." He offered Moriarty a stiff smile and left without further ado.

So this was the fellow giving bad characters to Sandy's old soldiers! Moriarty doubted he had any idea which man was which, much less if they'd performed their duties well or poorly.

Turner was watching with his lower lip caught between his teeth. "You're not seeing the captain at his best. He rides like a centaur and is fearless in battle. These cavalry men get a bit bored when we're at home."

"I understand. We aren't all made for doing sums and writing letters, are we?" Moriarty leaned forward to add, "But it's a good thing for Britain there are more of us than the centaur kind."

Turner chuckled. He glanced at the large mahogany clock hanging on the wall, which read twenty minutes to ten o'clock. "If you'd like to meet your class today, I could offer you a cup of tea in the meantime."

"I'd like that. Lemon and two lumps, if you have it. Just the sugar if there's no lemon."

"We're reasonably well supplied."

Turner went out through the front door this time, returning in a few minutes with a tray holding two cups and a plate of digestive biscuits. The tea was terrible, far too strong. They must have brewed it in a metal pot and left it on the back of the stove. But it was sweet enough, and the biscuits weren't stale.

Once Turner had resumed his chair, Moriarty asked, "Is Captain Greenway in charge of the whole barracks?"

"Goodness no!" The corporal seemed shocked at the depth of ignorance implied by that question. "A regiment is commanded by a colonel. Ours is Colonel Samuel Oxwich. You won't see him today, I'm afraid. Mondays, he meets with his superiors at the War Office."

"Ah." Moriarty's face took on the preternatural calm he had learned growing up in the vicarage in Miswell. Between his mother's acid tongue and his father's verbal traps, he'd learned from an early age to show the least expression when he was the most perturbed.

He recognized the name Oxwich, of course. That was the old villain who'd had Sandy cashiered to cover up his own embezzlement. He'd also been on that crooked board of directors, hadn't he — the year Moriarty met Angelina. She'd been stalking them, trying to find ways to get into their libraries and search for an incriminating letter being used to blackmail her brother. A nasty business all around. He was proud to have had some part in resolving it.

Turner rattled on about the other officers, the number of soldiers, the types and sizes of armaments employed by the Middlesex Regiment. It wouldn't have meant much even if Moriarty hadn't been preoccupied by that infamous name.

They finished their tea at five minutes to the hour. "I'll walk you over to the classroom," Turner said. "And I'll have someone meet you at the gate on Wednesday. Shall we say five to ten?"

Moriarty agreed. As he followed the corporal across the large compound, he decided how he would structure his lessons in arithmetic. Forget about cards and times tables. These soldiers needed to learn how to calculate their own deferred pay.

He might never be able to prove that Sergeant Fowler and the others had been defrauded. But he could jolly well perform a sort of financial inoculation to make sure no other soldier in this regiment ever suffered the same fate.

TEN

Angelina dropped another letter on the small stack she'd written Monday morning. She'd sent thank-you notes to everyone, using the directions Mrs. Payne had supplied when she'd come down from her nap. The first note went to her, but Angelina had also written to Mrs. Reynolds, thanking her for introducing her to such a lovely group of people, and to Lady Chetwood, thanking her for making the polo match so much jollier. Her note to Mrs. Oxwich lavishly rejoiced in making her acquaintance. She'd laid it on pretty thick, knowing that imperious personage would take it as her due.

She'd thought that would be that. She'd been invited to play whist at the Oxwich home on Wednesday afternoon. Surely anything anyone wanted to say could wait that long. But no, Monday evening's post brought a stack of replies, including an invitation to the next weekend party at Chetwood House.

"*Do* bring your husband," Lady Chetwood wrote. We're all positively *thirsting* to meet him."

She'd winkled her way into their set, all right. Would she ever be able to winkle her way out?

She set her pen in the holder and sighed dramatically. "Let's hope that's the end of it, at least for today."

Peg looked up from her newspaper. "Livin' out in them big houses in the middle of nowhere? I'll bet those nobs write letters the way you and I stroll down the hall to visit another dressing room."

Angelina sat at the writing desk beneath the windows in the morning room, the cozy parlor on the ground floor behind the dining room. Peg sat nearby in an upholstered armchair reading the *Illustrated Police News*. James had gone out already, off to the London Library to learn about the structure of an army regiment. Apparently, he'd put his foot in it a couple of times yesterday. He hated to feel behindhand in areas that might be considered common knowledge.

That never bothered her. Ignorance had its uses. It made people feel superior, which tended to make them trust you. Funny how that worked.

"What are you reading?" Angelina asked.

"Something that's giving me a shiver. Yours ain't the only Hindu girl gone missing lately." Peg's ominous tone gave Angelina a shiver too.

"Let me see."

Peg folded the paper and handed it over. Angelina scanned the densely packed text and found a heading that read, "A Tragic Mystery: The River Claims Another Victim." The brief article reported that the body of a second Indian woman had been found at the West India Docks. She was dressed in the soggy remains of her native clothing, but no further clues as to her identity had been discovered. The police believed the woman, a stranger to our shores, went into the water near Limehouse. Whether of her own volition or through an act of violence, they could not — or would not — say. The body remained with the coroner, who declined to answer questions about a possible slayer of Indian women lurking in the heart of London.

"Good Lord!" Angelina cried. "That poor woman." She met Peg's eyes, which mirrored her own horror. "You don't think this has anything to do with my missing ayah?"

Peg shrugged. "I don't think nothing. Just seems a mite peculiar, you being on the lookout for an Indian woman when there's Indian women washing up on the docks."

"It is a mite peculiar." Angelina drummed her fingers on the desk, staring at the stained-glass window she'd installed to hide the small and unappealing yard. They had to light the gas in here, even in the morning, but it shed a pleasing colored light around the writing desk.

She sighed again. "Well, I can't just let it go, can I? I should at least speak to that coroner, if I can find him."

Peg snorted. "How d'ye plan to find the old cove without asking the professor?"

Angelina glared at her. "I can find things out on my own." She glowered at the painted glass, a lovely depiction of a tall stand of red flowers in a blue pot. Who could she ask besides James? She couldn't very well trot down to the police station in Limehouse and ask for directions to the coroner's office.

"I know!" She snapped her fingers. "It must be in the Post Office Directory." James kept a copy here in the morning room. She hopped up and found the large red volume on a shelf and carried it back to the desk. She opened it and began running her index finger down the endless list of entries. "Is it called the Coroner's Office? Or the London Coroner's Office?"

"How 'bout the Coroner's Office of London?" Peg looked skeptical. "Or it might be the fellow's name, for all you know. And what're you planning to do? Turn up at his door in a sober-looking hat and ask to see the drowned Hindu woman?"

Angelina frowned. Peg was right. Even if she could locate this beastly coroner, he wouldn't tell her anything. Ladies were to be protected from such sordid matters. She slammed the book shut. "This is James's way, not mine. Who do I know who would know who the coroner is? And would be willing to go with me to meet the bloomin' fellow?"

"Someone who deals with dead bodies," Peg suggested. And that lit the spark.

"John Watson!" Angelina clapped her hands together. "He's a doctor. And he trails around with Sherlock Holmes, poking their noses into all sorts of murders. They must be regular chums with the coroner. What's more, James consulted Dr. Watson for his case. It's only fair that I should do the same." She turned back to the desk and whipped out a fresh sheet of her personal stationery. "I shall write to him at once."

* * *

She had an answer an hour later. Dr. Watson must have been feeling a trifle bored without Holmes around to stir things up. He said he would be pleased to escort her to the office of Mr. Baxter, the coroner for the County of Middlesex, Eastern District, and would call for her in a cab at one o'clock. The coroner kept law offices on Cannon Street, east of St. Paul's Cathedral. Watson added that he would send a quick note requesting an appointment but didn't believe one was necessary, given the man's official function.

Name, title, address, and an appointment to boot! James couldn't have done better.

Angelina thought about wearing her funeral garb — a black dress and a black hat with a short veil. But Peg scotched that idea with one wry remark. "Want him to think she was your dearest auntie, do you?" So she wore her dark lilac with a sedate purple hat sporting just one short white feather amid the satin bows.

She and Dr. Watson chatted amiably on the journey into East London. He was expecting Holmes to turn up any day now, having received a letter postmarked Marseilles. "I predict exhaustion, along with a refusal to admit the condition."

"I've known actors like that," Angelina said. "They work till they're all used up — completely empty — but still they can't stop moving."

She filled him on the case of the missing servant. "She might have been at the garden party for all I know. There must have been a dozen Indian women drifting around. Apparently, everyone contributed servants to the event."

"Do you have a description of her?"

"She was about my height and had two gold teeth. That's the best I can do."

Watson patted her hand in a comforting way. "It's certain to be someone else. Your memsahibs live at the opposite end of the county. How could a stranger to London find her way to Limehouse?"

They agreed that Angelina should simply tell the truth — that she'd agreed to help an acquaintance search for a servant who had been missing for a couple of months. Why shouldn't she? Everyone knew good servants were liable to be poached by friends and neighbors.

Mr. Baxter expressed no surprise at her story. He agreed that it was unlikely her servant was the woman in his morgue, considering the distance from Staines-upon-Thames to the West India Docks. "Why, it's nearly fifty miles, as the river flows!"

"Then she couldn't have fallen in near her house?" Angelina asked. "Playing on the banks with the children, for example? They might have been too frightened to say anything until it was too late."

"Quite impossible, Mrs. Moriarty, I assure you. The body would've been found far upstream." Baxter rose to trace the deep curves of the Thames on the enormous map of Middlesex County pinned behind his desk. "She might have made it down to Chertsey Meads, but no farther. The river turns back north at that point. No, my experts tell me she couldn't have gone in farther west than Limehouse."

The coroner returned to his armchair and sat back. He was somewhere past forty years old, Angelina judged, with a broad face and curly black hair. He wore his thick moustache so long it nearly covered his mouth, but his dark eyes were friendly enough, considering the nature of their call.

"Do you have a description of this servant?" he asked.

"I'm told she's a little taller than me, so about five foot eight. She has a slender build. The employer said brown eyes and skin, but that could cover a range of shades, couldn't it?"

"Death and the river would alter those in any event," Baxter said gently.

"Oh." Angelina grimaced. "She probably had a red dot painted between her eyebrows, if that would still be visible. They all seem to wear that dot. She also had two gold teeth on the right side, one up and one down." She pointed as Mrs. Reynolds had done.

"Gold teeth, you say." Baxter's eyes slid toward Watson. "Not uncommon, by any means, though that configuration is quite specific." He frowned at Watson again, then leveled a solemn gaze at Angelina.

She knew what that look meant. Her heart sank. She'd never met Ganesa, but she'd been so eager to find her a piece of her heart had been given to the woman's well-being. Now that piece was broken.

The coroner cleared his throat. "We're going to want your friend to come down to identify the body."

Angelina shook her head. "I'm not sure she'd be willing. She won't thank me for burdening her with this."

"We can compel her," Baxter said. "And surely she would want to know if she valued this servant enough to ask you to conduct a search."

Angelina couldn't explain that that had partly been an excuse to meet a theatrical idol. "I won't be able to rest without knowing." She sighed. "I'll find a way to talk her into it. Is there a particular time?"

"When you have secured her promise," Baxter said, "send a telegram to this office. We'll send you the name and location of the mortuary where the body can be viewed. Don't delay, Mrs. Moriarty. Evidence is lost with time."

Angelina refused to think about that process. "I'll see her tomorrow. With a bit of luck, we'll be here in the late afternoon." She could broach the subject after the card game. "But what about the other Indian girl? The article in the *Police News* said a second Indian woman had been found in the river."

Baxter grunted, presumably at the loose-lipped journalist. "There was another one in May."

"Was she like Ganesa? I mean, like this last one? Do you think they could be related?"

"That would not be a suitable topic to discuss with a woman." He glanced at Watson.

Angelina managed not to roll her eyes. "I'll step outside for a moment. Will that do, Mr. Baxter?"

He accepted that solution, though he must have known Watson would tell her everything on the way home. At least he preserved his own sense of propriety. She stood in the entry hall, smiling stiffly at a clerk behind a cluttered desk and watching the pendulum in the wall clock swing from side to side. Before two minutes passed, the door opened and Watson emerged.

"Mr. Baxter asked me to bid you good afternoon on his behalf. He's a very busy man."

"I should think so." Angelina had to wait until Watson hailed a cab and helped her into it to hear the words deemed too delicate for her feminine ears.

Watson respected her enough not to beat around the bush. "Both women were pregnant."

"Good lord!" They stared at one another, not quite able to absorb the implications of that discovery.

"Worse," Watson said, "they were both strangled before they went into the water. That rather changes things, doesn't it?"

Angelina wrapped her arms around herself. It had turned quite cold all of a sudden. "It does indeed, Doctor. It does indeed. This jolly little case of mine is no longer a game. It might very well be a murder investigation."

* * *

James and Peg were pouring their first cups of tea when Angelina walked into the drawing room. She pulled off her gloves and tossed them on the console table. "Pour me a cup, won't you, darling? With extra sugar? I've had the most appalling afternoon." She unpinned her hat, set it on the table, and crossed to her favorite chair, sinking into it with gratitude.

The other two exchanged glances, deciding James was the "darling" in this instance. He fixed a cup, adding an extra lump. He set it on the table next to her chair and then prepared a plate of ginger biscuits and brought that over too.

"Thank you." Angelina tilted her face up, and he obligingly bent down for a kiss. "You're an angel."

"I'm a model husband." He winked at Peg and returned to his chair. "I hear you've been to the coroner with Dr. Watson."

Angelina blew on her tea and took a tentative sip. Delicious, but a tad too hot. "I'm afraid I've found my missing servant."

"So soon?" James pretended to collapse in utter dejection. "What's my punishment to be? *La Traviata?*"

Peg grinned. "Gilbert and Sullivan, or it won't do you justice."

"Neither, darlings. The game is over. I mean, it's not a game anymore." Angelina took a swallow of tea and then told them the grisly news. The playfulness on their faces disappeared, replaced by shocked grimaces.

"Are you saying that poor girl was murdered?" Peg asked, shaking her head in disbelief.

"Yes," Angelina said, a trifle tartly. "She was strangled before she went into the water, most likely by the brute who violated her."

James's scowl deepened. "This is a horrible end to your quest, my dear, but it's rash to speculate on motives without further facts."

"What else could it be?"

"I don't know. Many things." James scratched the fringe of hair at the back of his head. That gesture seemed to stimulate his thinking.

"How about this?" Peg asked. "Say she ran away because she hated her job or her mistress or England or all of it together. She followed her nose to the docks, wanting a ship home, and was murdered by some stranger. Limehouse is no place for a woman alone, especially not after dark."

"But what about the babe?" Angelina asked. "The coroner couldn't be mistaken about that, I shouldn't think."

Peg's lips twitched. "I forgot about the babe." She screwed up her face for a moment of intense thought, then said, "All right, then. She was having it on with one of the men servants. You said they looked handsome with their loose trousers and those big turbans. What other men would she meet out there in the wilderness? Then what always happens happened. She thinks it's the end of the world and throws herself in the river. And that happens often enough too." She nodded once. Case closed.

Angelina shook her head. "She was strangled, Peg. Don't make me say it again! Besides, why would she go all the way down to Limehouse? The coroner said there's fifty miles of river between Staines and the West India Docks."

"That sounds about right." James rowed miles on the Thames for exercise, so he knew its qualities from his own experience.

Peg's jaw jutted forward in her mulish way. "Put 'em together, then. She finds out she's pregnant and decides she has to go back to India. Maybe she wants her mother. Who wouldn't? She finds her way to the docks — which ain't that hard if you can lay your hands on a little cash, so don't go throwing that one at me. And then she's murdered by a cutthroat, like I said before."

Angelina frowned at her. She chose a biscuit and nibbled at it. That scenario was not impossible.

James, predictably, weighed in on the contrary side. "That is both possible and plausible, Miss Barwick. And I must point out that we do not know for certain that the woman found by the docks is the woman you've been looking for."

"I know it. First, there are the gold teeth." Angelina held up a hand. "Yes, many people have them, but not in those precise positions." She pointed at her cheek. "One up, one down, on the same side. Besides, my intuition tells me it's Ganesa, and that's good enough for me."

James's gaze slid toward the ceiling. He had far less confidence in intuition — hers or anyone's — than she did. Never mind how many times she'd been right.

Angelina wagged her finger at both of them. "I believe that poor woman was forced by her master. That almost happened to our very own Dolly and Molly, as you may recall. It almost happened to *me* in that house."

James's face darkened. The poor man had never lost the desire to go back and pummel that scoundrel into a bloody pulp, though he managed to tamp it down most of the time.

Angelina smiled at him but held her ground. "The papers yap on and on about dangerous workplaces for men — mines and factories and whatnot. Nobody talks about how dangerous a country house can be for a maidservant."

"That's true," James said. He looked abashed on behalf of his sex, though a kinder man had never lived.

"I've heard stories," Peg said darkly. "In the servants' halls, that year we was pretending to be Americans."

Angelina suppressed a laugh. *She* had pretended to be an American. Peg had successfully pretended to be a Cockney dressmaker, a role she had played since the age of ten. "Women are terribly vulnerable, especially when the rest of the household is corrupt. But if worse comes to worst, an English servant can run away. Run home, if they have one, or disappear into the city and take up other jobs. These Indian women can't even do that."

They sipped their tea and munched their biscuits in silence for a few moments. Honoring Ganesa, perhaps. Lured or coaxed so far from her home, only to meet the worst of fates.

James broke the silence. "Well, our bets must be cancelled. They're unconscionable under the circumstances. But you did win, my dear. You found your missing servant, assuming her former mistress identifies her. I have yet to find any concrete evidence of a crime, although I know what to look for now."

Angelina waved that away. "I can't exact my penalty under these circumstances. I don't have the heart for it."

"Can you get that Mrs. Reynolds to go with you to the mortuary?" Peg asked. "She didn't seem like the steely nerved type to me."

"She must do it. It must be done. We have to know. The authorities must know, for their records, if nothing else. I'll just have to persuade her somehow."

James asked, "Do you intend to carry on afterward? You've fulfilled your obligation."

"That's true." Angelina met his worried gaze. "But I can't leave it. I must know what happened to that poor woman." She finished her tea. "There's whist tomorrow at Mrs. Oxwich's house. She's the leader of them all. Perhaps I can tease something out of her."

Although she'd never met a woman less susceptible to teasing.

* * *

That night, Angelina pulled on the thin socks she wore with her frilly flannel nightie and climbed into bed beside her husband. James had on his long-tailed nightcap with the little tassel she liked to use to tickle his chin. She plumped her pile of pillows and snuggled against his side. He rested his head on the thin, firm slab he considered best for good posture.

He kissed her nose, a sign that this would be a night of rest. Then he raised himself on one elbow. "There is one other thing, my dear, while we're showing our hands."

"Oh?" Something too private to be discussed in the drawing room?

He proceeded to tell her an astonishing story of a beautiful face in a carriage window and a reckless chase along the Embankment. The face belonged to the love of Gabriel Sandy's life, an Indian dancer named Zuri Padmani. James had made a colored sketch of the coat of arms he'd seen on the carriage door. "I'll show it to you in the morning."

"I'll keep my eyes peeled." Angelina could scarcely credit the tale. It sounded like something out of one of Mrs. Radcliffe's novels.

"I'm sure it's a coincidence," James said, always ready to pour cold water on anything the least bit fanciful. "Miss Padmani was slated to marry a wealthy businessman. They must be here on business. It's only natural the man wouldn't want his wife gawking at cabmen."

"Hmm. I believe in coincidences — the ordinary kind where you run into someone you've been thinking about lately. That's usually because you've been in places you shared, so you think of them and they're still around and so you meet."

"The other kind exists as well. It's a fallacy to assume that correlation implies causation."

"Oh, James! Not in bed!"

He chuckled.

Angelina didn't. "I don't think this is one of those, not either kind. An Indian woman went missing and turned up dead. Now here comes another Indian woman in mysterious circumstances, apparently being constrained. But coincidence or not, I don't care. We must help Sandy find her, James. He's one of our dearest friends. We'll find her, you and I, and let him decide what to do next."

ELEVEN

On Wednesday morning, Moriarty marched upstairs to ready himself for his first day of teaching in — how many years? It seemed like a lifetime. He went all the way up to his aerie, as they called it — his study-cum-laboratory at the top of the house — and filled a valise with all the spare notebooks and pencils he could find. He'd forgotten to ask if the army would supply such classroom necessities.

He remembered to tuck his magnifying glass into his pocket. He wanted a close look at a discharge record book if he could get a few minutes alone in the office. Brant had said he made his copies from the original at the barracks. If there were any erasures or altered numbers to be seen, they would appear in that book.

And if he found nothing? He had no other plan of attack.

While he grieved for the tragic end to his wife's investigation, he couldn't simply drop his own. The bets were off and the game was over, but those worthy veterans deserved answers. And no one else was even asking questions.

* * *

As promised, a private met him at the gate and led him to another part of the central building. There he found a classroom equipped with twenty desks and a large blackboard at the front. His escort assured him that the men would supply their own paper and writing instruments.

As the huge clock on the rear wall struck the hour, the door opened and men in red jackets filed into the room. They filled most of the desks, though some of them found it a tight squeeze. These were grown men with thick moustaches, not schoolboys. Moriarty reminded himself not to make any attempt to be droll. That had never gone well with his undergraduates anyway.

Once they were settled, he introduced himself. "In future, let's make an effort to be seated *on* the hour, not four minutes after, shall we?" That startled some of them. Punctuality must not have been not considered a virtue in this barracks.

"Since I don't know what you know, and I can guess some of you know more than others, we're going to begin at the very beginning. I mean no disrespect." They liked that. "I simply must know where to start, and this is the best way to find out."

Without further ado, he picked up his chalk and walked them through the numbers from one to a hundred. Everyone could count, and everyone knew that a thousand was bigger than a hundred. Only three understood that it was ten times as big. Everyone could recognize numerals written on the board, like 24 and 365. When he asked about the significance of the latter number, several faces crumpled in doubt.

One man, a lance-corporal by his single stripe, held up his hand. "That's how many days in a year."

"Correct!" Moriarty nodded at him. No beaming or "bright boys" with this group. Some of these men were older than he was.

He left the times tables for the next teacher and moved directly to the main item on his personal agenda: money. Everyone knew there were twelve pence in a shilling. Most remembered that there were twenty shillings in a pound. None but the bright lance-corporal understood that there were thus two hundred and forty pence in a pound. That astounding fact left most of the soldiers shaking their heads.

"Two hundred and forty," several of them murmured, as if trying to fix the number in their minds. One raised his hand and spoke before being granted permission. "It don't make sense, but it don't make no difference neither. They don't pay us with sacks of pennies."

"It'd be easier for you if they did." It would be easier for them if they were in France with its rational and easily computed decimal system. "Then you could divide them into seven stacks for fifty-two weeks and be sure you'd gotten your full pay."

That led him to the next topic. "Everyone knows a soldier is paid a shilling a day. It's on recruiting posters all over Great Britain." That failed to raise a single smile. Ah, well. "If you're paid a shilling a day, how many shillings do you receive on Saturday?"

The answer should have been obvious, but every man shook his head. The lance-corporal folded his arms across his barrel chest and leaned back in his too-small seat. Moriarty gestured for him to speak his mind, and he said, "We know you want us to say seven shillings, Mr. Moriarty. Which comes to" — he raised his eyes to the ceiling for a moment — "eighty-four pennies. A good-sized sack."

That got a chuckle.

"But you don't think that's right, Lance-Corporal."

"No, sir, it ain't. Not once they take their bites out of it."

"What bites?"

That got a mixture of chuckles — bitter ones — and grumbles.

The lance-corporal took it upon himself to explain. "We pay for everything around here, 'cept our meals. Used to have to pay for them too, but the reforms took that off our back. But say you want a haircut. Eleven pence, thanks very much. Or what if your uniform needs mending? Two shillings, eight pence. And that's just the start."

Another one spoke up. "Tailor, shoemaker, damage to the barracks, even if we didn't do it." He shot a dark look at some of his fellows. "Sometimes we pay for things we never saw. Like when you first sign up, they give you your kit — water bottle, ammo pouch, gaiters, and suchlike. That's all well and good 'less something's missing. Then they take it out of your pay! You say, 'But I never got one.' Supply officer says you did. And there you are on your first payday with empty pockets."

"That doesn't sound right," Moriarty said. He couldn't imagine there being much of a market for army gaiters — unless the scoundrels were selling the goods right back to the army.

Another one chirped up. "And what about the fines? Fines for being late, fines for sass, fines for not getting a haircut."

Another one called out, "Fines for not knowing something nobody never told you."

The lance-corporal summed it up. "We're lucky to end up with half of that shilling."

Moriarty Lifts the Veil

Moriarty scratched the back of his head and gave his students a rueful grin. "Well, you've made my job more complicated." He glanced at the clock. "And I see our time is up. Next time be sure to have paper and pencil, each of you. We're going to focus on sums of money. I want you all to be able to calculate what's owed you on a given day. That's a useful skill in every walk of life."

Most of them nodded their approval of his lesson plan. He was off to a good start.

He asked one of them to walk him over to the regimental office. It happened to be empty, with that special silence that suggested desertion. Perhaps Corporal Turner had gone out for lunch.

This was the opportunity he'd been hoping for. Moriarty closed the door behind him and crossed to the shelves holding the big brown record books. He chose the last one, guessing it would be the most recent, and took it down. He set it on the unused desk and opened it at random. He'd like to have time to sit down and read each entry, searching for the names of Sandy's soldiers, but for now he'd have to content himself with a quick look for signs of tampering.

He'd barely pulled out his magnifying glass before he heard the door open behind him. *Damnation!* He dropped the glass back into his pocket and turned to see Corporal Turner glaring at him with his hands on his hips.

"May I help you with something, Mr. Moriarty?"

"Ah." Moriarty had been caught red-handed. If it had been the hungover Captain Greenway, he might have offered some lame excuse, but Turner had his wits about him. He closed the book and turned full around. "I have a matter of interest here, Corporal. A problem posed by some of your recently discharged soldiers. It's a delicate matter . . ."

The corporal's face remained stony.

Moriarty tried a sheepish smile. "I'm not good at this sort of thing, as you can see. But I have a feeling you'll be on my side once you hear my story. Could I buy you lunch and tell it to you?"

Turner's eyes narrowed, then his lips quirked in that wry smile that said Moriarty had got it all wrong again. "We don't have restaurants at Odstone. How about being my guest in the enlisted men's mess? It's not fancy, but it's noisy enough for a private chat."

"That would be fine."

Turner put the book back where it belonged and ushered Moriarty outside. "We don't lock the office during regular hours so men can leave messages or pick up packages and suchlike. There's nothing of value in there, and I don't think it ever occurred to anyone that someone might sneak in to study the record books."

"Strictly speaking, I did not sneak. I merely took advantage of an opportunity." Moriarty wondered how much he should tell this man. He radiated honesty, with his open expression and his candid manner. He did, however, work for Colonel Oxwich.

The mess hall was full and absolutely deafening. How could they have any kind of conversation in this thunderstorm? But Turner found a table in a corner behind a stout pillar and shooed the original occupants away. Once they were seated, the volume dropped to a tolerable level. No one asked them what they wanted to eat. A server turned up with plates of sausages and baked beans with a ladleful of stewed greens and a chunk of plain bread. He set them down without a word and came back with two mugs of bitter beer and napkins rolled around sets of utensils.

They ate a few bites to take the edge off their hunger. Then Turner raised his eyebrows at Moriarty, inviting him to speak.

"I had the impression the other day that you're not altogether happy with the way Colonel Oxwich runs this regiment. If you'll allow me to start my story with a question . . ."

Turner nodded, his mouth full of beans.

"Have you been with this regiment long?"

Turner swallowed. "I've been with the original Sixty-Sixth since before the merger. That was three years ago, after we rotated back from India." He shook his head. "You can't imagine the paperwork. Or the confusion."

"I won't try. Was Oxwich the commanding officer then?"

"No. We had Colonel Warner. Everyone loved him. But he decided the changes made it a good time to retire." Turner drank some beer and grimaced at the taste. "Why we can't have decent beer is one of the army's greatest mysteries. Anyway, I respected the old man. He was the decent sort — strict but fair. He ran things on the straight and narrow, which is how I like it. A man knows where he stands when everyone's playing by the same rules."

Moriarty Lifts the Veil

"I agree. But Oxwich isn't like that, is he?"

"Do you know him?"

"Only by reputation. Some incidents in his past that I've been made aware of by people whom I trust." Moriarty sawed off another slice of sausage and chewed it down. Flavorful, if a little coarse. He followed it with a swallow of beer and made up his mind. Leaning closer to his host, he said, "You must not breathe a word of what I'm going to tell you, Corporal."

"I can't argue with a superior officer or disobey a direct order, but outside of that, you can trust me." Turner tapped his chest.

Moriarty pushed his half-eaten meal aside and set his elbows on the table. He made a brief tale of his encounter with three soldiers on the street in Shoreditch, summarizing their belief that their discharge papers had been tampered with.

At the end, Turner gaped at him. "I know Nate Fowler. Know him well. Incorrigible? Why, he's as sound a sergeant as we've ever had!"

"My friend said much the same thing about all three men. We found two others, presently scraping out a meagre living at the Salvation Army, who had also lost their savings."

Turner frowned. "That's not right. Not for our men."

"I suspect the discharge records have been tampered with. I think Fowler's years of service were altered, for example. A stroke here, a stroke there, and the sums come out quite differently. Those characters couldn't be so easily changed, though."

"Captain Greenway would write whatever he was told, especially if the one doing the telling was the colonel. You're assuming he's in on this tampering scheme, I take it."

"Not necessarily, though it wouldn't surprise me. He's done such things before. And it adds up to quite a handsome sum. I estimate that well over a hundred pounds was stolen from the five men I've met. Who knows how many others have suffered the same fate?"

Turner let out a low whistle. "I don't know whether to be madder that they're doing it or that nobody offered to cut me in."

Moriarty smiled. "You're an honest man, Corporal. It's obvious at a glance."

"I suppose you want half an hour or so alone with that record book."

"Half an hour would be ample. Is it possible?"

"Don't see why not. I'll keep an eye out for Sergeant Brant. He comes around on Wednesday afternoons to check my work and take whatever needs copying to the War Office. Won't be discharges today. We haven't had any all week. But I'm guessing you don't want to tell this story of yours to him. Not yet anyway."

"Not until I know for myself if the books have been altered."

Turner finished his beer. "It's part of my ration. Be damned if I let it go to waste."

Then they returned to the office. "I think you're best sitting right where you were, Mr. Moriarty. I'll scout out the reports from the last maths coach for you in case Captain Greenway comes in. Doubt he will since the colonel's out today again."

"Is he out often?"

Turner shrugged. "More out than in, let's put it that way. He has a house on Officers' Row which he finds more comfortable for meetings than the office." He took down the latest discharge book and got Moriarty set up at the desk. Then he went to his own desk and pointed at the window. "I'll see anyone coming in plenty of time."

Moriarty thanked him, drew out his magnifying glass, and set to work. He started with June, looking for Fowler's name. It took him all of five minutes to find exactly what he'd expected — the number of years of service had been altered. The work was neat, nearly invisible to the naked eye, but as clear as a billboard under the glass. As he'd imagined, the number four had been changed to one.

He flipped pages into July until he found Daniel Digby's entry and turned the glass to the *Character* column. He saw no evidence of erasure, which would look like light scraping with a penknife. It was impossible to change "Good" to "Incorrigible" by adding a few strokes, and he saw no sign that such an attempt had been made.

He stared at the words, tapping his foot, waiting for some detail to emerge. And then he had it. "Do you have a sample of Captain Greenway's handwriting?"

"Many." Turner shuffled some papers and brought him a sheet. "Any luck?"

"Oh yes." Moriarty showed him the altered numbers under the magnifying glass.

Turner drew in a sharp breath. "That's purely diabolical! I'd never have noticed it either, even if I'd gone looking, which I never would. That glass is pure genius. Whatever made you think of it?"

Moriarty would rather sit through the complete works of Gilbert and Sullivan than add to Sherlock Holmes's growing fame. "It's standard equipment for consulting detectives." He tapped his finger on the altered number. "Thirty pounds difference. But how did our forger get his hands on the money? That's the part I can't work out."

"Good question. I know how it's supposed to work. If it's a modest sum, they pay it in cash on the spot, after the discharged soldier signs out. For larger sums, the men have the option of having it sent to the post office nearest their next address. Most men choose that route. They worry about carrying a wad of cash on the train into the sorts of neighborhoods where they're likely to find lodgings."

"That makes sense," Moriarty said. He pointed at a column headed *Forwarding Address*. "This must be it."

Turner nodded. "I don't know if it's possible, but maybe this fellow has worked out a way to misrepresent himself. He knows the right man won't be calling for that money."

"I might be able to test that." Moriarty pulled out his notebook and jotted down the addresses given for Fowler and Digby — lodgings they hadn't been able to afford. "Let's have a look at these *Characters*, shall we?" He held the glass over the word *incorrigible*. "Look at how neatly these letters sit on the line. Each one occupies its proper space in a nearly perfect rhythm."

"That's Brant," Turner said. "Here's Greenway. And you're right. They're as different as chalk and cheese."

Greenway had the spiky hand of a man educated in a public school. Legible, but not in the slightest bit schoolboyish. Such niceties were disdained. You could be pounded in the yard at recess and have your pudding stolen at dinner for being such a prissy little snot-rag. Greenway's hand also betrayed a taste for drink, having a distinctive rightward drift, which he corrected at random across a single line.

"Is it a regular part of Brant's job to assign these characters?" Moriarty asked.

"Not to assign them, but Greenway never minds letting someone else do his work. But why these men? What could he have against Digby? Or Webb, for that matter?"

Moriarty shrugged and gave the corporal a minute to search his memory.

"Best I can think of," Turner said, "is that Webb or Fowler might've given the captain a bit of lip. That'd do it, right enough. He could be slipshod when he had a sore head, and Fowler liked things done right. Though I can't see Daniel Digby sassing anyone."

Greenway hadn't given Moriarty the impression of a man capable of such a devious crime. Embezzling from the officers' mess, certainly. That money would come right under his hands. But painstakingly altering records in these densely packed books?

"What about Sergeant Brant?" Moriarty asked. "He appears to be the man in charge of these records. Does anyone else even look at them?"

"I do. I write in the basics, the bits we get at enlistment. Height, weight, that sort of thing." He pointed at a third style of writing evident on the page. "But I don't do the discharge fields. That's Brant, at Greenway's direction." Turner perched on the edge of the desk. "Greenway would sign off on anything. He disdains paperwork. He likes the perks of the adjutant's office, but he doesn't care for the work. He's one of those men who's better in battle than behind a desk. These books are Brant's bailiwick."

They looked at each other, not quite able to grasp the increasingly obvious point. "He was so helpful," Moriarty said. "He acted like a man with nothing to hide."

"That's his way," Turner said. "Always happy to explain the details and walk you through a complicated calculation. Cheerful too."

"Why not, if he's pocketing an extra hundred pounds a year?"

Turner shook his head. "That's a trainload of money, all right. But Captain Greenway didn't do this. It's not his style. And I didn't do it. That leaves Sergeant Brant, whether we like it or not."

Moriarty gave him a cool look, only half in jest. "Are we sure you weren't a part of this? You and Brant working together; that's the most likely setup."

Moriarty Lifts the Veil

"I can see that." Turner shrugged sheepishly. "Unfortunately, I've nothing to offer in my defense except my honest face."

"Brant has an honest face too, or so I thought." Moriarty wished his wife were here. She could read faces as easily as he read the *Daily News*. His every intuition told him to trust the man before him, who was now screwing up his face and staring at the ceiling in his effort to come up with some proof of his innocence.

Then Turner snapped his fingers. "I can show you my bank book. That'll prove I'm not taking in an extra hundred pounds a year."

Moriarty smiled at his naiveté. Any good embezzler would have two sets of bank books from different banks. "Don't bother. We've been examining these altered entries together now for what? Half an hour? During which time you've made no effort to mislead me or divert me to the obvious Captain Greenway. Instead, you've defended him, in a way. I'm going to trust you until further notice."

Turner grinned from ear to ear. "That's a relief because I don't have anything else. What do we do now, Mr. Moriarty?"

"I'm not sure." That was the pertinent question, wasn't it? He steepled his fingers, tapping the tips together. "We can prove that someone altered these books, to the detriment of soldiers whom we can produce in court — I think." That thought gave him pause. "I should consult with my friend, the former captain, before moving forward. In the meantime, let's keep this between ourselves. Keep an eye on these books, but otherwise carry on as usual."

"Will do. We sure don't want Brant to twig we're on to him. He takes that book to the War Office whenever there's enough new discharges to copy. He could toss it in the river if he wanted to and call it an accident."

"That would be a disaster." Moriarty hadn't considered that possibility. He hadn't considered any kind of consequences, not truly believing in the crime until he'd seen the proof with his own eyes. But Brant had probably realized his scheme had been discovered the moment a visitor turned up with an implausibly fine-tuned statistical study. What were the odds? He would doubtless remove these damning volumes the next time he visited the office at the barracks.

Moriarty sank into his chair, weighed down by the realization that he'd tipped his hand with his very first move.

TWELVE

Balmer Park stood as far above Mrs. Payne's crumbling manor as the Moriartys' terrace on Bellenden Crescent stood above the cheap East End boardinghouses Angelina had grown up in. The grand house presented a vast facade of yellow stone with four tall columns holding up a triangular Grecian whatsit in the center.

It was meant to look imposing, and it achieved its goal. Plain, dull, pompous . . . it did a good job of representing its residents at least. Angelina didn't like it. If James ever talked her into buying a country house, she wanted one of those rambling, red-brick confections with the round towers and the forest of chimneys. Something with charm — and perhaps a ghost or two.

A footman in a turban helped her from the cab and ushered her across a large entry hall with a black-and-white-tiled floor and a smallish chandelier. They clacked on through another hall built to accommodate a grand staircase with a beautiful iron railing. Angelina followed the man's supremely erect back through an octagonal room with a *trompe l'oeil* sky painted on the ceiling. There he turned right, opened a door, and waited for her to pass through.

This room was a humble rectangle, its walls painted a rich cherry red. An ornate chandelier hung unlit in the center. Vast paintings in the Renaissance style hung about the walls along with an enormous gilt mirror. One must always be able to check one's form at a social event, *doncher know*?

The sofas had been pushed against the walls to make room for three tables covered in green baize. Most of the women had arrived already. They stood near the rear windows with glasses in their hands. Gin and tonic for the old India hands, no doubt. Angelina accepted a drink and let herself be introduced to the women she hadn't met yet. Soon Mrs. Oxwich clapped her hands and summoned them to the tables.

Each place was marked by a small card. Angelina found hers at the same table as Mrs. Oxwich, Lady Chetwood, and Mrs. Reynolds. She breathed a sigh of relief. She hadn't been to many card parties, preferring outdoor games or dancing, and it hadn't occurred to her she might be stuck all afternoon with a group of women who knew nothing about missing servants.

She'd been partnered with Mrs. Oxwich. She'd have to be in top form to avoid earning the woman's contempt. No one ever confided in a person they disdained. Thank goodness for James's patient lessons in the game!

Silent Indian women replaced their watery drinks with fresh ones and put dishes of salted nutmeats on the table. Mrs. Oxwich picked up the deck of cards and shuffled them expertly. She dealt the first hand and turned over the last card — the nine of clubs. "Clubs are trump," she announced. "We play for a penny a point, Mrs. Lovington. I hope you find that agreeable."

"Certainly."

And the game began. Angelina took the first trick with a five of clubs, earning a tiny smile from her partner. Mrs. Oxwich held her gaze a tad longer than necessary, then lowered her eyelids in a slow, catlike blink.

A signal, obviously, but what could it mean? Angelina guessed that one blink meant the lowest suit, which must be diamonds since clubs were trump. So she led with her second-best diamond, an eight. That earned a catlike smile. The colonel's wife took the trick.

So cheating was the name of this game, eh? Angelina was not surprised. The men at the garden party had played croquet as if the Afghan War depended on it. Why shouldn't their wives play whist with the same competitive zeal?

Lady Chetwood and Mrs. Reynolds presented little challenge. They gossiped nonstop about the polo players and their current *affaires de coeur*, a topic on which they were well informed. They threw down cards almost — but not quite — at random. Apparently, the real goal of the game was letting Mrs. Oxwich win. The falseness in no way diminished her pleasure in the victory. She gave her shoulders a little shimmy every time she took a trick.

When the game ended — all points to the Oxwich-Lovington team — servants brought more drinks. Angelina let them replace hers, though she'd barely touched it. She only had to pretend to keep up until the others got too sozzled to notice. Which wouldn't be long at the rate they were going.

Mrs. Oxwich totted up the scores with a gold pencil. Angelina turned to Lady Chetwood and said, "These Indian servants are simply marvelous. I wish I had one."

"Why only one?" Lady Chetwood let loose a peal of laughter. "They're cheap at the price."

That won her a frown from Mrs. Oxwich. Too crass? But servants who spoke no English wouldn't be able to ask for as much as a native, would they?

Angelina had a flash of inspiration. Perhaps the best way to get time alone with one of the Indians for a quiet conversation was to bring one home. Sandy could come over and translate. She could learn how they came to England and what they thought their prospects were. If they gossiped as much below stairs as English servants, she might learn everything she wanted to know in one conversation.

She'd have to persuade one of the memsahibs to lend her a housemaid for a time. In their present condition, that shouldn't be too hard.

"But *honestly*," Angelina said, leaning forward with a touch of wobble, "I'm in the most *terrible* bind. My two housemaids are determined to leave at the end of the month, and I can't find *anyone* to replace them. They hated the city, so they never went out, which I found to be a great advantage. They're always available to fetch this or take that away. I've been *haunting* the servants' registries with absolutely no luck. Some of those women quite terrify me, to be perfectly candid. They have such *strict* ideas, but my household is rather irregular, as you can imagine. The life of an actress, you understand. I simply *must* have a flexible staff."

"No one is more flexible than our Indian girls," Lady Chetwood said, slurring her words a bit. "You train them to suit yourself. They're here to work, and they're grateful for a warm bed and three meals a day."

"That's more than they'd get back home," Mrs. Oxwich added. "We rescue them from lives of desperate poverty."

"Desperate," Mrs. Reynolds echoed in a near-whisper. She'd drunk so much her cheeks were flushed. "Some of them are quite nice as well."

"I'm convinced," Angelina said. "But I can't go all the way to India. Don't any of you have one to spare? A little one, perhaps?" She held her thumb and forefinger about an inch apart and grinned like an idiot.

Two of them laughed. Mrs. Oxwich managed a smile, and her dark eyes took on an interested gleam. "I may be able to help you with that, Mrs. Lovington. Let me make a few inquiries on your behalf."

* * *

The party broke up around three. There was still time to visit the mortuary if they didn't dawdle. The women went out to the portico to wait for their pony traps, still chattering at full speed. Angelina stuck close behind Mrs. Reynolds during the exodus. Now she moved in beside her, taking her arm to ask in a worried tone, "Is it possible to order a cab, do you think? I would've done it earlier, but I wasn't sure how long we'd be here."

"Let me offer you a lift," Mrs. Reynolds answered, on cue. Angelina pretended to be overwhelmed with her kindness.

One problem sorted.

The carriage arrived, and they got in. Mrs. Reynolds sank into the cushions with a sigh. "Could there be anything duller than whist? And why must we always drink so much?"

"They keep bringing fresh glasses," Angelina said. "I started letting them go three-quarters full."

"Wise woman." Mrs. Reynolds closed her eyes. "Forgive me if I fall asleep."

"Not quite yet, if you don't mind." Angelina put a hint of warning in her voice. "There's something you must know."

"What is it?" Mrs. Reynolds opened her eyes again.

"I've found your missing ayah, I think. Ganesa."

Mrs. Reynolds sat up straight, all trace of sleepiness gone. "You sound so ominous. Where is she? At Chetwood House? That's where all the pretty ones —" She pressed her lips together.

Pretty ones *what?* "Somehow, no one knows how, she ended up at the West India Docks."

"What do you mean 'ended up'?"

Angelina leaned forward, in spite of the rocking coach, and grasped both of the other woman's hands. "It's bad news, I'm afraid. She's dead."

"Dead? How?" Mrs. Reynolds pulled her hands free. "Are you sure it's her?"

"Almost. The description you gave me matches the coroner's."

"Coroner! What possessed you to look there?"

Angelina told her about spotting the notice in the newspaper. "I had the sinking feeling it might be her, so I asked a friend to go with me."

"How on earth could Ganesa find her way down to the docks?"

"I don't know," Angelina said, "though I mean to find out."

"Is that enough to identify a person?" Mrs. Reynolds asked. "Two gold teeth? There must be legions of Indian women in London."

Angelina caught her gaze and held it. "That's the next thing. The coroner wants you to come down and identify her. I know it's a terrible thing to ask, but there really is no one else. I'll be right there with you every minute."

Mrs. Reynolds rolled her eyes. "I'm an army wife, Miss Lovington. I've seen far worse things than a dead servant. Bodies float down the Ganges River all the time, naked, as often as not. It's horrible, but you get used to it in a horrible way. And soldiers come back from skirmishes covered in blood with limbs shredded by bullets or swords. Ghastly, but you get used to that too."

"Ugh." Angelina shuddered. "You're a braver woman than I am. I'll go with you anyway."

"I suppose you want me to go now, don't you?" Mrs. Reynolds stared out the window. "I'm longing for a nap. But my father always said, 'Do the hard things first.' Where is this place?"

"It's called the Montague Street Mortuary. I'll send a telegram from Staines to let them know we're coming. Then let's sit in the dining car and have a nice strong cup of tea. How does that sound?"

"Tea would be marvelous."

***

The journey took two hours, but they were much restored by tea with bread-and-butter sandwiches by the time they reached Liverpool Street Station. A short cab ride brought them to the mortuary. A police constable met them at the door and escorted them down a long whitewashed corridor reeking of carbolic soap.

They reached a cold stone room. Both women avoided looking at the bodies shrouded on tables placed in neat rows. A clerk from the coroner's office came in after them, his profession declared by his black suit and top hat. He carried a small black valise.

"I'm here to note the official identification or lack of same for the record." He smiled at them as if expecting an answer.

"Thank you," Angelina said, unable to imagine what else he might want.

An orderly led them to a table and turned down the top of the sheet. Mrs. Reynolds gasped and turned away. "That's her. That's my servant Ganesa."

"Very good," the clerk said in a soothing tone. "And her surname?"

"If she had one, I never knew it." Mrs. Reynolds took a step away.

The clerk went over to an empty table near the door and opened his valise. He drew out two long sheets of paper — printed forms with blank spaces here and there. He took a fountain pen from his pocket and filled in some of the blanks. Then he asked Mrs. Reynolds for her full name, along with that of her husband and their place of residence.

"Where shall we send the body for burial?" he asked, his pen poised above the form.

"Why ask me?" Mrs. Reynolds shot an aggrieved look at Angelina. She'd done her duty and now seemed anxious to distance herself from the whole affair. She hadn't even asked how Ganesa died. Granted, the corpse was hard to look at, but she had bragged about her toughness.

Angelina was just a bystander here. It didn't seem her place to bring up the cause of death if neither the coroner's clerk nor the orderly saw fit to do so.

The clerk politely but firmly led Mrs. Reynolds to the recognition that Ganesa's burial expenses were her responsibility. They agreed that the body should be sent to Ripley Park as soon as possible.

"I don't know *what* we'll do with it," Mrs. Reynolds muttered at Angelina. "We can hardly put her with the family. But there must be a graveyard at Staines somewhere."

While the clerk finished up his form, the constable took his turn. "We'll be wanting to ask a few questions, Mrs. Reynolds. You and your husband and the other servants. Someone will come out to see you in the next day or two. We'll want to ask who saw her last and where — that sort of thing."

Mrs. Reynolds tilted her chin in order to look down her nose at the humble policeman. "By all means, Constable. Ask whatever you like. Ask everyone. We're a closely-knit community, the officers and families of the Middlesex Regiment. If you mean to question servants, you'll want to visit some of the other households. I suggest you start with our commander, Colonel Samuel Oxwich. He'll want to be apprised of any police intrusions, at any rate."

The poor constable swallowed hard, his Adam's apple bobbing. His superiors wouldn't like poking their noses into the domestic affairs of senior army officers, half of whom probably had titles. Especially when the cause was a foreign pauper with neither name nor family.

Nothing would be done, Angelina predicted. Nothing official anyway. She sent a solemn vow toward the pitiful, shrouded figure. She would find out what happened to Ganesa. She'd find a last name to write on the poor woman's headstone and bring an armful of flowers to place upon the grave.

THIRTEEN

Moriarty spent the better part of Thursday trying to disprove the conclusion he'd reached with Corporal Turner at the barracks. Hours of searching through newspaper archives at the British Museum yielded one reference to a man named Jeremy Brant, though he must have been much older than the sergeant. The paper was dated 1865 — twenty-three years ago. His Jeremy Brant couldn't be much past thirty.

The article reported an inquest into an accident in Berkshire in which a man had been killed. Jeremy Brant, gardener at a nearby estate, had been among the witnesses. Sergeant Brant might be the son of this gardener. It would put him in the right social class for a common soldier. Alas, it shed no light on the man's potential for criminal activities.

Angelina was in the same state of suspended activity today. They had embarked on their respective investigations for a lark — a way to fill the time until the renovations at the Galaxy were completed. She'd gone shopping with Peg on Oxford Street. They would no doubt subject the officers' wives to the same scrutiny they gave the trinkets and bolts of cloth.

Moriarty had a confidante as well — Gabriel Sandy. In a way, Sandy was also a proxy client, standing in for his men like the good officer he once had been. It was high time for a report.

As he walked down the broad stairs in front of the British Museum, Moriarty checked his pocket watch. "Great Scott! Four o'clock already?" He popped into the nearest telegraph office and sent a wire to Sandy arranging a meeting at the Bear and Staff. The cabman often had his tea there before the start of his regular shift of work.

Moriarty walked the short distance to Leicester Square and laid claim to a quiet table. The Bear and Staff was a classic English public house — warm, dimly lit, and redolent of fried foods and fermented drinks. He ordered a pint of pale cask ale and drank a quarter of it down thirstily. Studying old newspapers was dusty work.

The barmaid brought him a bowl of roasted nuts, which he munched as he tried to reconcile the bright young officer he'd met at the War Office with a man capable of ruining so many lives. He must be desperate for money. Or perhaps Oxwich made him do it, having some dark means of compulsion.

"Here you are." Sandy suddenly loomed over the table. He shed his overcoat and hat and took the opposite chair. "You're lost in thought. Good news or bad?"

"Both. More bad than good." Moriarty waited until his friend was supplied with ale and a plate of fish and chips. Sandy shook malt vinegar liberally over his food and listened to a full account of the alterations in the discharge book, the comparison of handwriting samples provided by Corporal Turner, and the inevitable conclusion that Sergeant Brant was responsible for throwing Sandy's soldiers into poverty.

"You liked him, didn't you?" Sandy said. "I remember you being pleased about finding such a willing ally. Doesn't it seem odd that he would be so willing? He could easily have said he was too busy or claimed his superiors wouldn't allow him to take the time. That's one thing about the army — there's always someone above or below you to blame things on."

"That would have been the end of the line for me, it's true. I had no other path to pursue. But Brant seemed eager to help me. Volunteering to show me the record room, for example. I didn't ask for that. And why recommend me for the teaching job? He wrote a letter introducing me to Corporal Turner. He acted like a man with nothing to hide."

"Are you certain he's responsible?"

Moriarty shrugged. "Not at all. But the handwriting is fairly conclusive. And he is the only one with opportunity, apart from Corporal Turner." He took a thoughtful drink of ale. "Who is also eager to assist, come to think of it." He shook himself. "I can't suspect them both."

"Maybe they're both sick and tired of being under Oxwich's thumb. They could be in it together, laughing behind their hands — all the way to the bank."

The two men traded grim looks.

Moriarty said, "You could be right. Or maybe Brant wants to be caught. He might be under pressure from Oxwich. My interference would give him an excuse to speak out."

Sandy looked skeptical. "Or he's the kind of soulless, evil rotter who loves being clever, thinks of money as proof of his cleverness, and doesn't care who he hurts."

"Or that." Moriarty blew out a sigh. "Either way, what should we do next? I can demonstrate that the record book has been altered. Corporal Turner can explain how those books are handled and by whom. It's a safe bet that Sergeant Fowler and the other injured soldiers would testify. But for that, we have to bring a case to court. Do we have enough?"

"A few scratched-out spaces in a record book with a thousand entries." Sandy grunted, then mashed his peas to make them easier to fork up. "It isn't much."

"I'd like to know how Brant gets his hands on the money. Turner told me that most men have their deferred pay sent to the post office nearest their future lodgings. Safer than traveling through the city with a roll of bills. The army hopes they'll deposit it straight into a savings account at the post office."

"That's the whole point of the deferred pay program. What can you do?"

Moriarty frowned, tapping a finger on the table. "I wish I had more data. I need a lot more time with that book — hours, not minutes. I did write down a few addresses." He snapped his fingers. "And of course your men know what they put down. I can use my city directory and my big map to identify the nearest post offices."

"That's a start," Sandy said. "Then what?"

"If I could watch them, day and night . . ." Moriarty broke off with a frustrated growl.

"Sounds like a job for the police," Sandy said. "You'd have to start an official investigation. Besides, the army investigates its own crimes. Proper procedure is to lodge a complaint with the suspected offender's commanding officer."

"Who commands a colonel? A general?"

Sandy nodded. "I'm not sure who's in command of Middlesex now, but he won't thank you for making accusations against his officers. He might refuse to listen to you, especially if he's a crony of Oxwich's. You'd be better off going straight to the adjutant general. He's the one who would conduct the investigation in any event."

"Where will I find him?"

"At the War Office, I should think. But the first question he'll ask is why you didn't discuss it with his CO first."

Moriarty glowered at his friend. "You've come full circle."

Sandy chuckled. "That's the army for you." He put his knife and fork on his empty plate and pushed it away. He took a long drink of ale, setting the mug down with a sigh of satisfaction. Then he laid his palm flat on the table and gave Moriarty a challenging look. "Let's do it. Let's go beard the old villain in his den. Let's show Oxwich that book and rub his crooked nose in it."

"I suppose we must if we want to move forward." Moriarty grinned at Sandy's spirit. "The worst he can do is throw us out, and then we'll be within our rights to go over his head. But you shouldn't go. You're liable to be recognized."

"I intend to be recognized. I'm through skulking. I've spent seven years running and hiding. But seeing Zuri makes me think it's time to wipe the old slate clean and lay claim to my life again. I want that bastard to see me, see what I've made of myself. If I were Greenway's kind, I'd be rotting away in a seedy opium den in Rangoon. Oxwich could boot me out of the army, but he couldn't do me down." Sandy pointed his thumb at his chest. "I'm here. I'm thriving. And I want that evil son of a bitch to know it."

* * *

When he got home, Moriarty sent a telegram to Corporal Turner asking when Colonel Oxwich would be in his office. The answer came swiftly back: on Friday afternoon. Moriarty sent a note to Sandy's flat, knowing he'd see it in the morning when he came in from work. He suggested they meet at the gate to Odstone Barracks at one o'clock. He had his class at ten.

Moriarty Lifts the Veil

Then he set the problem aside to enjoy a peaceful dinner with his wife. They talked about the theater renovations, Viola's children, and the crowds on Oxford Street — anything but cast-off soldiers and murdered Indian servants.

The next morning, Moriarty went out to the barracks to teach his class as if nothing had changed. He stopped by the office to make sure Corporal Turner still had possession of that vital record book.

"I locked it in the bottom drawer of Captain Greenway's desk." The corporal dangled a small silver key, grinning wickedly. "Not the one with the bottle in it — the other one. Nothing in there but pencil stubs."

"Clever man. I should warn you, an old friend is stopping by this afternoon. The one I mentioned before — the former captain. We plan to have a few words with your colonel about the crimes going on under his nose. My friend tells me it's the necessary first step in an official investigation. You might want to make yourself scarce."

"That's bold! But I'll stay and watch your backs. I mean to hold on to that book until I can hand it straight to the adjutant general. Could be me next, you know, tossed out on my ear with 'incorrigible' on my character and not a penny to my name."

Today's lessons were more difficult than Moriarty had anticipated. He'd meant to start them on calculating their deferred pay. But every man he chose had some complicated exception. Good conduct pay, for example, for which an enlisted man was eligible after five years. Then he could earn another bonus five years later.

As he erased his first calculation to begin again, he wondered if any of the discharged men with altered characters had been granted good conduct badges. That might help prove that the record book was wrong.

He had lunch by himself in the mess, letting the noise drown out his thoughts. There was nothing left to plan or prepare.

He didn't recognize Sandy when the cabman first came through the gate. He'd shaved off that thick scruff of beard and trimmed his moustache, waxing it into narrow points. He'd had his hair cut too. His chin was noticeably paler than the rest of his face, but he looked like a member of the officer class.

"Great Scott, man!" Moriarty cried. "You must've left quite a pile on the barber's floor."

"If there were a market for ginger hair, they'd be rich." Sandy shook his hand more heartily than usual. Then he stood a moment to look about the barracks with the air of a man returning to a long-abandoned place he had both loved and hated. Moriarty could imagine looking around in just that way if he ever went back to the University of Durham. He'd been happy there . . . until the end.

Several heads turned as they crossed the yard. A man in a blue officer's uniform stared openly. "Gabriel Sandy?" He sounded like he'd seen a ghost.

His companion gave him an elbow. "Impossible. He's long lost. Besides, this is the last place he'd turn up, with old Oxwich sitting in the big chair."

The first man shook his head as if clearing his vision, and they walked on.

Sandy gave a wry smile. "Not quite forgotten, then."

Corporal Turner greeted Sandy with a nod, then handed Moriarty the book. "He's in his office. Captain Greenway's in there, but go on ahead." He pointed toward the door at the rear of the office.

Moriarty caught Sandy's gaze. "Ready?"

"Never been readier."

Moriarty led the way. He knocked once and opened the door without waiting for a response, revealing a man past the middle years with a weak chin and a salt-and-pepper moustache sitting at the desk. The epaulettes on his blue uniform bore two gold diamonds beneath a red crown. Captain Greenway, with his habitual dark circles and disgruntled air, stood a couple of feet away.

Both men scowled at Moriarty as he strode into the room. Greenway sputtered, "I say, you can't just —" But his words were lost under Oxwich's outraged cry as his eyes lit on Sandy.

"You!" he roared.

"Me," Sandy replied, a wry smile quirking his lips.

"I thought you were dead."

"You were wrong."

"What do you want?"

Moriarty held up the discharge book. "We're here to apprise you of ongoing acts of malfeasance in the disbursement of deferred pay to discharged soldiers."

Moriarty Lifts the Veil

Greenway frowned and blinked rapidly. They'd lost him already. "Discharged soldiers?"

Oxwich shot him a dark look. "Get out, Greenway." He tilted his head toward the door. "Now."

Greenway tucked his chin, offended, but he turned on his heel and left without another word.

"Where'd you get that book?" Oxwich demanded.

Moriarty almost laughed out loud at the stupidity of the question. "Here, of course. It normally reposes on a shelf in the outer office."

"I mean, what are you doing with it? What do you know about deferred pay?" He should have looked imposing, with his brass buttons and the portrait of the second Duke of Cambridge hanging behind him. Instead, his pinched nose and twitching moustache made him look like a cornered rat. His black eyes darted nervously from one opponent to the other. He'd betrayed his guilty knowledge from the moment he ordered Greenway from the room, and every question only dug the hole deeper.

"We know quite a bit," Sandy said. Anger crisped his accent, bringing out the aristocratic tones of his upbringing. "We bumped into my old batman the other day, along with some other good fellows. They're living on the streets, Oxwich, hand to mouth, thanks to that book." He jabbed a finger toward the brown volume. "Daniel Digby, the most dutiful man in Her Majesty's service, was discharged, wrongly, with ignominy. He can barely stand the shame of it. He also lost fourteen years of deferred pay." He strode forward to stab his finger onto the mahogany desk. "I mean to get it back for him."

Oxwich glared at the finger as if it were a knife. Then his gaze slid toward Moriarty. "You're that new maths coach. You can't know anything."

Moriarty smiled at him as if he were a dim student who'd finally got one right. "That would suggest that I know a fair bit about mathematics. But not much is needed other than to note the disparity between pay owed and pay received."

"You can't prove anything." Oxwich sat back and crossed his arms.

Now Sandy did laugh out loud. "Spoken like a guilty man. You don't know my friend, Professor Moriarty. He never stops digging until he finds the truth."

"I've been studying this book," Moriarty said in a conversational tone. "To the naked eye, it seems well enough." He pulled his magnifying glass from his pocket. "But with this, I found clear evidence of tampering. Years of service have been altered — another way to reduce a soldier's discharge pay. Worse, characters have been altered to turn worthy men like Daniel Digby into scoundrels."

"No one will hire them," Sandy said. "To say nothing of their pride."

"That's Greenway's job," Oxwich said. "I've nothing to do with the characters." His face took on a crafty look. "Are you telling me Captain Greenway's been mucking about with those records?"

Too late for that.

"No," Moriarty said. "We're suggesting Sergeant Brant has been doing it. Allow me to show you a few examples." He walked over to stand beside the desk and laid the book where the colonel could see it. He turned to the page he'd marked with a slip of paper and held the glass over one of the rows. "Do you see the scraped patch beneath the number forty-seven? You can see how the four has been changed to a one. And note the differences in handwriting in the *Character* field from one row to the next." He pointed out features of the inked characters that betrayed the work of two different hands. "It's rather reckless," he observed, more to himself than the others. "I have many examples and am confident I'll find more. This is evidence that will hold up in a court of law."

Oxwich shoved the book away. "It's nothing to do with me."

"It's your regiment," Sandy said. "You're in charge. Crimes committed on your watch are your responsibility."

"Nonsense. There are a thousand men in this regiment. I can't be held accountable for every slip and stumble." Oxwich puffed dismissively at the book. "Looks more like a prank to me. Someone wants to put egg on Greenway's face. It's a bad turn for the poor sod who's leaving, but it's hardly a crime. Besides, none of those men are innocent. Your batman earned his character, one way or another."

"A prank?" Moriarty could hardly keep from shaking some sense into the old fool. "By my calculations, the stolen pay adds up to over two hundred pounds a year."

"Two hundred!" Oxwich shouted. "By God, I'll —" He snapped his lips closed too late. His face displayed shock, not indignation. He'd been cheated by the wily Sergeant Brant.

FOURTEEN

When Angelina went down to the dining room for lunch — with Peg again, instead of her husband, who was out bearding a lion in his den — she found a letter on a silver salver waiting for her. She showed it to Peg. "It's postmarked Staines."

"Looks like you're back on the job, then, ducky."

Angelina slit the top of the envelope with the silver knife Rolly had thoughtfully provided. "I just hope it's not an invitation to another whist game. Once is enough for me."

It wasn't. It was a summons — politely phrased but unmistakable — from the Honorable Mrs. Oxwich. She believed she could satisfy Angelina's request this afternoon at two o'clock, if she would undertake another journey to Balmer Park.

Angelina left her ham with melon slices waiting while she got up and went to the writing table in the morning room to pen a response. She applied the stamp with a firm thumb, went back to the dining room, and rang for Rolly. "Pop this down to the postbox, won't you?"

She read the short letter from Mrs. Oxwich to Peg, who asked, "What's this request of yours?"

"I believe she means to give me one of her servants."

"It'll be the worst one," Peg warned.

"I don't care." Angelina grinned as she picked up her knife and fork. "We've got the daily char to do the actual work now. Once we get this woman home, we'll find a way to talk to her. And then we'll get to the bottom of this Indian business once and for all."

Peg regarded her with a knowing eye. "Just be sure you remember you're hiring a maidservant, not adopting an orphan child. Don't forget to haggle."

* * *

The journey to Staines seemed to grow shorter every time she made it. The footman in Hindu dress met her cab and led her to a room at the front of the house — another expensively appointed parlor, this one decorated in buttery yellow and snowy white. No fires had been lit on this warm afternoon, and the tall windows filled the room with a clear light. The footman directed her to a group of silk-upholstered sofas.

Angelina sat at the end of one of them with her hands in her lap, tapping her thumbs together while admiring the plaster ornamentation on the ceiling. After a minute or two, Mrs. Oxwich appeared, followed by two Indian women in their native garb. The first one was tall and stunningly beautiful. She had a perfect oval face with wide almond-shaped eyes ringed with thick lashes. Her warm olive skin showed no wrinkles, but something about her poise made Angelina put her in her mid-twenties.

The second one couldn't be a day over fourteen. Shorter and darker than her companion, her cheeks still held a childish plumpness, though her uptilted eyes and shapely lips promised better looks in the future. Angelina blinked twice as she recognized her. This was the girl who'd been weeping in the dining room at the garden party. She didn't look weepy today. Those rosy lips were pressed tightly together, and the glittering black eyes held a mulish glare.

Not perhaps the *best* expression for a well-trained maidservant.

Angelina rose and gave Mrs. Oxwich's extended hand a weak squeeze. She painted a smile of delight on her face. "I *knew* this must be what your note was about! You're a lifesaver, Mrs. Oxwich, you really are. I hadn't expected two, but I'll confess we could use them. So long as they don't mind sharing a room?"

"Why would they mind?" Mrs. Oxwich sat on the sofa. "But Zuri" — she gestured at the tall one — "is only here to translate."

Zuri? Could this be Sandy's long-lost love? If so, she had not married that wealthy merchant. Far from it. Angelina determined to find a way to talk to her.

But this was not the time. She resumed her seat at the other end of the sofa. The Indians remained standing, backs straight, hands folded passively.

Mrs. Oxwich gestured at the younger one. "Harini will be going home with you today. I'm afraid her English is still limited, but she's quite bright. In a household with no one to help her, she'll soon get the knack."

No one to help her? That sounded dire. Rolly would learn Hindi before it came to that. Angelina wondered if the child spoke any French.

Mrs. Oxwich addressed Harini now, speaking slowly, as if to an idiot. "You're going home with this memsahib. Her name is Mrs. Lovington. She is very, very nice. She lives in a fine house in London, in a very respectable neighborhood."

Zuri translated. Her voice was mellow, and the language had a pleasing lilt.

"You will live in Memsahib's house from now on," Mrs. Oxwich continued. "You will keep it clean and tidy, just as I taught you. Very clean. In exchange, you will be well treated and given your bread and board."

Harini faced Mrs. Oxwich but kept her gaze turned downward. Her posture showed compliance, but her eyes flashed as she listened to Zuri's murmured translation. Anger? Resistance? Was she upset to be leaving this house and the other Indians?

Angelina's intuition told her there was more to it than that. She wouldn't hire an English woman who showed signs of a rebellious temperament, but she wasn't actually hiring a maidservant. She just wanted to get the girl into her house, find someone to translate for her, and find out what the devil was going on out here. They'd work out what to do with her after that together.

Mrs. Oxwich said, "Do you have any questions for Harini, Mrs. Lovington? Now would be the time for anything the least complex."

"Complex?" Angelina tittered, stalling.

Where do you come from? How did you end up here? Have you been mistreated? Have any of the men bothered you? None of the questions she wanted to ask could be uttered here.

She smiled with as much warmth as she could muster at the sulky child. "We'll get to know each other at home, won't we, Harini? I think you'll like it there."

She received a cool look in response. This girl was no servant; not unless the lower classes in India were very different from those in other countries. Who was she?

Angelina wanted to speak to Zuri but couldn't think of any excuse to draw the woman aside. So she fell back on a reliable ploy — playing the flibbertigibbet. It confused people or annoyed them. Either way, it put them off their guard.

She batted her eyes at Zuri. "You're a pretty one, aren't you? And such a clever translator. I can tell. I know someone who speaks your language, as it happens. *Such* a lovely sound, isn't it? Almost like music. He was a captain somewhere or other. Cavalry, I think. He loves horses, I know that much. His name is Gabriel Sandy. He lived in India for simply years. Did you know him?"

Zuri's eyes widened in recognition. Then her gaze flicked toward Mrs. Oxwich, and Angelina remembered too late that Sandy's name would be familiar to the colonel's wife as well. *Blast!* But she had to soldier on.

She answered her own question with a little bark of laughter. "Of course not! How could you? Silly me. India is *enormous*, they say."

Zuri smiled politely, then said something in Hindi to the other girl that took rather longer than that fatuous remark. Harini puffed out a short, high-pitched note of disdain. She had a nerve, this one! Mrs. Oxwich glared at her repressively. In that moment of distraction, Zuri gave Angelina one clear nod and mouthed the words, *Yes, Gabriel.*

Angelina trilled a laugh. "You really *must* come and visit us at Bellenden Crescent in South Kensington to see how your friend has settled in. We're at Number Twenty-Eight. Our servants' hall is very pleasant, and we have a French cook. He makes the most delicious curried eggs. That's Indian, isn't it? You could have tea. Indians drink tea, don't they?"

"Thank you, Memsahib." Zuri folded her long hands together and bowed her head. "You are most kind. Perhaps one day you will come to Chetwood House. My memsahib has a very fine garden; you will wish to see."

"I *adore* gardens! I'll make a point of it." Angelina smiled so broadly she nearly strained a muscle in her cheek. "In fact, I'll be

Moriarty Lifts the Veil

there Saturday next with my husband for the party. I'm told the charades are great fun."

"Yes, Memsahib," Zuri said. "All the sahibs and memsahibs enjoy them."

Mrs. Oxwich eyed them both with impatience. "That's settled, then, isn't it? You girls may leave us now. Go up and fetch Harini's bag." She clapped her hands sharply.

"Yes, Memsahib," Zuri answered for them both. They bowed to Angelina and then to Mrs. Oxwich, then filed silently from the room.

"What lovely creatures!" Angelina said. "That little one will be a delightful addition to our home. I can't wait to train her to serve canapes at parties. I'll be the envy of all my friends!"

"I'm glad you think so." Mrs. Oxwich shifted toward Angelina and folded her fingers. "If you're satisfied with the offering, then it's time to discuss the terms."

"Oh! *Terms.* Yes." Angelina turned toward her a trifle and folded her fingers together too. "I've been paying my housemaids sixteen pounds per annum each — with livery, bed, and board, of course."

Mrs. Oxwich nodded. "That is the usual rate for a maid of all work. Now consider paying that princely sum every year for ten years. You've spent one hundred and sixty pounds just to have your beds made and your fireplaces cleaned."

Angelina wondered where this was going. "That's a great deal of money."

"Harini is young and healthy. She has no distractions; nothing to draw her away. No family, no friends, no connections of any kind. She will remain in your house, becoming ever more attuned to your daily needs, for the whole of her working life. That could be twenty years or even thirty."

"Oh my stars! I never thought of it that way." The poor creature! Most housemaids worked until they met a beau and married. They used their saved-up salaries to lease a tea shop or enter a trade. Few of these Indian women would ever find their way into that cozy corner of British life.

Mrs. Oxwich leaned forward, pressing her point. "Assuming you never raise her wages, which you would have no reason to do, you would be out nearly five hundred pounds by the time she retired."

"Five hundred pounds!" Angelina exclaimed. "Heavens above! If she saved it all, she could retire in splendor."

"They're never very sensible about money." Mrs. Oxwich's lip curled. "Think what your husband could do with that amount by investing it."

"James is *very* clever about money." Angelina simpered like an idiot, although that was nothing but the truth.

"I thought he might be, having bought himself a theater on Leicester Square." Mrs. Oxwich smiled in a way that made Angelina feel like a small bird seated next to a large cat. "My offer will save you three hundred pounds over the life of your servant."

"Three hundred pounds?" Angelina let her genuine puzzlement show. "I don't understand."

"I am offering you that healthy young woman for the modest rate of two hundred pounds."

Now Angelina was completely baffled. "That's rather high for a finder's fee, isn't it? The agencies only charge ten percent of the first year's salary."

Mrs. Oxwich let out a dry chuckle. "It isn't a finder's fee, Mrs. Lovington. It is the total cost of acquiring the servant."

"Total cost of acquiring," Angelina echoed in a whisper. "I see." The girl was for sale, like a horse or a piano. She struggled to find her voice again. "I'm afraid I don't have that much money with me."

Mrs. Oxwich unbent so far as to pat her knee. "Your note is good enough for me. Your husband can transfer the funds directly from his bank to mine."

Her bank? Did she not share one with the colonel? "My note?"

Mrs. Oxwich produced another smile as she opened an embossed leather box that had been waiting on the marble-topped table. She drew forth a sheet of paper and handed it over.

Angelina pursed her lips, playing a featherbrain pretending to be shrewd. The note, about four inches by six, read, "I, blank, promise to pay the sum of two hundred pounds into the account of the Honorable Mrs. Samuel Oxwich at the Imperial Bank in Lothbury Street, London. This sum will be remitted no later than the twenty-fifth of October 1888. An interest charge of six and one-half percent will be charged each day thereafter. Signed, blank, on this day, blank."

"My, this is very official," Angelina said. "I suppose the blanks are for my name?"

"And today's date." Mrs. Oxwich took the paper from her and laid it flat on the table, then handed her a pen. She watched while Angelina wrote her name in plain letters in the first blank and then scrawled her signature in the second one. She hesitated over the third, and Mrs. Oxwich prompted, "The seventeenth of August."

Angelina filled in that blank as well and returned the pen. She swallowed down a bitter taste. She felt filthy. She'd just purchased another human being.

* * *

Harini said nothing, sitting silent and stony-faced all the way home. Angelina gripped the girl's unwilling hand as they navigated the station at Waterloo. When they finally reached Bellenden Crescent, she took the girl's elbow to guide her up the steps.

Rolly had the door open before they reached the landing. "Afternoon, Missus," he greeted her, staring wide-eyed at the Indian girl.

"This is Harini, our new —" What was she? Slave? Refugee? She was certainly not a housemaid. "She's a guest for now. Let's put her in the big room on the third floor."

"Right away, Missus." Rolly bounded down the steps and returned with a well-worn carpet bag. Angelina thought of the two good-sized trunks that held Dolly's and Molly's possessions. She'd bet this lost child owned exactly one change of clothes and one winter coat.

They trooped up to the third floor and into the guest room. This used to be Peg's room and was comfortably furnished with a bed big enough for two, a good-sized wardrobe, and a chintz-covered slipper chair. A mirror hung above a painted dresser, and light shone through the front-facing window, but the place felt bare. Angelina had put a vase of flowers in the maid's room across the corridor, expecting to put the newcomer there.

"This is your room," Angelina said brightly. "Don't worry, it will look homey enough once we unpack your things." And find some other ones. A colorful quilt would do wonders.

"It's a lovely room," Rolly said, as he set the bag on the floor. "It's never cold, not even all the way up 'ere." His gaze kept returning to the red dot on Harini's forehead.

Harini ignored him, which wasn't easy. That took practice, that complete self-possession. Where had she learned it?

Angelina poured some water into the basin on the washstand. She gestured at it, then rubbed her hands together over the bowl. "Would you like to wash up a bit?"

Harini gazed at the bowl in silence. The girl's haughty pose didn't fool her for a minute. Angelina could only imagine how she would feel if this calamity had befallen her.

"Let's go down and have some tea. I'll bet Antoine's got something lovely for us to eat." Angelina smiled with all her might.

She beckoned the girl back down the stairs, pausing on the first-floor landing. "Like to use the lavatory, ducky?" She didn't bother to mince her words since they wouldn't be understood.

She opened the small door and gestured again, feeling like a demonstrator at a department store. Harini raised her eyebrows, which made Angelina fear for a moment that she didn't know what the room was for. But then she nodded, went in, and closed the door herself.

"Well, that's one less thing to worry about." Rolly chuckled, but Angelina shook her finger at him. "We don't know anything about this poor child."

The water flushed and the girl came out. She stood waiting for the next thing, hands by her sides, her expression perhaps a touch less wary than before. Nothing bad had happened yet. Perhaps tea and biscuits would make her comfortable enough to tell her story — if they could find a way to understand it.

"Let's go down to the kitchen, shall we?" Angelina held out a hand, which was met with disdain. She sighed and led the way down to the basement. She found Antoine sitting at the servants' table, marking up a cookery book. He rose when she entered.

"Good afternoon, Antoine. I'd like to introduce you to our guest. Her name is Harini. She's from India." She turned toward Harini. "This is Antoine LeClerq, our wonderful chef. You'll eat very well while you're in this house." She rubbed her tummy and hummed.

Moriarty Lifts the Veil

Harini gazed at him with an unreadable expression. He bowed and said, "Welcome." When no response came, he shrugged at Angelina.

"She doesn't seem to speak any English, although she must understand a little. Let's try your language, shall we?" She looked at Harini and asked, *"Parlez-vous français?"*

A small light lit in the girl's dark eyes. "No."

"She speaks Hindi, I believe," Angelina said. "Mr. Sandy speaks that language. I'd best send him a telegram. We may have a while to wait."

"If I may propose an alternative," Antoine said. "I play écarté on Tuesday evenings with a few friends in the vicinity. Mr. Kumar, the grocer, is Indian. He speaks many languages. Perhaps this child's is one of them."

"Oh, Antoine, I could positively hug you!" Angelina grinned as the chef took a few steps back. She turned to Rolly. "Run and see if this Mr. Kumar would be kind enough to pay us a visit. Straightaway, if possible. Tell him we have an urgent need for a translator who speaks Hindi."

Rolly still dropped most of his Hs, but he make them if he tried. "*Hhh*indi," he repeated. "Got it. Back in a flash, Missus." And off he went.

"Perhaps we could have some tea while we wait," Angelina said. "And I'll bet our guest would like a piece of that treacle tart you gave me for lunch. I've no idea if she's eaten anything today."

"Bah! We cannot have that, Madame. Not in my kitchen."

Angelina pulled out a chair for Harini, then sat down beside her. Antoine served their tea, setting the sugar, milk, and lemon on the table so they could suit themselves. Angelina added her usual splash and two lumps to her cup, then held the tongs over the sugar bowl. "Do you like sugar?"

Harini nodded, so she dropped a lump into her cup. She picked up another one and held it until she got a second nod. This was something, questions and nods. Far better than fear and suspicion.

While Harini sipped her tea and ate her tart, she gazed around the servants' hall with interest. The name was a bit grand — the room wasn't more than twenty feet on either side. Colorful theater posters decorated the walls, and a group of comfortable chairs sat before the brick fireplace. There was a deep armchair for Antoine and chintz-covered rockers for the maids. Peg had a larger chair with plump cushions, a small footstool, and a good lamp for sewing. Rolly had a padded stool where he could spread a canvas on the floor and enjoy the warmth of fire and company while brushing mud from hems or blacking shoes.

All in all, it was a pleasant space that spoke of a staff living in comfort and harmony

After an interminable amount of time — all of twenty minutes — Rolly came huffing through the back door leading a short, dark-skinned man with a fine black moustache. Of an indeterminate age, he had a full nose in a round face and a warm demeanor. Angelina liked him at once.

Antoine performed the introductions, and they exchanged a few pleasantries about the sunny weather. Then Angelina presented Harini. Mr. Kumar asked her a few questions in the same lilting language Zuri had used. Harini answered in an aggrieved tone. He folded his palms together and gave her a deep bow, then turned to Angelina.

"This young woman is not a servant, Mrs. Moriarty. On the contrary. She is a princess, the daughter of Rajah Chand of Jaswan, which I believe is in the Punjab."

"Oh my stars!" Angelina gaped at the girl. She pulled out a chair and sat down with a thump. "Oh my stars." She shook her head and patted herself on the chest, then said, "You'd better sit down too, Mr. Kumar. And of course, the princess. Rolly, let's all have more tea, and then you and Antoine should join us. I suspect this is going to be a long story."

Once they were settled, she said, "Please tell Her Highness — is that right?"

Mr. Kumar smiled. "Her proper title is 'mahila,' which is like 'lady' in English."

Angelina nodded. "Then please assure Mahila Harini that no one expects her to do any kind of work in this house. She is safe here and will be treated with respect and kindness. I bought — I brought her home because I think there's something queer going on out there with those memsahibs and their Indian servants, and I couldn't think of any other way to find out what. But let her tell her story first, if she's willing. How did she end up here?"

Mr. Kumar translated all that, and the girl burst into tears so wrenching Angelina cried along with her, clasping her pudgy hand. After a few sniffles, more tea, and an additional slice of treacle tart, the tears subsided. Harini even managed a real smile. Then she began to talk, her eyes shifting from Angelina to Mr. Kumar.

It was a true Gothic nightmare, straight out of Mrs. Radcliffe's work. Harini, being a typical fourteen-year-old in many ways, had chafed at the restrictions her father placed upon her. She could never leave the palace without a small retinue, including an eagle-eyed governess and a looming bodyguard. She couldn't go anywhere interesting and was forbidden to visit the teeming, endlessly fascinating marketplace.

One day, she heard some guards talking about an exhibition of horsemanship to take place at the English Club. She loved horses, and she loved to see the English officers in their bright blue uniforms with their funny flat hats strapped under their chins. She wanted to see this exhibition. Her father forbade it, but she was determined. She made her servant trade clothes with her and slipped out of her carriage on the way to the temple.

For a short but glorious while, she ran free, unrecognized, through the streets of the city. She found the English Club quite easily and slipped inside the walls. People were streaming in one direction, so they must have been going to the exhibition. She walked along with them, sticking to the outer edge, meaning to worm her way to the front when they reached the field. But she was distracted by two English ladies with their arms linked, strolling under an arch into a garden. She decided to follow them while she had the chance. English ladies fascinated her, though she'd had few opportunities to observe them. She couldn't understand how they could look so normal from the front and yet have such enormous backsides.

Angelina's eyes must have popped because Harini broke off. She explained, through Mr. Kumar, that she now knew about the wire cages they wore under their skirts.

She resumed her tale. She slipped into the garden, skulking along the shrubbery like a thief, following the two ladies. She wanted to see them sit down on one of the stone benches that dotted the long, curving garden. But they turned abruptly to go into the house. Harini wasn't sure which way to go, so she kept on along the garden path. Next thing she knew, a meaty hand grasped her by the shoulder and gave her a shake.

"There you are, you naughty girl!" An older woman, Indian and very ugly, scowled down at her. "Don't you know they are leaving? We must hurry now and get you into the wagon."

Harini protested vigorously, threatening the old witch with her father's wrath, but the woman only shook her harder for lying. She could barely set her feet flat on the ground, the woman gripped her arm so tightly. Harini struggled and cursed, but was no match for her captor. She was dragged to a large wagon covered with patched canvas.

The old woman shouted, "I've got her," and several hands reached out to drag her inside, where she was shoved into the farthest corner. She tried to shout her name, but someone slapped her, hard.

"Your parents paid for this, you wretched ninny. You'd best sit quietly and do as you're told. Bad girls are punished here, you know."

She obeyed from that point forward, feeling for a long time as if she'd fallen into one of those confusing nightmares where strangers direct you along twisted paths. Once the ship set sail, she lost all hope.

"When did she arrive in England?" Angelina asked.

Mr. Kumar repeated her question, then answered, "She isn't sure, but it wasn't long ago. The other Indian servants have been trying to take care of her and relieve her of the worst labor. Most of them wanted to come here. Most had always been servants and didn't mind getting their hands dirty or waiting for others to eat first. Everyone missed the smells and sounds of their native land, but most were content with their new lives. They were never hungry here. Things could be worse, they said."

Angelina nodded. "Tell her I'm glad Mrs. Oxwich chose her for me. I couldn't have kept one of the willing ones. I can't explain it yet, but I wouldn't feel right about it. Since there's no question of keeping a rajah's daughter, I'm spared that difficulty."

Mr. Kumar gave her a knowing look, perhaps guessing at the unspoken part. Then he translated and gave a small chuckle before relating Harini's reply. "It wasn't luck, she says. She's the worst servant Mrs. Oxwich has ever seen. Everyone said so. She didn't even know how to dress herself until she came to this cold, wet country."

Angelina laughed. He laughed with her. After a moment, Harini joined in. Angelina wondered how long it had been since the princess had enjoyed that simple release.

"Tell her she is welcome to sleep in the room we showed her. Rolly will keep an eye on her. I suppose she should have her meals upstairs with the professor and me, being a foreign dignitary. Although, if she would rather come down here, she may. Otherwise, she's free to do as she pleases. I would advise her not to go out on her own yet. My husband will doubtless have some ideas about how to remedy her situation. I imagine she wants to go home."

Once Mr. Kumar had translated all of that, the poor, lost child burst into tears again.

FIFTEEN

Gabriel Sandy paced back and forth across the sitting room of his flat in Shoreditch, arguing with his young assistant, Zeke. Really, he was arguing with himself, but the lad made a handy sounding board.

"I didn't finish it," Sandy said. "I never said what I went there to say. But Oxwich looked so stunned — so guilty — when Moriarty mentioned how much money the embezzler was taking that we decided to leave before he could muster a defense."

"Get the goods and get out quick." Zeke nodded his approval. "That's the first rule." He huddled in the big armchair in the front room, wrapped in a blanket, his brown hair sticking up. He'd heard Sandy pacing and come to see what the stir was about.

Normally, they would both be asleep at this hour. It was just on six o'clock, and they seldom got home from work until past two. But Sandy had tossed and turned, the words he'd wanted to say to Colonel Oxwich echoing in his mind. He'd finally given up, gotten up, and dressed to go out.

"I can't close that chapter of my life until I've had my say. Made my peace with the old bastard." He tapped himself on the chest. "I want him to know he didn't harm me. In fact, he did me a favor. I like the life I have now much better than the one I had before."

"Me too." Zeke snuggled into the chair and closed his eyes. "Go tell 'im, Guv'nor. Give 'im what for."

Sandy grinned down at the lad. He'd plucked him from the street, clad in rags and nearly starving, but still possessed of that unsinkable Cockney spirit. The British cavalry could use more of that.

He glanced out the window. Gray, as always, in the East End, but with the flat sheen that signaled sunshine out beyond the city. It would be chilly for another hour or two. He pulled his greatcoat from the rack by the door. As he shrugged it on, he gave the sitting room a critical review. The wallpaper had darkened where gaslight struck it and had faded where sunlight from the skinny window fell. The yellow-and-white pastoral pattern was dreadfully dated, but at least it hadn't starting peeling.

He'd bought the furniture at second-hand stores, so nothing matched and every piece bore dents and scratches. The place was roomy enough for him and Zeke, but once Zuri joined the family — if that was what she wanted — the flat would feel crowded. There was no hope for it. He would have to find better digs.

* * *

Sandy walked through the gate at Odstone Barracks behind a group of enlisted men who had a slanging match going on with the guard. He eyed Sandy's civilian clothes without interest, tossing one last insult after his chums as he shoved the logbook at the visitor. "Gabriel Sandy. Weren't you here Friday?"

So he did pay some attention. Sandy nodded. "Business with the colonel. Bit of follow-up today. Won't be long."

The guard shrugged, signaling that it wasn't his job to say yea or nay. He logged them in and logged them out, and that was all.

Sandy didn't bother stopping by the barracks office. He knew where Oxwich would be on a Monday morning — napping in his house in the officers' quarters. Some habits never changed. He'd have some grand mansion out in the country where his wife could live in the style she preferred, but he'd keep a place in the barracks for entertaining military visitors, maintaining a spare wardrobe, and catching a few winks.

Signs directed him to Officers' Row. The houses weren't marked, but Sandy spotted a sergeant walking toward him. "Colonel's office?" he asked when the man drew within speaking range. "Last on the right," the fellow answered in an oddly deep voice.

The door was unlocked. Nothing odd about that in barracks. Sandy let himself in, then stood for a moment in the entry hall, listening. He heard a light snore sounding somewhere upstairs and hoped Oxwich hadn't gone up to lie down. He didn't like the idea of confronting a man lying on a bed.

Sandy looked around the hall, his lip curling at the wealth of Indian and Afghan artifacts. Oxwich must've looted half the Punjab on his way out. He'd bought a few gorgeous silk tapestries for color — or his wife had — but showed a preference for weapons. Gleaming swords with jeweled handles and scimitars with curved blades engraved with the spiraling characters of Arabic writing crowded the walls. A few spaces were empty. Perhaps they'd been sent out for cleaning.

The door on the right hung open a few inches, revealing a tall bookcase. The library, no doubt. Sandy pushed the door open and stepped onto the plush Persian carpet. He noticed the top of a black-haired head lolling against the side of a wingback chair. No snoring: that was a small surprise. One would expect the old reprobate to snore like a band saw. No sound of breathing either. In fact, the room was absolutely silent and held an unpleasant, coppery smell.

A shiver ran down Sandy's spine as he approached the chair. Oxwich lay still, his head resting on one of the wings and his mouth agape. He seemed dead to the world. Then Sandy saw the ivory-handled knife sticking out from the colonel's chest. A thin trail of blood darkened the blue uniform.

"Great God Almighty!" Sandy's body convulsed as if he'd taken a punch to the gut. He backed up, turning away to gulp down his rising gorge. He mastered himself and turned back. He was loath to touch the body to feel for a pulse, but it clearly wasn't necessary. The man was dead.

Sandy rubbed his face, staring at the hideous sight until the horror subsided and his wits returned. Who had done this? It couldn't have been long ago. That blood looked wet. Fresh. The knife had undoubtedly come from the display on the walls in the entry hall. Yes, there was the scabbard on the floor beside the chair.

A clock chimed somewhere in the house, reminding him that time was passing. This must be reported to the military police at once. Sandy took one step toward the door and stopped.

He couldn't do it. How would that look? He was a stranger. Or no, not a stranger. He was a former officer with a long-standing grudge against the murdered man, one that many people at Odstone knew about.

But what kind of coward refused his duty at such a time?

He'd hesitated too long. Footsteps sounded on the stairs and approached the study. "Time to wake up, Colonel." A sergeant walked in and stopped abruptly. "I know you," he snarled. "Gabe Sandy, the thief! We thought you was dead."

The recognition was mutual. Sergeant Billy Yates had been Oxwich's tool from the start. He'd managed the embezzlement from the officers' fund and planted the evidence convicting Sandy of the crime.

Yates didn't wait for an answer. He walked around the chair, saw the dreadful sight within it, and cried, "Bloody hell, man! What have you done?" He glared at Sandy, dashed out the front door, and started shouting for help.

There was nothing for it. Time to run and run fast. Sandy raced into the hall, turned around twice, then ran toward the rear of the house, bursting out the back door. He sprinted down the alley and took the first turn that led away from the main gate.

He slowed to a fast walk, breathing hard, his nerves jangling. He remembered this feeling, reinforced by the army uniforms and the utilitarian style of the barracks. His old training drew on the fear, turning it into fuel for his body and focus for his mind. He turned and turned again, always navigating away from the gate. There would be another gate at the rear for large deliveries.

He spotted a saddled horse waiting placidly in front of a house. He scanned the street but saw no one. He trotted over to the beast and mounted it. His heart soared as he kicked his heels and clucked his tongue. He always felt better — stronger and more alive — on the back of a horse.

He saw an empty wagon rolling ahead of him and followed it. As it neared the gate, he nosed right up to it as if he were part of the team. He waved casually at the guard, trotted around to walk beside the wagon for a few excruciating minutes, then kicked the horse into a gallop, riding hell-for-leather to the train station.

He slowed to a walk as he approached it. He dismounted and threw the reins to a boy lounging against the railing. "Mind him, won't you? Back in a tick."

He sauntered into the station, shedding his coat as he walked. He folded it inside out and slung it across his arm. He wished he could stuff it into a rubbish bin, but he'd need it tonight.

The departures board showed many trains for Waterloo, but that was too obvious. When they came after him — which they would, in a matter of minutes — that was where they'd go. The next train leaving the station went to Reading, a bigger station than piddling Staines. He'd find better options there.

He jumped aboard just as it was pulling out. No one shouted, "Stop that train!" or raced along the platform shooting furious glances into the windows. He found an empty seat and sat down, heaving a sigh of relief. There must be a world of confusion back there, with Yates howling about an old enemy and men running to see what the noise was about. Someone might take after him, but they'd run toward the main gate, not deeper into the barracks. They'd question the guard and demand to see the logbook. They'd find his name there, sure enough, but by then he'd have made it halfway to the station.

When he reached Reading, he took the first train heading away from London. This one was going to Manchester via Oxford. They'd never look for him there. In Oxford, he turned back to London. The excitement had long since worn off, and exhaustion overtook him. He slept all the way to Marylebone. Refreshed, he strode down Baker Street and took the Underground to Aldgate.

Now he was only a short walk from his flat, but he couldn't go there. By this time, the place might be full of police. Zeke could cope. In fact, he would run for Professor Moriarty as soon as he worked out what had happened.

But Sandy couldn't go there either. He couldn't go to any friend. Besides, he had a better option, thanks to his years of driving a cab from the East End to the West and back again.

He directed his feet toward the Seven Dials. His best hope now was to lose himself in the wilderness of the worst slums in London.

SIXTEEN

Moriarty had entered his home on Friday evening eager to tell his wife about the confrontation with Colonel Oxwich. He'd practiced the story in his head on the train home. But his success — which seemed more modest and inconclusive as he spoke — was soundly trumped by Angelina's purchase of an Indian princess.

Who could compete with that?

It was a harrowing tale, from the point of view of the princess. Moriarty could only imagine the nightmare she'd endured, scooped off the street during her one brave bid for freedom and imprisoned in a house five thousand miles from home, where no one cared if she lived or died. Her parents must have been tearing their hair out.

He'd also been looking forward to a quiet weekend, perhaps with a long stroll in Hyde Park while the weather held. He wanted to study his great map of London to locate the addresses he'd copied from the discharge book and identify the nearest post offices. He couldn't think of any other way for Brant to lay his hands on those stolen funds than to present himself under the cheated soldier's name. It seemed far-fetched, and he didn't know how to test it, but it was all he had.

But their regular household routine was cast aside while Angelina, Peg, Antoine, and Rolly devoted themselves to amusing Harini. One example would illustrate them all. Late Saturday morning, Moriarty heard screams emanating from the second-best bedroom, which Angelina used as an oversized dressing room. Given their recent discoveries of murder and theft, he naturally feared the worst. He raced upstairs and threw himself against the stout door, sending it banging into the plaster wall. He barged into the room, fists raised, and then stopped, gaping at the tableau before him.

His wife stood with her hand clapped over her mouth to contain her bubbling laughter. Peg stood with her arms full of flouncy fabric, some dress being readied to go over the head of the princess. Harini stood before the long mirror wearing nothing but frilly combinations, a shining wire bustle, and a look of purest indignation.

They'd been playing dress-up; that was all. Moriarty backed out and closed the door, his cheeks burning with embarrassment. Howls of laughter chased him up the stairs to his private retreat on the top floor.

Later that afternoon, Mr. Kumar, a neighborhood grocer, came to tea to translate for Mahila Harini. Moriarty did not consider himself any kind of a snob, but he wasn't accustomed to receiving grocers in his drawing room. Fortunately, his participation in the conversation was seldom required, so he spent the time calculating the average social rank of a grocer and a princess. It came out somewhere around the level of a knight, which put a former professor and his actress wife at a distinct disadvantage.

Ah, well. He hadn't expected kidnapped princesses when he married Angelina, but he'd known his life would never be mundane. For the most part, he embraced the challenges.

* * *

By Monday morning, Moriarty was glad for an excuse to leave the house after breakfast. He meant to meet his class at Odstone; no reason to leave his students in the lurch. He also wanted to check in with Corporal Turner. He was anxious about those discharge books — his only real evidence against Brant. They sat openly on a shelf in the regimental office. They could be taken outside and burned, every one of them. Such a rash act would be hard to explain, but less difficult than pleading against embezzlement charges before a judge.

He logged in at the gate at five minutes to ten. He'd beguiled the time on the train by working out more exercises using money. He planned to elicit a typical weekly budget and teach them how to extrapolate that to a monthly plan.

The men enjoyed correcting one another's notions of necessary and optional expenses, entering into a lively debate. They'd barely gotten started when a hubbub arose outside the windows. One of the soldiers flung up the sash and leaned out to ask what was happening.

"The colonel's been murdered!" someone shouted back. "The villain's escaped, but our men are hot on his trail."

Moriarty's first thought was of Sergeant Brant. But no, that didn't seem like his style. He'd been as cool as the proverbial cucumber that day at the War Office, though he must have suspected at once that his scheme had been detected. But who else had a reason to kill Oxwich? One of the cheated soldiers, perhaps? A chill ran down his spine. Not one of Sandy's friends, he hoped.

He dismissed the class and jogged across to the regimental office. Soldiers were running in all directions, so his hasty pace went unremarked. He found Corporal Turner standing in the middle of the room with a half sheet of yellow paper in one hand. He looked stunned, as if he'd never seen a telegram before.

Moriarty said, "I've dismissed my class. They're saying Colonel Oxwich has been murdered. Can that be right?"

"It sounds insane, but it's true. Within the hour, I'm told, judging by the condition of the body. Stabbed through the chest with one of his own knives." Turner stared blankly through the window. "He collected them, you know. From the Punjab, most of them."

"Great Scott! Where did it happen?"

"In his house on Officers' Row. He always goes there to take a nap on Monday morning. He tends to stay up late on weekends."

"Who could have done such a thing?" Moriarty's stomach clenched with the fear that his brazen accusations on Friday had somehow provoked this violence.

Turner tilted his head to give him a queer look. "They say your friend did it — Mr. Sandy. Sergeant Yancy, the colonel's batman, found him standing over the body. He knew him from India. There's no doubt about his identity."

"Impossible." Moriarty shook his head, as if to shake those dire words out of his ears. "Simply impossible." But why had Sandy come here today? He'd given no hint about any such plan on Saturday — not one word. "Who's in charge of the investigation?"

"Officially, the military police. But this is well beyond their scope. They break up fights, mainly, and toss rowdy drunks in jail for the night. I wired Scotland Yard the minute I heard the news." Turner flourished the telegram. "Inspector Forbes will be here soon."

"Where is Mr. Sandy now?" Moriarty asked. "Have they taken him into custody?"

Turner shook his head. "He scarpered. Ran like the wind, according to Sergeant Yates. Out the back door, into the streets. Found a horse somewhere and rode off. To the station, we assume. Captain Greenway mounted up with a couple of military policemen and went after him, but it's too late. He'll be on the train to Waterloo by this time."

"I suppose Scotland Yard will take up the chase in London." One telegram would have a team of constables waiting on the platform. But Sandy would know that. Where else would he go?

Turner went to stand by the window, gazing toward the gate, as if expecting the man from Scotland Yard to appear at any moment. If the inspector had caught a departing train and prevented it from making any intermediate stops, he very well might.

Moriarty went over to the shelf containing the discharge books and counted them. All seemed to be in order. "I know this seems trivial under the circumstances, but I'm worried about these books. Do you still have the one we've studied under lock and key?"

"No fear, Mr. Moriarty. No one knows it's there. And Brant hasn't been here either. I lock up for the weekend, though of course Captain Greenway has a key. Hard to imagine him coming anywhere near this place on a sunny Saturday, though. He'd have been off watching a race somewhere."

"Good. Good." Moriarty hesitated, then asked, "Would you mind if I waited for the inspector with you? I know I have no role here, but Mr. Sandy is a good friend. And I can't help thinking this murder has something to do with our accusations on Friday."

"Dear Lord, I hope not! I'm as much to blame as you." Turner waved at a chair. "To be honest, I'd welcome the company. We've never had a murder before, not in my time."

Moriarty took down a discharge book and sat at the desk to study it, working backward. This one held the records from 1887. He found a few suspect entries and jotted the men's names, addresses, years of service, and characters into his notebook. He only managed to examine a few pages before Turner leapt up from his chair and straightened his jacket. The man from Scotland Yard had arrived.

A moment later, a soldier opened the door, saluted Corporal Turner, and left. A man in a brown jacket and striped trousers, neither of best quality, walked in. He wore a bowler hat, and his thick brown moustache wanted trimming. He nodded at Turner. "I'm Inspector Forbes from Scotland Yard." His keen brown eyes shifted toward Moriarty, then widened in recognition. "You're that fellow Sherlock Holmes brought me out to arrest. Place called Hainstone House, couple of years ago. Some lord got himself strangled in his own library. Professor something, wasn't it?"

"Moriarty. I was proven innocent on the spot, as you may recall."

Forbes blew out a dismissive breath. "Never forget it. Dashed waste of my time. Confounded nuisance, that Holmes. Thinks he's the be-all and end-all of criminal investigation, but he's wrong as often as not. 'Course, those aren't the cases that make the papers, are they?"

"No, I don't suppose they are." Moriarty held out a hand.

Forbes gave it a sound shake. "You're the one discovered the real murderer, aren't you? Nice work. Tricky business." He gave Moriarty an assessing look. "Come with me now, if you've the time. I could use another pair of eyes — ones connected to a working brainpan, that is. These army coppers could just about find a horse in a bathtub, with a little help."

Moriarty gladly assented. He'd been wondering how he could insert himself into this investigation. Now here it was, handed to him on a platter, thanks to the arrogance of Mr. Sherlock Holmes.

The soldier who had opened the door guided them through the barracks to Officers' Row, a short street lined with neat brick houses. The colonel's house was easily identified by the crowd in the street and the officers standing around the door. Inspector Forbes showed them his card, and they stood back to let him in. Moriarty nodded at them as he passed, hoping no one would recognize him as the maths coach.

A man wearing sergeant's stripes met them in the hall, introducing himself as Sergeant Yates, Colonel Oxwich's batman for many years. Moriarty recognized the name from Sandy's account of that sad affair in India. The sergeant looked bewildered and sounded hoarse.

Forbes elicited his account of the critical events. He claimed to have been napping upstairs. The colonel played hard on the weekends, right up through Sunday night, and liked a bit of catching-up time on Monday mornings. That habit was well-known in the barracks, as it should be. Wouldn't be much of a rest if men came barging in every two minutes, now would it? Yates caught a few winks himself as a rule, waking when the clock on the landing chimed the half hour. Then he'd splash a bit of water on his face and go down to wake the colonel.

He recounted his surprise at seeing Gabriel Sandy standing in the library. Like everyone else, he'd thought the man had died years ago or disappeared into the East. His surprise had turned to horror when he saw what had been done. He'd run out front and raised a shout, but Sandy had escaped through the rear door. Yates knew better than to leave the house unguarded, so he'd kept shouting until men came to see what the noise was all about. That got things moving, but by then Sandy had disappeared.

Forbes asked if anyone else had been in the house that morning. The answer was no. There weren't any other servants when the missus wasn't there, which she seldom was. And no, the door was never locked during the day. Why would it be? They were in the middle of an army barracks, for pity's sake!

The knife was a Choora dagger, a gift of the amir. Very old and very valuable, the colonel said. Yates pointed at the empty place on the wall where it had hung.

"Would it take much strength to wield it?" Forbes asked.

Yates shrugged. "Drive it into a man's belly, you mean? Not much. Sharp as needle, that knife. It was made for piercing armor, they say, back in olden days. And I keep all the weapons in top condition. The colonel was proud of that collection." The batman's eyes grew moist. At least some one would miss the corrupt commander.

The door to the library gaped open. The carpet bore evidence of many feet coming and going, but the body had been left undisturbed. Peering past the inspector's shoulder, Moriarty saw the ivory handle of a knife jutting forth from the dead man's chest, right up in the hollow under the rib cage.

"There doesn't seem to be much blood," he said, noting the dark stain down the navy wool jacket.

"Knife plugs the wound," Forbes answered. "He's past bleeding now." He laid two fingers against the neck and then raised one of the lifeless hands. It fell limply back onto the armrest. "Not cold, but not warm either. Rigor hasn't begun." He turned away from the corpse. "Cause of death: stabbing. Time of death as attested by Sergeant Yates: shortly before 9:45. Could've been a mite earlier, but no earlier than nine o'clock, when the sergeant went upstairs. We'll let a doctor work out the rest."

"That's a narrow window," Moriarty observed. "Less than an hour."

Forbes grunted. He stood with his hands on his hips, shifting his gaze from the teacup on the table beside the armchair to the newspaper dropped on the floor. Moriarty noticed that it was the *Morning Post* — a predictably conservative choice for an army colonel.

"What's this?" Forbes asked. He stooped for something behind the chair, lifting up a man's overcoat by one lapel. "Odd place for a coat." He turned his head to call for the sergeant. "What's this doing here?"

Yates frowned, leaning away from the thing. "That's the colonel's overcoat. That should be hanging on the rack in the hall. Where'd you find it?"

"Here, bundled up behind the chair."

Moriarty went around to get a better look at the area in question and pointed at a pair of gloves lying on the carpet. "Were those his as well?"

"I suppose so." Yates shrugged, mystification writ clear in every line of his body. "How did they get down there?"

Forbes had been gingerly examining the coat. "Looks like blood here on the cuff. I'll wager we'll find more on those gloves."

"Ah," Moriarty said. "I see. The killer pulled on his victim's coat and gloves in order to protect his own clothes. Then he just left them here. Why not?"

Forbes shot him a dry glance, noting the anonymous "killer" when they had a solid suspect. But Moriarty wouldn't believe Gabriel Sandy had murdered a man in his sleep if he'd watched him perform the deed with his very own eyes.

He left the other men inspecting the garments for other clues and wandered over to the desk. The mahogany surface was empty, apart from a silver basket containing invitation cards, an ornate silver desk set, and a single sheet of paper placed squarely before the chair. Moriarty moved around the desk to read it.

"Stay out of that," Forbes warned, dropping the coat and striding toward him. "You're here to observe only."

Moriarty took a step back. "I wondered if he might have had an appointment for this morning. It appears that he did."

Yates shook his head. "He never made appointments for this time Mondays. I told you that."

Forbes walked around the desk and picked up the note to read it aloud. "Confirm Monday morning, nine o'clock. We'll sort things out. Not worried. All good things must come to an end." He grunted. "It's signed 'Jeremy Brant.'"

"Ha!" Moriarty said, attracting another sharp look from Forbes.

Yates said, "That don't make no sense at all. Why would Brant come here, 'specially on a Monday? He knows better'n that."

"Who is he?" Forbes asked.

"He's our liaison with the Army Pay Office. He don't work regular here on the barracks, just comes out once a week or so. And that's to the main office, not here." Yates's lip curled. "That's where the pay books are, ain't they?"

Forbes's dark eyes flashed. "You'll keep a civil tongue in your mouth, Sergeant, or you might find yourself charged with this crime."

"Me?" Yates's mouth fell open. He took two steps backward toward the door. "Nobody's been more loyal to the guvnor than me. Not even 'is own wife!"

Moriarty thought it unlikely that this man had done the deed. He'd be cutting off the hand that fed him, for one thing. And he didn't seem stupid enough to commit a crime that could so easily have been laid to him had it not been for the accident of Sandy's visit.

Forbes echoed his thought. "I'll give you the benefit of the doubt — for the moment — because you're the only man who could be counted on to be here during the critical time. Convenient for you, to have that other fellow turn up out of the blue." He glanced at Moriarty. "If that's what happened. And now we've got this other sergeant to look into."

"I appreciate your willingness to consider alternatives, Inspector," Moriarty said.

"Doesn't mean I think your friend is innocent."

"Captain Sandy — or whatever he is now — hated the colonel," Yates said. "Hated him like poison. There was trouble back in Jaipur. Turned out Sandy was stealing from the fund when it came his turn to be Officer of the Mess. He was guilty, plain as day." Yates pointed at himself. "I'm the one caught him out, as a matter of fact. He was tried right and proper and cashiered on the spot. He tried to blame me and the colonel for it, right up to the bitter end."

"When did all this happen?" Forbes asked.

"Must be six, seven years ago."

"That's a long time to hold a grudge," Moriarty said. "He's built himself a new life in that time. A good life. He's not a vengeful man, Inspector."

"Maybe so, maybe not." Forbes gave the library a last, long look, then said, "I had to sign in at the gate. Is that true for everyone?"

"Even officers," Yates said. He'd brightened considerably after contributing that motive for Sandy.

Forbes nodded at Moriarty. "Then let's go see who came in when."

The guard spread the entry log out on the table in his small hut. Moriarty pulled out his notebook and pencil, then chuckled as Inspector Forbes did the same.

"Do you mind?" Moriarty asked, holding up his pencil.

"Suit yourself."

The record was clear and gave Moriarty the first glimmer of real hope. Sergeant Brant had signed in at 9:15 and out again at 9:40. Ample time to walk to Officers' Row, stab the colonel, and walk back.

Sandy signed in at 9:35. Moriarty pointed out that he'd entered his own name. "Would a man do that if he'd come to commit murder?"

Forbes snorted. "You've no idea what men do when they're bent on killing. Plan everything down to the last detail, then leave their monogrammed handkerchief at the scene. Besides, if he was part of this regiment, he would expect to be recognized. No point in signing a false name."

"Brant didn't go to the office," Moriarty said, "according to Corporal Turner. I asked because he's implicated in an ongoing embezzlement scheme that I've uncovered."

"Oh, have you?" Forbes looked almost amused — a bad sign.

Moriarty soldiered on. "I believe Colonel Oxwich was a party to the scheme. In fact, Mr. Sandy and I came here on Friday to confront him with it. The colonel was dismissive, to put it mildly, but his manner confirmed my guess."

"I need something stronger than a manner, Professor."

"I know. I'm working on it. But if Oxwich told Brant about my accusations, the sergeant may have decided his best chance to get away free was to kill the only man who could point the finger at him. That would account for the note on the desk, need I remind you. I submit that Sergeant Brant is a more likely suspect than Mr. Sandy, whose grudge, however legitimate, must have grown cold after seven long years."

"Or festered, Professor. Some men never forget and never forgive. And he was caught red-handed, if you'll forgive the expression, right over the body. More damning, in my view — he ran, instead of standing up for himself." Forbes shook his head. "Give me all that and I don't much need a motive."

SEVENTEEN

James came home from the barracks that afternoon with the most appalling news: Colonel Oxwich had been murdered in his library, and Gabriel Sandy was the leading suspect. Oxwich had been a vile, corrupt, uncaring man, but Angelina had never wanted him killed. She wanted a big trial and a public scandal to cover his face with shame.

"Are you hungry?" she asked her husband after the first telling. There would be more discussion of this — much more — but the poor man looked so haggard, and he'd missed lunch.

"Starved. I had a dry ham sandwich on the train, but I would love a proper meal."

They went down to the dining room, where Rolly soon delivered a dish of curried eggs with boiled potatoes and a green salad, along with beer for the master and lemonade for the missus.

Angelina let him enjoy his food for a few moments in peace. Then she smiled and said, "We have guests for tea this afternoon."

"Mr. Kumar again?"

"No, but isn't he just the most delightful man? I had a note this morning from John Watson, inviting himself to tea . . . with Sherlock Holmes."

"Oh no, Angelina! Not today, of all days."

"I could write and put them off, but Watson said Holmes might be able to shed some light on my Indian servant problem. I do want to know what happened to Ganesa. He's been in India — Holmes, I mean. For several months, apparently. He's brought home an Indian servant puzzle of his own. Watson thinks they may be related."

"That sounds vague."

"Doesn't it? But Holmes might know something about the Indian side of Mrs. Oxwich's slave-trading game."

James focused on his eggs. After a few bites and a swallow of beer, he relented. "All right, then. Let them come. But not one word about the murder. Let's not even mention Sandy's name."

"Absolutely not. That's a separate matter altogether and none of Mr. Nosy's business." She let a moment pass in peace and then picked up the original subject. "It's lucky Inspector Forbes remembered you so favorably. Last time he saw you, you were wearing a pair of his iron bracelets."

James smiled at the memory. "That wasn't one of our best days, was it, my dear? But it appears Forbes kept up with that case. And yes, we're lucky to have him instead of a stranger. I like him — so far. He seems willing to consider alternatives. A less intelligent man might decide that one suspect was all he needed and disregard everything else."

"Sergeant Brant sounds like a much more plausible candidate than our Sandy. He had a great deal to lose if Oxwich decided to throw the blame on him."

"Which he would do, if Sandy's history is any indication." James mashed some potato to soak up the last of the curry sauce.

Angelina sipped her lemonade thoughtfully. "Are we certain Sandy didn't do this terrible thing?"

"My dear! How can you doubt him?"

She shrugged. "He truly hated that odious man — with good reason. Oxwich cast him out of a career he loved, humiliating him in the process. That dishonorable discharge cost him his family, don't forget. His father disowned him. And worse, it cost him the one true love of his life, that dancer, Zuri. Maybe seeing her again reminded him of everything he'd lost."

"He had every right to hold a grudge. I'd forgotten about the dancer. He doesn't show his feelings much, does he? He buries things. Bottles them up. It isn't healthy."

Angelina bit back a grin. That was the pot calling the kettle black.

"But murder, my dear. I shouldn't think the man was capable of such an act."

"Shouldn't you?" Angelina placed her hand on his. "You nearly allowed a man you hated to be murdered right before your eyes. He had done you so many grievous wrongs already. What if Lord Nettlefield had succeeded in separating me from you forever?"

James met her eyes, remembering the dangerous days of their extraordinary courtship. Then he nodded. "You're right. It is possible."

Angelina smiled. "It doesn't mean we won't defend Sandy for all we're worth. Tomorrow I'll find a way to reach him, to make sure he has money and knows we're with him. I have lots of old friends in the East End, and Rolly should be able to find some of Sandy's lads."

"Well-deserved grudges aside, this was the act of a coward, killing a man in his sleep. I wouldn't do that, however much I hated the brute. I don't believe Sandy would either. Brant's a far better suspect. I intend to pursue that alternative with everything in my power."

"I have every confidence. But do try to get it sorted by Saturday, darling. Don't forget we're spending the weekend in the country."

* * *

The door knocker sounded at precisely half past four. Angelina wondered how they managed it. Did they stroll around the block, watches in hand?

Never mind. All was ready. She'd changed into a sedate purple costume with a jacket and a shallow bustle, sparsely trimmed in lavender lace. James changed as well, into a dark gray suit — an older one. He claimed it was for his own comfort after the dust and unpleasantness of that morning. He reminded her not to breathe the slightest hint about the Oxwich murder, as if she could have forgotten.

She extended a welcoming hand as Watson entered the drawing room. "So good to see you again, Doctor. It's always a pleasure." He was the image of a family doctor with his kindly gaze and drooping moustache. He took a genuine interest in everyone he met — a benign one, unlike his companion.

"And Mr. Holmes," she said. "My goodness, you *have* been spending time in tropical places!"

She hadn't seen the detective since last year. The days had not been kind to him. Always slim, he now looked almost skeletal. His suit hung loosely on his rangy frame. His face was brown as a sailor's, and he'd added a thick, brushy moustache with a bristly short beard.

"An obvious deduction, Mrs. Moriarty, since Watson has already told you I've been in India." His hauteur had not diminished, however.

"Merely a remark, Mr. Holmes. Nothing more." James and Watson were talking amiably, so she held on to Holmes's hand and leaned in to murmur, "Peg has a lotion that will fade that tan for you. Then you'll be able to remove those hairpieces. They must itch like fury! She also has an ointment that does a better job of removing spirit gum." She rubbed her finger over her upper lip to demonstrate and winked.

Holmes regarded her with such a droll mix of embarrassment and disgruntlement that she had to laugh, just a little. She patted his hand. "Never fear, Mr. Holmes. Your secret is safe with me."

He gave her a sour look and went to shake James's hand. They treated one another with a wary accommodation. They had a great deal in common, both being men of exceptional intelligence and thirst for knowledge, but both were also proud, independent, and poorly schooled in the social graces. They would never be friends; hopefully, they would never truly be enemies.

Angelina got the men seated in chairs around the tea table. She put Holmes closest to an open window with a large ashtray nearby. If he couldn't smoke, he'd become even more agitated. His jacket smelled frightfully of tobacco and something peppery. His pupils were somewhat dilated too. She wondered if he'd picked up another nasty habit while traveling.

The samovar sat on a side table near her. She poured tea, passing the cups around while chatting with Watson about the pleasant weather they'd been enjoying, speculating about how long it could last. They both knew how small talk irritated the other two, which added a bit of zest to the routine. She gestured to the assortment of small cakes and bread-and-butter sandwiches, inviting the gentlemen to serve themselves. Once this was accomplished, she nodded at Watson. "Much as we always enjoy seeing you gentlemen, we do have a topic of particular interest this afternoon. A rather sad one, I'm afraid."

Watson nodded. "I told Holmes about our visit to the coroner last week. It's a bad business. Very bad indeed."

"Watson wasn't clear about your involvement, Mrs. Moriarty," Holmes said.

Angelina gave him a brief resumé of Mrs. Reynolds's visit and her peculiar request. "At the time, I thought it mainly an excuse to meet me and see my home. She's an admirer, by her own confession."

"But why would she think you could solve her problem?" A tense note in Holmes's voice warned that he already knew the answer.

"A mutual friend, an actress, had told her about some of our successes. We've solved a few little puzzles for people, mostly in theatrical circles." Angelina offered him a teasing smile. "Rather like what you do, Mr. Holmes. In fact, I believe that's where the professor got the idea. He says it keeps his mind sharp."

"I can speak for myself, my dear." James gave her that fixed look that said, *Stop it, whatever you're doing.*

Holmes's lip curled. "Imitation is the sincerest form of flattery. I suppose I was bound to attract counterfeiters at some stage."

Watson chuckled. James sipped his tea with the air of a man waiting for a train. No one could be as impassive as James Moriarty when he chose.

Angelina shook her head at both of them and carried on. "I expected to spend a few afternoons poking about some attractive country houses, eventually discovering the coveted ayah in someone else's nursery. If Peg hadn't noticed that paragraph in the newspaper, I suppose I'd still be looking."

"That was a stroke of luck," Watson said, then caught himself. "Not for that poor woman, of course."

"Nor for whoever put her in the river," Holmes said. "Now they have me on their trail."

"A twist they could never have expected," Angelina said. She didn't know if she was relieved or disturbed by that declaration. Holmes was tenacious and as bold as brass. He'd keep digging until he uncovered the truth. He'd be better — faster, smarter, braver — than she was too.

But now that her dear friend Sandy was caught in that circle of corruption among the Middlesex Regiment, she didn't want Holmes getting anywhere near it.

On the other hand, there were more young women at risk of the same dire fate. She must do everything she could to save them, including bringing Sherlock Holmes into the fray. She'd just have to hope their friends in the East End could keep Sandy hidden until everything was resolved.

"What brings *you* into this situation, Mr. Holmes?" Angelina asked. "Dr. Watson hinted that you had a story to tell us that might prove relevant."

"Highly relevant, I should think." Holmes patted his breast pocket — perhaps unconsciously, perhaps as a subtle hint.

Either way, Angelina understood. "You may smoke, if you wish. You'll find an ashtray at your elbow."

"Thank you." Holmes lit a cigarette with a hand that trembled ever so slightly.

Angelina noted a crease on Watson's brow. The consulting detective had come home in less than perfect health.

Holmes took a long draw on his cigarette, turning his head to expel the smoke in the direction of the windows. He leaned back in his chair and embarked upon his tale. "Now that it's all done, I can give you the whole story, at least in general terms. You may not know that I have an older brother named Mycroft."

"I've heard of him," James said, "from my friend Sir Julian Kidwelly. I believe they move in similar circles of influence."

"Intersecting ones, at any rate," Holmes said. "Mycroft is one of the brains in the darker reaches of the Foreign Office. He sent me to India to track an arms-trafficking operation. Out-of-date English Snider-Enfield rifles had been turning up in the hands of Pathan tribes, some of whom were shooting at English soldiers instead of at each other. Having excellent French, I disguised myself as a French rug merchant. I left Marseilles in May and followed the smugglers' trail down the Red Sea and around the Arabian Peninsula. I spent a month in Muscat, getting to know the vendors, both legitimate and otherwise. Then I journeyed into the Punjab with three mules loaded with rugs. I picked up quite a bit of the local dialects along the way. By the end of July, I had sorted out the arms dealers and identified their leader. I delivered him, along with full documentation of his confederates and the path along which the guns traveled, to the viceroy, who happened to be in Delhi at the time."

Moriarty Lifts the Veil

"That sounds like an extraordinary adventure." James was impressed and let it show. Angelina rewarded him for his generosity with a smile — and by shoving the almond tartlets closer to his hand.

"It's a pity Watson wasn't with me," Holmes said. "He could've gotten a whole book out of it."

"Oh, I'll get that book," Watson said, his eyes twinkling. "One chapter at a time. The almanac says the rain is coming back. We'll be stuck indoors for many a long evening."

"Capital!" Holmes said. "I would hate to deprive the reading public of your wit." He stubbed out his cigarette and took a sip of tea. "To continue. While I was in Delhi, recovering from my weeks in the rough, I met Rajah Chand of Jaswan. He had learned of my *unique* talents" — he shot a dark look at James — "from the viceroy and requested a private meeting. The rajah was distraught about his daughter, who had been missing for a month. No trace of her could be found."

A shiver ran up Angelina's spine. She recognized the name. It took all her skill to keep from glancing down toward the basement, where Harini sat playing piquet with the cook at this very moment.

Holmes broke off to give her a brief, searching look. Good heavens, the man's intuitions were acute! Angelina smiled at him blandly. "Do tell us you found the poor girl in the arms of some humble, yet honorable, young man."

"Nothing so predictable," Holmes said. "The princess was last seen in Jaipur, where the rajah keeps a small palace. He said that she had been going through a rebellious phase, chafing at the demands of her station. She slipped away from her attendants one afternoon. They've been duly punished, but no one has seen her since. I believe she changed clothes, donning a servant's garb, in order to sneak into the British Club. There was an exhibition of horsemanship that afternoon, and I was told the princess loved horses. From there, she simply vanished. The rajah offered me the emerald ring he wore on his left hand to find her and bring her home again."

"I suppose you started your search at the club," James said. "She can't have actually vanished. With a good enough description, you'd find someone who remembered seeing her there."

Holmes didn't deign to respond to that obvious remark. "The rajah gave me a miniature painted some years before, but weeks had passed by that point. Memories had grown hazy. I disguised myself as a street vendor to explore the area around the club. I learned of two other girls who had disappeared around the same time. Following that trail, I discovered that some parents had sold their daughters to the English as servants."

"Why, that's barbarous!" Angelina gasped. Harini hadn't mentioned that.

Watson shrugged. "We may think so, but it's not uncommon in some parts of the world."

"For some of these girls," Holmes said, "a life of service to a decent mistress is the best of a short list of bad options."

"But what if the mistress isn't decent?" Angelina said. "Or the master?" Mrs. Oxwich was an Englishwoman. She should have refused such offers, regardless of local customs.

"You must have found out something about this princess," James said to Holmes, "or you wouldn't be here now. We're agog to hear the rest of your story."

He sounded ironic. Still baiting Holmes. Hadn't he twigged to the identity of the missing princess? Angelina batted her lashes at him to tell him to behave himself.

Holmes smiled thinly, taking the taunt as a compliment. "By adopting a variety of disguises, including eye doctor, missionary, and water-seller, I gradually uncovered a slave-trading ring being operated by one of the army officers' wives. Her main confederate is the wife of the Assistant to the Secretary for Transport and Railways. As part of the Indian Civil Service, she's nearly always in India. I can't be perfectly certain until I close the circle here in England, but I believe the rajah's daughter was taken to England by a memsahib as part of her retinue. But which one? And where is she now?"

He paused to light another cigarette. Angelina took the opportunity to offer more tea, which everyone accepted. Rolly slipped in and carried away some empty plates, sliding a new one filled with an assortment of tiny sandwiches onto the table.

Holmes blew a mouthful of smoke toward the window, displaying his gaunt profile. Angelina saw that tiny crease on Watson's brow again. The detective really was far too thin. But that inner hum of nervous energy hadn't diminished. On the contrary, between the tobacco and whatever else he was taking, it seemed to have increased. He tapped one heel repeatedly on the floor. He'd never been fidgety before.

"Where was I?" Holmes asked himself. "Ah, yes. I returned to my natural guise, traveled to Bombay, and gained access to the records of English families returning to the home country in the past month. I was able to determine which ones had departed during the week of the princess's disappearance. Two in particular caught my interest. The wife of an Indian Civil Service officer had gone home to enroll her three children in school, traveling with an unspecified number of servants. The wife of an army officer had returned with a smaller group on the same ship. I booked passage on the next boat for Portsmouth, a freighter with few amenities. I was three weeks behind the princess, but I had greatly narrowed the field of search."

He paused for another drag on his cigarette, perhaps to give them time to interject questions or objections. No one did. "I followed the civil service man's wife to her estate in Norfolk. Two days of inquiries around the neighborhood assured me that there had been no increase in the number of Indian servants in her household. No one was the least secretive about it — another clue. So I shifted my attention to the second family, that of a Major Payne, resident of a somewhat run-down country house not far from Odstone Barracks." He met Angelina's eyes. "Have you met a Mrs. Payne among your circle of officers' wives?"

"I have. And I knew she had recently returned from India. I went to a garden party at her house last week. There were Indian servants everywhere, many brought from the other houses, I was told. And now that you remind me, some of them did seem to be new arrivals. At least, they were being trained by the others, I thought."

"Intriguing," Holmes said. "I decided to pose as a missionary once again. A useful disguise. One can turn up anywhere, and no one pays any mind. I rented a small room in West Bedfont, the nearest village, and borrowed a safety bicycle from the postman. Then I started making the rounds of the larger houses in the district, collecting funds for orphans in Delhi."

"How did you do?" James asked.

"Not as well as one might expect among people who know the place." Holmes grinned. "Though I can be quite persuasive. Have no fear, Professor. The funds have been wired to an orphanage. I collected a few pounds and got a few doors closed in my face. The servant at the Paynes' house — an Indian man — gave me two shillings and a scowl. I watched that house for several days with a telescope from the woods nearby. I saw women in saris — the traditional dress — coming and going about their chores, but none that resembled my portrait of Harini."

Angelina didn't dare look at James. She wanted to hear the end of Holmes's story before revealing their great secret.

Holmes paused, as if sensing a change in the tenor of the room, then went on with his tale. "At last, I attempted to visit a large house called Balmer Park."

He flicked a sharp glance at Angelina, who must have blinked at the name.

"I've been there too," she confessed. "Colonel Oxwich and his wife live there. I don't believe they have children. If they do, they're long since grown and gone."

"There are no children in the house," Holmes said. He knew she'd thrown out that irrelevant information for a reason but evidently had no idea why — not yet. "I learned a great deal about these families, as you shall soon hear. I had barely gone halfway up the drive when I was approached by a very large Sikh. He told me in firm, if broken, English to go away and not come back. He watched me as I pedaled back down the avenue of lime trees.

"Naturally, that aroused my suspicion. Why set a guard if you have nothing to hide? I had already discovered that Mrs. Oxwich was the leader of the wives in India. One could safely assume she would retain that dominant role here as well. So I found a concealed spot in the woods above the house and set up my telescope. One day, I was rewarded by three Indian women emerging with baskets of wet laundry, which they proceeded to hang from lines in the field behind the kitchen garden. One of them did next to nothing, merely standing by the huge basket with her hands folded. She looked to be about the right height and skin color, with the round face of the young princess. I felt certain I had found my quarry at last. Still, I had no authority to barge in and demand her release. I returned to London to consider my next step. There Watson related his visit to the coroner with you, Mrs. Moriarty. He told me the body found in the Thames had been identified by one of the wives in Mrs. Oxwich's circle. That will give me a way in."

He'd stubbed out the last cigarette some time ago. Now he rubbed his hands together. "I visited the coroner myself today. The body has not yet been buried, so I was able to conduct my own examination with the coroner's assistant. Unfortunately, she'd been in the water too long. There was nothing more to be learned." He smiled at Angelina. "Although perhaps you're not aware that she was strangled?"

"Dr. Watson told me." Angelina shuddered. "That poor woman. Does that help you identify the murderer?"

"No," Holmes admitted. "But her condition gives us the motive, and that gives me the place to start — Balmer Park and the Oxwiches. What can you tell me about the colonel?"

Angelina blinked at him, mouth ajar, just for a moment. She couldn't allow that line of questioning to develop. She forced a smile. "I've never met him. But I do know someone you might care to meet."

She rose and rang the bell for Rolly, meeting him at the door when he appeared. She murmured a few words in his ear, at which he grinned and said, "In a jiffy, Missus." Then she turned back to the men. "More tea, anyone?"

James was giving her a burning look. She nodded at him with a slow blink. Watson wore the expression of a man about to receive a birthday treat. Holmes fairly writhed in his chair, he was so distressed at not having predicted this turn of events.

In a minute, Rolly returned, towing the princess by the hand. "It's all right," he assured her before slipping out again.

Angelina laid a light hand on the girl's shoulder. "Mr. Holmes, I believe this is the young lady for whom you have been searching. Mahila Harini, this is Mr. Sherlock Holmes."

Holmes bounded to his feet and strode toward them, astonishment written across his face. Harini shrieked at his approach, crying, "No, no, NO!" The one English word she'd mastered. She clung to Angelina like a drowning woman clinging to a piece of wood. James dashed over to stand between her and the terrifying stranger. He put his hands on his hips in a creditable show of masterly protectiveness.

"It's all right, darling," Angelina said, but Harini only shrieked again.

Holmes rolled his eyes at James, but he stepped backward. He held up both palms to show his peaceful intent and spoke to her in Hindi. Angelina caught the words "Rajah Chand." Holmes reached into an inner pocket and drew forth a gold ring with a carved black stone, glinting in the rays of the afternoon sun. He handed it to Angelina, who passed it to the frightened child.

Harini studied it closely, turning it around and around. Then she clutched it to her breast and burst into tears. *"Mere pita! Mere pita!"*

Watson translated quietly. "She's saying, 'My father. My father.'"

Angelina's lip trembled as her eyes filled with tears. At last, the lost little girl had been found.

Harini flung herself at Holmes, wrapping her arms around his neck. The shock and dismay that flashed across his angular features was worth the two hundred pounds Angelina had sacrificed to make this moment possible.

She let him suffer for a moment, then moved in to disengage the princess from the sleuth. She took Harini's hand firmly in hers and smiled at her. "Tell her that all will be well, please, Mr. Holmes. But how will we get her home?"

He spoke a few more words in Hindi, then led Harini around the table to take his chair. He remained standing beside it while Angelina returned to her seat. James, never to be outdone, stood behind her chair.

Watson heaved a deep sigh. "That was the most satisfying ending to a long and troubling story that you could ever have contrived, Mrs. Moriarty. I feel fortunate to have been here to witness it."

"I'll have to bring her home myself," Holmes said. "I can't risk her with anyone else. But I'll need a respectable woman to travel with us." He cocked an eyebrow at Angelina.

"Absolutely not," James said.

Angelina flapped a hand at him. "I have a play opening in three weeks, Mr. Holmes. I'm afraid it's out of the question."

Holmes shrugged. "Merely a thought. She clearly likes you. But I'll find someone at the Ayah's Home."

"What's this?" James asked.

"A house on Jewry Street in Aldgate where Indian serving women wait for a return passage. Most of them eventually get picked up by an English family to manage the children on the long journey."

"I wonder if Ganesa ever found her way there," Angelina said. "This is the first I've heard of the place."

"I'll ask," Holmes said, "though it doesn't seem likely. There is one small detail to discuss. Two, actually. First, I imagine you would prefer to make the selection of companion yourself, Mrs. Moriarty. The princess is accustomed to being waiting on. She'll want servants of her own."

"We've done our best, but we're a small household." Angelina welcomed the task. Aldgate was dangerously near Whitechapel and the places Sandy might be hiding. She didn't want Sherlock Holmes spending any more time in the East End than was necessary. "And the second detail?"

"Someone will have to pay their passages. I don't have that emerald ring yet."

James smiled. "I'll pay, for as many ayahs as you like, if they're willing to travel second class. I'll pay your passage too, Holmes, so the princess will have company at her table. It'll be worth it to get this house back to normal."

Watson chuckled as Angelina said, "Oh, *James!*" *So* typical of her husband to make a generous offer sound like self-centered crankiness.

EIGHTEEN

Moriarty received a wire on Tuesday morning from Inspector Forbes, inviting him to call around at Scotland Yard that afternoon. The inspector would have time then to hear about the embezzlement scheme that purportedly had some relevance to the Oxwich murder.

Moriarty went at once to the post office on Gloucester Road to wire his response. He would be there on the dot. He recommended the inspector send a constable or two to collect the evidence supporting his claims from the regimental office at Odstone Barracks. Corporal Turner knew which books to take. Moriarty would do it, but he feared someone might later claim that he had altered the books himself.

The reply came almost at once: "Agreed." The police must have their own telegraph system in house.

The headquarters of the Metropolitan Police lay in Westminster, opposite the Horse Guards on one side and the Board of Trade on another. Like the War Office, Scotland Yard had spread far beyond its original building, colonizing a whole row of lesser structures. Fortunately, the sergeant at the front desk summoned a constable to guide Moriarty through the labyrinth to the warren of small offices granted to inspectors.

Forbes called, "Come in," when the constable knocked on his door. He remained seated while Moriarty entered the cramped room. "Good afternoon, Professor. Leave the door ajar, if you would. No air otherwise. Sit anywhere you like."

There was only one chair — plain, pine, and armless — not heaped with papers. It stood squarely before the cluttered desk. Moriarty took it. "I see your man brought the whole shelf of discharge books."

"Better off here than there. Corporal Turner said you'd only had time to look at the two most recent ones. If there is an ongoing scheme, we'll want to know when it started."

"Agreed." Moriarty removed his hat, setting it atop a tilting stack of papers. "Is there any news on the Oxwich case?"

"Bad news for your pet theory, I'm afraid. I went over to the War Office yesterday to interview Sergeant Brant. He can't explain how his name got into the entry log, but he has an iron-clad alibi for Monday morning. He was at his desk."

"How can that be certain?" Moriarty asked. "A man can slip in and out of his office without notice on occasion."

"Not for three hours, which is what it takes to travel out there, spend twenty to thirty minutes, and return. And I saw the room he works in. It's one long gallery with rows of desks, three men to a row. You couldn't sneak out for a cuppa without six men noticing. And no one did. I asked."

"I've seen it too." Moriarty reviewed the place in his mind, searching for a gap through which his suspect might have crawled. He couldn't find one. "Then who signed his name in the log?"

"That's a poser, all right. If it was meant as a prank, it's a dashed odd one with devilishly bad timing. I questioned the guard again on my way out. His description fits Brant well enough — average height, slender build, brushy side whiskers, round specs. But he refused to swear to it, claiming he didn't know the man well enough for that. Can't say I blame him. Over a thousand men live in that barracks, to say nothing of a steady stream of visitors all day long."

"What about the train stations?"

Forbes nodded. "A man with sergeant's stripes and round specs got off at Staines at the expected time. Not worth checking Waterloo. Too busy."

"It must have been Brant, Inspector. Nothing else makes sense."

"It wasn't Brant, Professor. Not unless he has a twin brother." Forbes gave Moriarty a wry smile. "Which he doesn't. I asked about that too."

Moriarty gave up for the time being. There was something else going on here, but he could only tackle one challenge at a time. "Shall we have a look at those books?"

"Which do you want?"

"Let's take the one from this year. I have two specific cases I want to show you."

Forbes found the right volume and handed it to Moriarty, who cradled it in his left arm as he flipped through the pages. "Ah. Here they are."

He got up and went around the desk to place the open book before the inspector. "We'll start with two men, Corporal Tommy Hale and Private Charlie Appleton. I've met them. They're working at the Salvation Army headquarters on Whitechapel Road." He ran his finger down the page to the entry for Private Appleton. "As you can see, these entries contain a wealth of information about each man's time in the army. We have his physical description, his former trade, tours of duty abroad, and expected future place of residence."

"Fascinating," Forbes said, his gaze shifting from side to side as he scanned the two-page rows. "I'm glad to know about this, Professor. Could come in handy if we're ever in pursuit of a military man."

"I hadn't thought of that." Moriarty gave a short laugh. "Well. Today we're interested in these two columns: years of service and character. The record here says that Appleton served seven years."

"Isn't that the usual term?"

"It is, but Appleton told me he served two more, for a total of twenty-one. That's not the sort of thing a man could forget. This record's been altered."

Forbes bent forward to peer closely at the page. "It does look a bit fuzzy."

"It's more than that. A number's been scraped out." Moriarty pulled out his magnifying glass and handed it to the inspector.

He re-examined the record with the superior vision afforded by the instrument. "By gad, you're right! You can see the marks of the knife as plain as day." He leaned back and looked at the glass itself with a chuckle. "Lestrade bought himself one of these things. Says Sherlock Holmes won't leave home without it. Thought it was a foolish notion. Now I might get one for myself."

"I'm finding it indispensable," Moriarty said. "I'll confess I got the idea from the same source."

Moriarty Lifts the Veil

Forbes returned to the book, placing his index figure on the altered record. "All right. Someone erased fourteen years of this soldier's life. Where does the embezzlement come in?"

Moriarty explained the concept of deferred pay, skimming over the complexities of good conduct bonuses and the rises for promotions. "One of the reasons I wanted to start with Private Appleton is that his history is uncomplicated by such things. He's a simple man with little ambition. He seems content with the Salvation Army now. But he was cheated, Inspector. Instead of collecting thirty pounds at his local post office, which he could then easily deposit in a savings account, he was handed a ten-pound note as he left the barracks."

Forbes let out a low whistle. "Twenty pounds missing, eh? That's a lot of money. And you're saying there are many of these altered records."

Moriarty nodded. "Take Corporal Hale." He flipped the page and found the corporal's record. "Change 'Good' to 'Incorrigible,' as you see here, and the soldier's deferred pay is withheld as a punishment. Hale swears he never did anything to deserve a bad character, and Appleton supports that claim. Hale was cheated of upward of twenty pounds, thrust onto the street with no means to start a new life."

Moriarty held the glass over the altered character. "To the naked eye, the row merely appears slightly worn, as if the writer's sleeve had rubbed upon it. But with the glass . . ."

"Plain as day." Forbes scowled. "That's an outrage, as well as a crime." He leaned back in his chair. "Well, you've convinced me, Professor. But are you certain Sergeant Brant is responsible?"

Moriarty tucked his glass back into his pocket and returned to his chair. "He's the only one with full access to both sets of books — the originals at the barracks and the fair copies he makes at the War Office."

"Or he innocently copies out whatever he's given," Forbes said with a challenging grin. "Seems to me Corporal Turner and Captain Greenway are in the best position to alter these records. They have constant access and no supervision, as far as I can tell. I wasn't impressed by the discipline at that barracks."

"When the commanding officer is corrupt, the men are bound to feel it, even if they don't see it happening with their own eyes. Small, easily sold items slip into pockets, and blind eyes are turned. Numbers are fiddled to come up a bit short. That sort of thing spreads like a disease."

"It is a disease, my way of thinking," Forbes said. "But why not Turner and Greenway? Turner seems like a decent fellow, but so did Sergeant Brant."

"It won't work, Inspector. If those two were running the game, why bother to alter the records at all? They could write whatever they liked the first time around and not bother with re-inking numbers or scraping out characters."

Forbes pointed a long finger at him. "True. Hmph. But how does Brant get his hands on the money?"

"I can't prove it yet," Moriarty said, "but that's next on my list. I believe he must have the stolen funds forwarded to the post office nearest those expected future addresses. I have some, ah, confederates keeping an eye on him this week."

Forbes shook the finger at him now. "Not against the law as such, but mind your step." He closed the discharge book and laid a hand on it. "I like solid evidence. Something I can see and show to a judge. You make a good case, Professor. But —"

The door flew open, banging into the back of Moriarty's chair. He twisted around and saw the aquiline features of Sherlock Holmes and leapt up to stand with his back against a cupboard with his fists raised.

"You!" Holmes bellowed, pointing with his long arm fully extended. "You *knew*!"

"What's all this?" Forbes demanded. He got to his feet as well and stood with his fists on his desk as if staking his claim. "Lestrade, what is he doing here?"

"I'm sorry." A smallish man with a protuberant nose and a shallow chin slid past Holmes to stand next to the desk. "He came to see me, then heard your voices down the hall. I couldn't stop him."

"Call for a constable, then," Forbes said.

Holmes ignored them. His color was high, even under the tan. He riveted his glare on Moriarty. "You sat there yesterday sipping

Moriarty Lifts the Veil

tea, letting me rattle on about my visit to Balmer Park, knowing all the while that its master had been brutally murdered by your friend Gabriel Sandy!"

"That's not proven, nor will it be," Moriarty said. "Sandy never did it."

"You'd say that whether it were true or not. You'd say anything to protect one of your henchmen. But you can't deny you knew about it. You were there! You withheld information pertinent to my investigation, leaving me to find out about it from the morning papers!" Holmes thundered those last words.

Now Moriarty understood his true crime — getting the scoop on the great detective.

"What are you doing here, Mr. Holmes?" Forbes asked again.

"This man's a criminal, Inspector," Holmes said, leveling that pointing finger again. "And a harborer of criminals. He's got a forger in his basement."

The inspectors traded doubtful frowns. That one hadn't gone down well.

Holmes didn't see them, being so focused on Moriarty. "Have you searched his house for the fugitive? He's probably sitting in that basement playing cards with the forger as we speak. Or he's squirreled away in the Galaxy Theater, also owned by the professor here. You could hide an army of murderers in that place. Don't ask the staff — they'll lie through their teeth if the master tells them to."

Moriarty gauged the rising level of incredulity on the policemen's faces and tried a different tack. "Does Dr. Watson know you're here, Holmes? I understand he prescribed rest until you've fully recovered from your long journey."

Holmes gave a disdainful snort. "Have you asked Moriarty about his friend? Did he volunteer anything — anything at all, like Sandy's home address or his occupation?" That piqued the inspectors' interest.

"He has not been forthcoming on that front," Forbes admitted.

"Then I'll tell you." Holmes crossed his arms. "He's a cabman who owns his own rig. Two horses and a hansom cab. He lives in Shoreditch, not far from the Empire Theater of Varieties. I don't know the precise address, but there's a public house called the Two Bells on the high street frequented by cabbies. They'll know."

"That's very helpful, Mr. Holmes, thank you." Lestrade's voice held a note of oily admiration.

"Cabbies won't tell you anything," Forbes said with a sneer. "They'd never peach on one of their own."

"The publican might." Lestrade lifted his weak chin in defense of his hero.

Moriarty wasn't worried about this line of inquiry. Sandy was too smart to go home. He was more concerned about constables turning his own house inside out. How would they explain Harini? He must send a wire to Angelina as quickly as possible, and another one to Sebastian at the Galaxy. They couldn't have a troop of bobbies turning over pans of flash powder or unsettling the weights under the trapdoors.

"Look at him, Inspectors," Holmes said. "You can see the gears turning under that high, bald dome. How will he get out of this? Where can he hide his accomplice until he convinces you to drop him and chase after his chosen red herring?"

"Wait a minute, Mr. Holmes," Forbes said. "Are you trying to tell me the professor here had something to do with Colonel Oxwich's murder?"

"He might have, Inspector. He might have. For all we know, he hired someone to impersonate that sergeant he's working so hard to convict."

"For God's sake, why?"

"He has a history with Oxwich, or rather, his wife does."

"Holmes." Moriarty filled his voice with warning. "Leave my wife out of this."

Holmes gave him that menacing shark's smile. "You can't pretend there's no connection. Draw the lines, Inspectors. From Oxwich to Sandy to Moriarty. His wife has reason to hold a grudge of her own. Since I'm a gentleman, I'll let you question her for yourselves. But in the meantime, you'd be wise to lock this man up where he can't communicate with his criminal network."

Forbes swiped his hand through the air. "All right, that's enough. You're not yourself, or at least I hope not. No, sir. You fooled me once with a convoluted tale about Professor Moriarty. Luckily, that was proven wrong before any harm was done. But I won't be fooled again."

Holmes drew himself up to his full height, towering over Lestrade. "Very well, Inspector. Your colleague and I will pursue the Oxwich case without you. Lestrade, away!" He swept out the door with as much drama as could be managed in the restricted space.

"You've got your consultant," Lestrade said to Forbes. "I've got mine. We'll see which one leads us to the truth."

Moriarty exhaled a long breath. This was an ugly turn. It was hard enough to persuade Forbes to consider Brant a suspect without that half-mad sleuthhound baying in his ears.

NINETEEN

"I'm worried about Holmes, darling." Angelina slathered marmalade on her toast. "Not just the wild things he said about you, but his health. I asked Watson about the peppery smell clinging to his jacket at tea. He said it was betel nut. You chew it, and it perks you up like a cup of Italian coffee."

"That's the last thing Holmes needs." James cut a piece of kipper. "Why would a man with his preternatural energy need to dose himself with stimulants? He smokes like a chimney and drinks tea like a man dying of thirst. He even takes cocaine when he's nothing better to do."

"Perhaps he suffers from low spirits. He does seem to have a cynical cast of mind. And he has no uplifting hobbies or interests. He doesn't paint or read novels or do abstruse mathematical calculations just to keep his hand in." Angelina beamed at her brilliant husband.

"You may be right. Perhaps that's why he turns to morbid fields of study." James pointed his fork at her. "But we must be both on our guard, my dear. He knows we'll do whatever we can to protect Sandy."

Angelina nodded. "I wish Watson could pack him off for a rest cure. He'll only muddle things up, and they're muddled enough as it is. I think you're missing a motive for Colonel Oxwich's murder."

"How so?"

"I don't know. But I wouldn't murder my partner just to keep him from squealing. I'd simply take all the money I could round up and scarper. And don't forget that two of Mrs. Oxwich's Indian servants were fished out the river with babes in their bellies. Maybe the colonel had something to do with that."

"I had forgotten. How beastly of me! But who would seek revenge for those women? Another servant?" James took the last slice of toast and buttered it thickly.

"It's possible. Maybe one of the Indian men was in love with Ganesa. I'll bet they come and go from the barracks all the time without notice, bringing along forgotten things from home." Angelina warmed to her idea, which none of the men had thought of.

"They'd still have to sign in at the gate."

"Not if they can't write. I'll bet they pass right through without so much as a 'good morning.'"

James gave her the look that meant she'd stumped him, but he would refuse to admit it. "The police may come to search the house today. How do you want to manage that?"

"I'm taking the princess to Wilton House. They've more space and far nicer rooms. I'm sure Badger can drum up an undersecretary who speaks Hindi."

Badger, properly known as Lord Brockaway, was a Somebody in the Foreign Office, as well as the protector of Angelina's younger sister, Viola. She didn't live in his mansion in Mayfair — that would put them both beyond the pale. But she and their two small children lived in a lovely flat nearby and had free run of the big house. One never said it in so many words, but they were waiting for the long-estranged Lady Brockaway to die, preferably quietly in her hotel in Nice.

"Good," James said. He'd be glad to have her out of the house. The poor girl burst into tears at the drop of a handkerchief, which was trying for any man. "She'll be safer there too."

"I've already written to Viola," Angelina said. "We'll go first thing after breakfast. Then I will plant myself in our drawing room with my hands on my hips, scolding the bobbies if they touch the slightest thing."

James smiled at that image. "I'll warn Antoine. Perhaps he could spend the day with a friend. We could go out for dinner, couldn't we? Be a nice change of pace."

Antoine had been hiding from the French Sûreté since he'd first come to London two years ago. They'd doubtless forgotten about him in that time, but he still flinched at the mere mention of the police. He'd never survive a search of the house.

Rolly brought up the post. James tossed the usual advertisements aside, then picked up a plain white envelope, the sort you could purchase at any post office.

"It's from Sandy," he said, as he unfolded the single sheet.

"Thank goodness!"

"Is 'e all right?" Rolly asked, adding her plate to his tray.

"He's fine." James nodded at Rolly. "You should listen too — you're mentioned." He read the letter aloud. "I'm safe and sound among friends. Don't worry. The bluebottles won't get far in these parts, and I stay on the move. I trust you'll sort it out in short order so I can get back to searching for Zuri.

"I can use the Royal Mail, God bless our gracious Queen. You can reach me through my lads. They'll be around, ones that Rolly knows. Just send him out to the post office or the grocer with your note. They'll work out the exchange. Our three veterans can also be trusted.

"And now the more delicate subject. I could use some money, about twenty pounds in small coins, if you can manage it. The best thing I can think of is to send it to the stable in a box of horseshoe nails. They should come from Lewis and Son, Ltd. Zeke and our three friends can take it from there.

"I can't tell you both how grateful I am for your friendship. There's no one else in the world I could ask for help at such a time. Someday, perhaps I'll be able to repay you.

"Your loving friend, Gabriel Sandy."

"Some day!" Angelina dabbed at a bit of moisture in the corner of her eye. "We're in his debt a thousand times over."

"Indeed, we are." James started to refold the letter, then stopped. "I suppose I should burn this." He rose, gathered up the advertisements, and tossed the whole lot onto the fire. He stirred the burned fragments with the poker to be sure all was ash.

"Well," Angelina said, pushing back her chair. "I've got a busy day. What will you be doing?"

"I mean to find out how Brant is collecting the money he steals. Sandy's lads have been watching him. I hope they'll have some news. Which means my first task should be to send Rolly out to buy a paper at the stall near the grocer's." He smiled at her. "I know it's no joke, but all this does feel rather cloak-and-dagger, doesn't it?"

"Theatrical, I was thinking. I wish you good hunting, darling. Try not to be too late getting home tonight."

* * *

Mr. Tweedy was dispatched to the ironmonger after stopping at a bank to change a twenty-pound note into coins. He was happy to volunteer, having thus far had no role in the Moriartys' sleuthing adventures. Like the others, he was restless, waiting for the theater to re-open. James worried that his face was too well-known, being one of London's most beloved comic actors. But sometimes the best way to hide something was to doll it up and put a funny hat on it. No London bobbie would question Timothy Tweedy. They were more likely to ape some of his famous routines and beg for an autograph.

Leaving the money in his capable hands, Angelina turned her attention to moving the suspicious Harini to Wilton House. Pantomime failed to convey the intended meaning, though she and Rolly did their level best. Harini clung to the bedpost as if they were trying to throw her into the street. They finally had to summon Mr. Kumar, still wearing his grocer's apron, to explain the plan.

She remained tense until their cab drew up to the marble steps and a liveried footman descended to help her out. Once inside, each fresh sign of luxury stripped away a layer of doubt. By the time they reached the Blue Bedroom, with its fifteen-foot ceiling and its silk-curtained bedstead, she was positively beaming.

The wife of an assistant to the undersecretary in the Department of Indian Affairs met them in the hall. She'd been sent to translate, being perfectly fluent in Hindi. When she explained that the opulent bedchamber was to be Harini's sanctuary until they could work out how to restore her to her father's home, the child burst into tears — for joy this time.

Angelina waited for the shower to subside, then smiled warmly at the princess while speaking to the assistant undersecretary's wife. "When the mahila has had a chance to rest and recover, I hope she'll be willing to tell me more about her experiences in the Oxwich house. I'm especially interested in what happened to a woman named Ganesa."

Harini's round face sobered as she caught that name. Angelina quirked an eyebrow and was granted a small nod of acknowledgment before she left.

Getting Antoine out of the house was nearly as difficult. Torn between his fear of police and his attachment to his kitchen, he kept turning back from the door to fuss with something else.

"You will starve," he said. "You cannot eat a cold lunch."

"Of course we can," Angelina said. "The professor will be out, so it's only Peg, Rolly, and me. You've left us enough cold meats and cheeses for an army. We'll manage splendidly."

She finally coaxed him into his coat and pushed him out the door with a copy of *Les Misérables* under his arm. His plan was to sit in the darkest corner of the Hereford Arms reading until someone came to fetch him.

Angelina nipped back into the kitchen and stole a piece of lemon tart, devouring it in three big bites. She dusted the crumbs under the worktable. Now she wanted a cup of tea. She shifted the kettle over the low fire at the back, feeling like a sneak thief in her own house. She'd barely found the packet of tea and got the pot ready when the coppers came.

The heavy *boom-boom-boom* on the front door knocker sounded an unmistakable command. Angelina pulled the kettle off the heat, ran a smoothing hand over her hair, and went upstairs to meet the intruders.

She gave Rolly a tight smile. "Might as well let them in, else they'll knock the door down."

Sherlock Holmes led the pack, striding into the hall with a proprietary air. He was followed by a lean little man with close-set eyes who kept one careful step behind Holmes, forcing him to peer around the taller man. Two constables in helmets and blue uniforms brought up the rear.

Holmes introduced the little man as Inspector Lestrade. James had mentioned him as the sleuthhound's puppet. She greeted him with a cold nod.

"We're looking for a tall man with ginger hair," Holmes told the constables. "Though he may have dyed it."

Angelina gave him a withering look. "You can't honestly believe you'll find Mr. Sandy skulking under a bed. This is harassment pure

Moriarty Lifts the Veil

and simple, Inspector, and don't think my husband won't be having words with your superiors about it."

Lestrade quivered like a rabbit caught between two large dogs, but he was clearly in thrall to Holmes. "We've our job to do, Mrs. Moriarty. Best let us get on with it."

"I'll know if he's been staying here, Mrs. Moriarty. The least sign speaks volumes to me, as you well know. The professor is welcome to watch and learn, if he likes."

"Piffle. He's out searching for Colonel Oxwich's murderer. As you should be instead of indulging your unseemly curiosity."

That had no effect. Holmes seemed to have convinced himself that Sandy had come here to hide, even though that would have been the stupidest choice. He'd be better off in a room at the Savoy. Surely Holmes knew that.

"We'll start with the basement," Holmes said, striding toward the stairs. His lackeys trailed behind him.

Rolly got out in front as they entered the kitchen, planting himself protectively before the iron range and the rows of gleaming copper pans that hung beside it. "One mark on these pans and you'll be in the soup."

"Where's your French chef?" Holmes asked as he strolled about the room with his hands behind his back.

"Shopping, I should think." Angelina affected an air of unconcern. "If you'd warned us when you were coming, I'm sure he would have stayed to offer refreshment."

"No doubt." Holmes strolled on into the servants' hall, giving the group of chairs by the hearth special attention. His dark eyebrows flicked up and down, but he made no comment.

The three policemen trailed him pointlessly. They were only here to legitimize his insufferable intrusion into his archrival's home.

"Who is your superior, Inspector Lestrade? His name, I mean."

Lestrade blinked at her. He'd evidently failed to credit her earlier threat. "Chief Inspector Wright."

"Thank you."

"Don't worry, Lestrade," Holmes said. "We're on safe ground. When searching for a fugitive murder suspect, all places of possible concealment, however improbable, must be inspected."

He led the men down the hall, opening each door. No ginger-haired murderer lurked within the narrow confines of the scullery or the pantry. Antoine had left his room spotless. His bedstead and dressing table gleamed with wax, and the whole chamber smelled of lemons.

Rolly bounded ahead to stand in the middle of his room, hands on hips and eyes blazing. That small but cozy domain was the first place he'd ever been able to call his own, and he guarded it fiercely. Angelina had never looked inside since he'd taken possession. She was pleased to see how neat it was and surprised to see a small portrait of the queen hanging on the wall.

The constables seemed to respect the lad's dignity. They barely peeked inside. Besides, there wasn't room in there to hide a cat.

Back upstairs to repeat the ritual in the dining room and morning room. No cabman's overcoat hung on the rack, no copies of the *Sporting Life* lay folded beside an armchair. So up they went to the first floor to inspect the front and rear drawing rooms.

"You had tea in this room two days ago, Mr. Holmes. If you'd wanted a tour of the house, we could have given you one then."

"I didn't know then what I know now." Holmes's eyes narrowed. "You and your husband deliberately concealed your knowledge of that murder from me. *Me!*" He poked himself in the chest.

True enough, for excellent reasons. "Oh, that's what's got your nose out of joint!" Angelina wrinkled her nose at him in mock playfulness. "We beat you to it, by the simple coincidence of the professor teaching his class. Crafty of us, wasn't it?"

"I don't believe in coincidence."

"Don't you? Your world must be a very tangled and nefarious place, Mr. Holmes."

Angelina cocked her head to study his face anew. So thin, so brown, and so outlandish with that false beard and moustache. He looked like a man who'd been sleeping in the woods, spying on people with a telescope. His pupils were still a little dilated, and he moved his head in small jerks, like a bird, as he examined clues visible only to him.

By this point, the constables were reduced to entering a room and standing in the middle of it with their hands at their sides.

Moriarty Lifts the Veil

Lestrade strolled about with his hands behind his back, imitating his idol, but it was obvious he didn't really notice anything.

They climbed the stairs to the landing, where Rolly opened the door to exhibit the water closet. Then on to the second floor, where Angelina endured the indignity of four men tramping through her bedchamber and her dressing room. Lestrade made a point of looking under both beds and opening every cupboard door.

"Touch one of my gowns with your greasy fingers, Inspector, and I'll hit you with a galloping great cleaning bill."

Lestrade startled and thrust his hands into his pockets.

None of the rooms on the third floor was occupied now that Harini had gone. They found Mrs. Shawe, the daily char, in the guest room, polishing every fingermark or speck of soot from every surface.

Holmes watched her work with a cold eye. He waved the constables and Lestrade off to the other bedrooms, staying behind to ask in a quiet voice, "What's become of the former occupant?"

"Moved on to finer accommodations in Mayfair until her relations can be notified." He would know she meant Wilton House, which meant Lord Brockaway would now take charge of the missing princess. "Don't worry, you'll still get your emerald ring. His Lordship feels the rajah will want to come collect his child himself."

"Satisfactory," Holmes said and let the matter drop.

The last floor was a single large room under the sloping eaves of the roof — James's aerie, his private retreat where he could read journals or engage in statistical studies without interruption. Holmes waved the constables back down. "Wait in the front hall, if you please." To Lestrade he said, spreading his hands wide, "This is where the master criminal weaves his webs."

"There are no webs, Inspector," Angelina snapped. "My husband is a scholarly man, a mathematician who takes an interest in financial crimes. His network, if you choose to employ that fanciful term, consists primarily of the reading room at the British Museum and the libraries of the Royal Society. He exposes crimes, he doesn't abet them."

Unless the criminal was his wife or a member of his wife's family or a very close family friend. She held an exasperated expression on

181

her face while that last thought ran its course to keep Holmes from reading her mind.

Lestrade looked about the room with admiration, taking in the telescope, the huge map of London spread atop the long table, and the welcoming chair with just the right lamp set at just the right distance from the tiled fireplace.

"Wish my office was fitted out like this. I could solve a lot more crimes on me own."

Angelina treated him to a benign smile. "Would you give us a moment, Inspector? We'll catch up with you on the way down."

Holmes granted his permission with a slow blink. James called him a sleuthhound, but in many ways the detective was more like a cat — swift, ruthless, and utterly self-possessed.

He raised his eyebrows at her.

"You've invaded my home for no reason, Mr. Holmes. It's done now, and that's that. You can repay me by answering a question without prying into my reasons for asking it."

"Fair enough."

"If you had the chance to uncover something ugly, truly ugly, which you only suspect at present but have a very strong feeling about, by spending a weekend with the suspects on their own ground, how would you go about accomplishing this great uncovering?"

He followed that tangled speech without difficulty. "At the Oxwiches' house?" A reasonable guess, given the present circumstances.

"No. But someone in that circle. It's related to the Indian women, as you've undoubtedly guessed. But don't ask me my plan because I don't have one. I'm asking you."

"Well. I would play my expected part for a while, then contrive some excuse to retire early — a headache usually suffices. Then I would disguise myself as an invisible person, like a servant in a sari and veil, and lurk about, listening at keyholes and spying through windows. You'll have to take some risks to get close to the heart of this ugly thing, whatever it is. They won't be torturing their servants in the drawing room, at least not with the curtains open."

"I thought as much. It just seemed a bit mad to dress up in a costume and sneak around in someone's house."

Holmes chuckled. "That's Watson's view of most of my investigative techniques. But you're an actress, Mrs. Moriarty. It should be well within your range."

"Thank you, Mr. Holmes. My fledgling plan seems slightly less impossible." Ideas had bloomed in her mind at the words "sari" and "veil."

Holmes gazed down on her with something almost like collegial sympathy. "Do be careful, however. Persons who traffic in human flesh are not generally known for their clemency."

TWENTY

Wednesday morning's mail brought an invitation from Inspector Forbes for Moriarty to accompany him on his visit to Mrs. Oxwich. Purely routine, but sometimes the grieving widow held a vital clue somewhere in her memory.

Moriarty suspected the invitation derived from Forbes's competitive nature. If Lestrade had a consulting detective, then by gosh, Forbes would have one too. But on the train, Forbes confided that he'd made the offer to make up for Lestrade's outrageous intrusion the day before.

"It was out of bounds," Forbes said as the train pulled out of Waterloo Station. "You'd be within your rights to lodge a complaint, which wouldn't do the service any good. Besides, your house is the last place your friend would hide."

"That's what my wife told them. But the search was merely a ruse. Holmes has an idée fixe about me, especially when he's in one of his agitated phases. We've learned to take it in stride."

Forbes shook out his newspaper and added, "We do need to talk to Mr. Sandy, however. Surely you can understand that."

"Of course." Moriarty opened his copy of *The Economist*. He'd finished *The Times* at home. Then he returned Forbes's level gaze. "But I have no control over the man, and I honestly do not know where he is."

They read their papers in silence for the rest of the journey. They took a cab from the station to Balmer Park. Moriarty's stomach clenched as they came in sight of the great house. Its three stories of honey-colored Bath stone declared a history of wealth and influence. How much of that wealth had been founded on the sale of human beings? Or was Mrs. Oxwich the first in her family to enter that despicable trade?

Angelina had described the woman as a dark-haired Queen Victoria with a slight Bristol accent. That turned out to be quite apt. The widow looked tired, with dark hollows under her dark eyes. She had undoubtedly had many unpleasant duties to perform in the past two days, given her late husband's prominent position.

She received them in a yellow-and-white drawing room. She sat in the center of the sofa while the two men took the armchairs opposite her. Forbes apologized for the intrusion, assuring her it was purely routine. "I must ask, Mrs. Oxwich. Did your husband have any enemies that you know of?"

"Enemies? Certainly not." She seemed aghast at the idea. "Unless you count Ayub Khan of Afghanistan, though I believe he may be dead." She spoke without a trace of humor, as if she thought there was a real possibility that the former Afghan ruler had sent an assassin to murder her erstwhile military opponent.

Forbes nodded and jotted something in his notebook. "I know this is painful, but I must ask where you were on Monday morning, between 9:15 and 9:45?"

"Home, of course. Where else would I be?"

"Can anyone vouch for you?" Forbes asked.

She frowned so deeply her chin doubled. "Any of the servants. You have only to ask."

At that moment, an Indian woman appeared bearing a tray with tea and small cakes. She set the refreshments on the low table and glided away again without ever raising her eyes. Moriarty watched her surreptitiously, not wanting to betray his interest. Angelina had said most of them spoke little English. Could any of these servants in this house actually give testimony?

Mrs. Oxwich poured tea and offered the cakes. While the men sampled them, she said, "I'm told a former officer named Gabriel Sandy has been charged with my husband's murder."

"No charges have been made as yet," Forbes said. "We haven't been able to question him."

"Why not?"

"We haven't apprehended him yet. But rest assured, it won't be long. He can't evade the entire Metropolitan Police force forever."

Moriarty doubted that. The police had little influence in the city east of St. Paul's. Or Sandy might decide to abscond to some lesser metropolis until a more pressing case wiped his name from the top of the list.

Mrs. Oxwich's expression reflected Moriarty's skepticism. "I knew him, of course. Gabriel Sandy. In India. He was in my husband's company. He was the worst sort of young officer. His father forced him to enlist, as I recall, hoping the army would teach him discipline. It works for some. Others find new ways to misbehave. Captain Sandy spent most of his time playing polo, gambling, and visiting houses of ill repute. He built up a considerable debt, which his father quite correctly refused to pay."

"Gambling debts?" Moriarty asked. Forbes shot him a warning glance. He should leave the questions to the policeman.

"Oh yes. He was caught embezzling money from the officers' mess. An attempt to cover those debts, presumably. Or to buy gifts for that little dancer he'd fallen in with. A fancy term for another occupation, if you'll pardon the observation. Sandy tried to throw the blame on my husband, but he was cashiered in due course. I believe his family disowned him, and rightly so." Mrs. Oxwich ended her brief, yet devastating, character assassination with a long sniff.

Lies, all lies. If Sandy had been so addicted to gambling as to steal to pay his debts, he would've shown some sign of that vice here in London. And yet, while he liked to watch horse races when he got the chance, he never risked so much as a shilling on the outcome.

Forbes had taken copious notes during that diatribe, but his face showed no trace of his opinion. Now he turned a page and changed the subject. "We found a note from a Sergeant Jeremy Brant on your husband's desk, arranging an appointment for that morning. Do you know anything about such a meeting?"

Mrs. Oxwich's black eyebrows rose. "No, I don't. But the colonel often held meetings in the barracks residence, Inspector. It's quieter than the regimental office."

"Do you know anything about this Sergeant Brant?"

"No. Is he one of ours?" Her expression remained politely attentive as she lifted her cup and took a sip of tea.

"He's the liaison from the Army Pay Office, according to Corporal Turner."

"Well, if Corporal Turner says it, it must be true. He's the one who really runs the regiment, you know." Here she offered the first

Moriarty Lifts the Veil

small smile. "I fear I know very little about the administrative routine in the barracks. Why shouldn't Sergeant Brant make an appointment with the colonel?"

"Sergeant Yancy swears no such meeting took place. Sergeant Brant denies having made any such appointment, although he logged in at the gate at 9:15 and left thirty minutes later. He did not visit the office. I'd like to know what he did do. His visit overlaps the estimated time of death."

Mrs. Oxwich frowned, drank some tea, then placed her cup carefully on the table. "Are you suggesting that those two men — Captain Sandy and this Sergeant Brant — collaborated in the murder of my husband?"

Forbes cocked his head, his pencil suspended above the page. "That seems unlikely, given what I know so far. Sergeant Brant has a solid alibi, but the guard saw someone who resembled Brant enter the gate and sign the book. That contradiction alone makes Brant — or whoever entered the barracks using his name — a suspect, along with Mr. Sandy and Sergeant Yates."

"Yates! Goodness gracious, Inspector. You can't suspect Billy Yates. He's been with us for ages. There's no reason for him to kill the goose — I mean rock the boat — now."

A faint twinkle in Forbes's eyes told Moriarty that he'd caught that revealing slip. The goose that laid the golden eggs — by embezzling discharge pay, perhaps?

The inspector asked, "Are you sure your husband never mentioned Sergeant Brant?"

"Well." Mrs. Oxwich picked up her cup, drank a sip of tea, and returned the cup to the table. She licked her lips as she glanced out the window, then returned a worried look to the inspector. "I don't know the man and don't wish to slander him unjustly, but my husband did tell me the most appalling story on Friday afternoon. Gabriel Sandy and another man — the new maths coach, I believe he said — barged into the colonel's office making wild accusations about irregularities in the discharge records. Well, that's Captain Greenway's concern. He's in charge of everything to do with the enlisted men. But these men seemed to think the Army Pay Officer was cheating the men of their savings, with my husband's approval.

It's complete nonsense, of course. My husband regarded the men who served under him as members of his own family."

"So you don't think that sort of theft would be possible?" Forbes asked.

"I have no idea, Inspector. But I do wonder . . . Could it be possible that this Brant had been blackmailing my husband? If he really was stealing those funds, I mean. After those horrid men left, the colonel would've summoned his pay officer straightaway to answer a few sharp questions. Any attempt at bribery or blackmail would've made him all the more adamant. He might have threatened to bring it all before the adjutant general."

Forbes was nodding as he wrote his notes. "That's an interesting idea, Mrs. Oxwich. If Brant feared the colonel would open an investigation, he'd have a pretty good motive for stopping him."

"Why wait two days?" Moriarty asked. "The colonel could have met with Brant's superior on Saturday morning, if he'd been so concerned."

"At the War Office?" Mrs. Oxwich scoffed. "On a Saturday? Nonsense. But my husband would never level such a serious charge in haste. He would want to confirm his impression of what had or had not been implied on Friday afternoon, quietly, man to man. Monday morning is the time for that sort of thing. The colonel always retired to the residence to catch up on the newspapers. It's important for a man in his position to keep abreast of world affairs, you know. Yates pretends to read his paper too — he's always aping the colonel — but he inevitably falls asleep. My husband said his snores could be heard throughout the house."

"We're looking into Sergeant Yates as well," Forbes said.

Mrs. Oxwich quirked her lips. "I'm sure you know your business, Inspector." She shifted forward, placing her hands on her knees as if about to rise. Time to go.

As they got to their feet, she said, "It's a good thing you came to me to hear the truth about that sorry business in Jaipur. You'd find a variety of opinions in the officers' mess, I shouldn't doubt. We thought Captain Sandy had scuttled off in shame and lost himself out there in the East. But truthfully, I'm not surprised to learn that he's turned up again and gone back to his old tricks. I suspect you'll find that he and your Sergeant Brant were working together on that new scheme. They must have had a falling out, as thieves inevitably do, and tried to throw the blame on each other. Mark my words, Inspector. Catch the one, and you'll catch the other."

TWENTY-ONE

"I still don't think it's very plausible." Angelina addressed the remark to the open pages of *The Times* since all she could see of her husband were the hands holding the paper and the legs beneath it.

The Moriartys were sitting in the morning room. Angelina had penned a short note to Sandy warning him about the impending box of nails. She'd also told him that since their house had now been searched by Sherlock Holmes and his police lackeys, there was no reason Sandy shouldn't come live in comfort on their third floor. She doubted he would accept the invitation, but she felt better for having given it.

"What's not plausible?" James asked from behind his paper.

"That your Sergeant Brant would commit such a dramatic murder. If he knew the man's habits well enough to catch him napping, why not doctor a packet of his favorite tea and leave it in the office? He's clearly a patient man, by his methods."

"Too chancy. Might kill Corporal Turner or someone else." James turned a rustling page.

Angelina scowled at the newspaper. "That would depend on how special the tea was, wouldn't it? But the two crimes don't fit together, James. That careful selection of victims and painstaking alteration of records with lots of excruciating calculations — that sounds like something you would do if you were an Army Pay Officer with a lust for money. But strolling boldly into a crowded barracks to drive an ancient ceremonial dagger into your sleeping victim's chest? That's pure theater. That's something I would do if I hated or feared the man so much I simply had to kill him."

Now James lowered his paper to give her that furled-brow look that meant she'd switched his train of thought onto an unexpected track. "*That* is a very interesting observation, my dear." He chewed on the fringe of his moustache, his dark brows furling more deeply. "Very interesting indeed." Then he glanced at the clock on the mantelpiece and snapped his paper closed. "But I have to catch Brant either way. Which means I ought to be getting up and going out."

He suited his actions to his words, dropping a light kiss on her forehead as he left. That wasn't quite the full-throated acclamation of her idea that she felt it deserved, but it was doubtless the best she would get. On those terms, she'd take it.

* * *

She'd barely written half her daily letter to Viola when Rolly bounced in with a telegram on a silver salver. "It's from Wilton 'ouse, Missus!"

Angelina tore the thin sheet open and scanned the short message. "It appears I've been summoned to speak with royalty." She smiled at Rolly's gaping mouth and added, "Our princess, remember? Harini. It would seem she's ready to talk."

Viola and the children were out, taking their morning airing in the park with the nannies. Just as well. The little poppets were so adorable; Angelina could squander an hour or more petting them and listening to their doting mother's detailed account of their activities.

Spared that distraction, she followed the footman straight up to the Blue Bedroom. There she found Harini clothed in what one assumed was her accustomed splendor. She'd only been here for one day, but she'd already managed to have a new costume made. Where in London had she found that *gorgeous* length of Indian-patterned silk? She looked every inch the princess, wrapped in sumptuous red fabric trimmed in gleaming gold. She wore a pair of huge gold earrings and had rimmed her eyes with kohl, making her look older. She'd restored the red dot between her eyes as well, which made her look more exotic.

All in all, it was a complete transformation.

Harini watched Angelina take in her new look with a gleam of satisfaction in her dark eyes. She seated herself in a silk-upholstered armchair and then gestured grandly for her guest to take the low, armless seat before her.

Angelina accepted the lesser position without a qualm. At least she hadn't been obliged to lower herself, bustle and all, onto a footstool. She folded her hands in her lap. "Thank you for seeing me so soon, Mahila."

Harini nodded graciously and spoke a few words in Hindi. The translator, Mrs. Undersecretary — her name had never been mentioned — said, "I also am eager to see justice done to the villains who stole me away from my father's home."

"We will do everything we can. Does Her Ladyship know what happened to Ganesa? I know she was in a different house, but perhaps there was gossip in the servants' hall?"

Mrs. Undersecretary relayed that in Hindi, then listened to a long answer. She nodded and turned to Angelina. "The mahila says that yes, she knew Ganesa and liked her. The ayah was kind to her when they met, which was often because the English women have parties all the time. They have no children and no subjects or lands to manage. They are idle and fall easily into wicked pastimes."

That had been Angelina's observation, though she hadn't put it in quite the same terms. "What happened to her?"

Mrs. Undersecretary said, "This is all gossip. It may not be true. But the mahila believes it is true because of the way the others talked. Ganesa was very pretty. When the children of her mistress went away, she was more in the company of her mistress, often in her bedchamber with her clothes and cosmetics. The husband saw her more, they say, and liked her. She became pregnant, they said, by the master. She did not wish to make her own memsahib sad, so she came to Oxwich Memsahib seeking a remedy. Oxwich Memsahib ruled the others. That one said, yes, she knew what to do. They say she took Ganesa away in the carriage with Rajesh to go into the city of London. The memsahib and Rajesh returned, but Ganesa did not."

Angelina nodded, fleshing out that tale with what she had learned. Mrs. Reynolds must have suspected something like this had happened to her ayah but hadn't wanted to admit it to herself. She was skilled at hiding her feelings. She hadn't really seemed that worried when she'd come to enlist Angelina's help.

"Who is Rajesh?" she asked.

The translator elicited the answer. "He is the tall manservant of Oxwich Memsahib. He is not like the others. He is paid, they say, in English money, and can come and go as he likes."

"I see." And what a useful henchman he must be for a woman responsible for dozens of lost, stolen, deceived, or otherwise helpless servants. Angelina asked the translator, "Does she know that Ganesa is dead? I don't wish to startle her, but the body was found recently in the river. I believe Mrs. Oxwich and her man murdered her."

Mrs. Undersecretary quailed. "Oh mercy! I can't tell her that. She's only a child."

But Harini had watched the exchange with her hard, bright eyes. Now she snapped her fingers and made a summoning gesture.

"She wants to know," Mrs. Undersecretary said, surrendering. As she performed her duty, Harini's eyes narrowed. She nearly spat her response. "She says you must question the servants in the Oxwich Memsahib's house, especially the women. They are no happier than she was, though they were Shudra caste — servants — and accustomed to the work. They will tell you about Rajesh and the things he does for that memsahib."

"They will all be questioned," Angelina promised. Surely this was enough to get the attention of the police.

But Harini hadn't finished. The translator listened to her with growing horror on her face. Then she turned to Angelina. "I can barely stand to listen to it, much less repeat it to you. But she wants you know that worse things happen in that house. Ganesa's sahib wasn't the only one who used his servants in that way. Oxwich Sahib was worse. That is the real reason the memsahib sent her away. And me also."

The translator faltered. Angelina said, "It's all right. The princess is very brave to tell her story. Without her courage — and yours — these horrible people can never be stopped."

Harini said something else, which sounded like something in the same vein. The translator drew in a deep breath, found her own courage, and carried on.

"She said her cheeks are still round like a child, but she is no longer a child. She is a woman. Oxwich Sahib is a very bad man, bad in his heart. He thinks the women in his house are there to serve him however he likes, whenever he likes. The princess was warned from the start to avoid him, especially at night, but the women had to climb the stairs past his door to reach their beds. Sometimes he would wait for them, hiding in his dark doorway. Or he would catch one in his library when she came in to clean and lock the door so his wife would not know.

"They tried never to be alone, but it is difficult. The memsahib is very strict about the work. She did not like the use her husband made of them. He caught this darling child once, pushing her into a corner and groping her with his horrible fat hands, but the memsahib came up and clapped her hands, very loud, the way she does when the servants do something wrong. He let her go and went away. The memsahib did not punish the girl, though she was very angry. Mahila Harini went down to the kitchen, where the cook explained it to her. Oxwich Sahib spoils her trade, you see. She brings servants from India, trains them in English ways, and sells them for much money to the other memsahibs. But a servant with a child in her belly is no good to her. She cannot work. She cannot be sold. She cannot be sent home because then all would be known there as well. She must be taken away with Rajesh and never seen again."

Angelina met the translator's eyes, mirroring her expression of disgust and anger. "Tell the princess that I mean to put a stop to it — all of it. I don't know how yet, but I will do it."

After hearing that translated, Harini nodded. Then a bright smile broke across her face. She spoke, and Mrs. Undersecretary translated. "She says that when her father comes to collect her, he will kill Oxwich Sahib for you. He will want to do it in any case."

Angelina laughed. "Wouldn't that be simpler? But I'm afraid it's already been done. It appears one of his former colleagues beat you to it." She rose, performed a deep bow to the girl in the gorgeous draperies, and excused herself.

She smiled as she pattered down the marble staircase. She'd found a motive for Oxwich's murder that beat covering up a bookkeeping crime all hollow.

TWENTY-TWO

Moriarty walked up to the post office on Gloucester Road and asked to speak to the postmaster. He said he was preparing to send a cousin a largish sum of money and was concerned about how the cousin could identify himself when he collected it. He hadn't been living in that town for very long and wouldn't be recognized by the staff.

"Does your cousin have a passport?" the master asked.

"Not to my knowledge."

"Can he present anything bearing his name and address, like a bill from the coal-man or a library subscription card?"

Moriarty frowned, surprised. "He has his army discharge papers."

The postmaster beamed at him. "Why, that's perfect! Don't worry, sir. Your cousin won't have any trouble."

Nor would Sergeant Brant. He could simply make a copy of his victims' papers for his own use. The system seemed hopelessly inadequate, but what could be done? One couldn't rely on personal acquaintance anymore. People moved around too much nowadays. In a city like London, one could leave one's past behind by merely shifting from north to south or east to west. Methods that relied on trust were painfully easy to exploit.

* * *

Moriarty wrote a longish note to Gabriel Sandy and handed it to Rolly. The lad would go in and out of a few shops on Gloucester Road and be relieved of the letter in the process. Moriarty had just finished a solitary luncheon — Angelina had been unable to resist spending an hour or three with her sister and the little tots — when

Rolly appeared at the dining room door with an air of irrepressible excitement.

"They're 'ere, Perfessor. Two o' Sandy's boys. They've got somefing to report."

"I'll be right down. Put them at the servants' table and ask Antoine to give them some lunch."

Moriarty hastily finished his chicken salad, then collected some paper and pencils from the desk in the morning room before jogging downstairs.

He found Rolly setting glasses of cold milk before two boys. Their hands and faces looked freshly scrubbed. Both had the pinched faces of children who rarely had enough to eat, but their eyes were alert and intelligent. One was either very young or small for his age, being something under four feet tall. Rolly had added some cushions to his chair. He introduced the waif as Scooch, "Because 'e can squeeze through small places."

"Very apt," Moriarty said as he took a chair opposite. Surely the child had another name, but perhaps it was safer to use these *noms de guerre*. Then again, Rolly had no idea what his mother's surname had been. He barely remembered her.

The other boy was taller, needing no extra boost to clear the table. His name was Dipper, which even Moriarty knew was the slang term for a pickpocket. The boy wore a top hat and a grubby scarf around his neck, knotted in a once-fashionable style.

Antoine brought plates of thick chicken sandwiches and set them before the boys. He must have seen that pinched look too and would never allow anyone — child or man — to leave his domain hungry. Then he went back to fetch cup of tea and a plate of ginger biscuits for the master.

Moriarty gestured for Rolly to join them at the table. This was a conference, not a social call. "I assume you're the lads who've been keeping an eye on Sergeant Brant for me."

They nodded, mouths too full to speak. Rolly wagged a finger at them. "Every detail now. Let the perfessor decide what's important. You can take turns."

One boy ate while the other reported. They'd been following Brant since Friday afternoon, at Sandy's request. Lots of toffs around the War Office and every kind of uniform you'd ever hope to see.

Moriarty Lifts the Veil

Brant was easy enough to spot, though, thanks to those side whiskers and his shiny round specs.

He lived in a neat lodging house on Bedford Street not far from Covent Garden. On Saturday, he'd left his house wearing a tan checked suit with a straw boater and gone to Waterloo Station. He'd boarded a train bound for Windsor, leaving the boys on the platform. They'd never been out of London and weren't sure what the world was like out there. The streets might be empty, for all they new, with no friendly crowds to blend into. Besides, they hadn't the coin.

Moriarty commended their decision. These urchins would've been picked by a local constable in a matter of minutes. He did not fail to note, however, that Brant could have gotten off at Staines, instead of Windsor, and gone from there to Balmer Park. He might have been summoned by Colonel Oxwich to discuss the threat of discovery.

The boys continued their report. Sergeant Whiskers, as they called him, left each morning at 8:45 and walked to the War Office, arriving as the bells at some nearby church struck nine. He stayed there all morning, as best they could tell. They couldn't follow him inside, but they'd taken turns circling the building and never saw anyone coming or going through a different door. They reckoned it wasn't allowed, being the army and all.

Brant had his lunch at a chophouse a few streets away, the same one every day. Then he went straight back to the War Office. At four o'clock, he left in a great throng of other clerks. Dipper had to climb up on a wall to spot their man. Half the fellows coming out were wearing red jackets. The job was ticklish, but they were up to it. They followed him back to his lodging house, where he remained until dark. Then they decided to chuck it and find a place to sleep nearby.

Moriarty wondered if they'd had anything to eat during all that time. He didn't like to ask — these boys had their dignity — but he'd make sure they had some coins in their pockets when they left. They were working for him, after all. They deserved a fair wage.

So much for Monday and Tuesday. Things changed on Wednesday. Brant left the office at noon, as usual. This time, however, he was carrying a brown valise. He usually left that in the office when he went out at noon. He walked to Haymarket Street and lunched in an oyster house, not his usual chophouse. Afterward, he walked east instead of going back to Pall Mall, up to Clerkenwell Road and down a narrow street called Saffron Hill to a lodging house of a very different stripe.

There was mold growing on the front steps, and the windows looked like they'd never been washed by anything but rain. Brant entered through the front door without knocking. He spent a little more than a quarter of an hour there, by the church bells, then came back out wearing a different red jacket. This one had frayed cuffs and patches on the hem. He also seemed to have a left an arm upstairs, because one sleeve was pinned up empty.

"How is that possible?" Moriarty asked.

The boys smiled at his ignorance. "You 'ides your arm inside," Rolly said, "like this." He stood up to demonstrate, unbuttoning his blue livery coat, pulling his arm out of the sleeve, and letting it hang by his side. It was a bit of a struggle, but he managed to get it buttoned again by himself. "It's easier if you pin the sleeve up first, of course." He limped around the room a bit, swinging his empty sleeve.

"Where did you learn that trick?" Moriarty asked.

Rolly shrugged. "It's good for begging. They give you more when they feel sorry for you." He restored his arm to its sleeve and straightened his jacket.

"I see." Moriarty turned to the regimenters. "Are you certain this man was Sergeant Brant?"

Dipper gave him a withering look. "We been watching the bloke all week, Perfessor. We knows our job."

Brant went directly to the post office on Farringdon Road — the nearest one to his second lodging. The bells chimed once before he came out looking pleased with himself.

"We wondered why 'e was so perky," Scooch piped in his childish voice. "So when 'e got to 'olborn Road, Dipper picked 'is pocket."

"Always a good crowd there." Dipper grinned, showing a missing tooth. "What d'ye reckon I got?"

Rolly have him a doubtful look. "The perfessor ain't likely to — "

"Don't worry," Dipper said. "I put it back a few blocks down the road. It were a big wad of bills, Perfessor. I counted twenty-five quid!"

Moriarty Lifts the Veil

Rolly cackled with glee and punched the boy in the arm. "Now, there's a neat trick! First you robs him, then you gives it back. And 'ere's the poor mark strolling along, never the wiser."

Dipper preened at the praise. It must take a great deal of confidence in one's prowess to risk discovery again in order to restore your victim's goods. And considerable strength of character not to keep the money and say nothing about it.

Moriarty's esteem for these clever urchins rose. He dug into his trouser pockets for coins and divided the three or four pounds between the boys. "Good work, lads. I'd like you to show me that house on Saffron Hill. I want a word with the landlord or lady, if possible." He glanced at his pocket watch. "But I'd like to have a representative of the Metropolitan Police with us, if I can arrange it."

"The beak!" Scooch cried. "Wotcher want dem for?" Both boys looked dismayed.

"Wot if one of our mates sees us working wif a copper?" Dipper said, his voice laden with foreboding.

"Can't be done, Perfessor," Rolly said. "Might as well brand 'em on the cheek. There's nuffink lower than a squealer out there on the streets."

"Sorry," Moriarty said. "I hadn't thought of it from that angle. Well, you lads can hop off once you show me the house. I'll have the constable wait at the top of the lane for my signal. Will that do?"

The boys exchanged looks all around, then nodded. "I can stay wif you," Rolly said, "seeing as 'ow I'm retired from my former trade."

"That's settled, then." Moriarty rose and rubbed his hands together. "I've got a telegram to send. Then how would you lads like a piece of pie? I'm sure Antoine's got something nice tucked away in his cupboards."

Broad smiles met that suggestion. Moriarty went up to the morning room to compose a telegram to Inspector Forbes, requesting the company of Constable Gus Norton, if he were available. If not, anyone would do. The constable should meet him at the corner of Clerkenwell and Saffron Hill in one hour to further the investigation of Sergeant Brant.

Rolly returned with a response in the affirmative in fifteen minutes. Then they went downstairs to join the others in slices of fresh raspberry pie.

Moriarty sipped a cup of China tea while the three boys stuffed an astonishing quantity of pie into their bellies. He asked them questions about their lives on the street and was treated to a lively course in small crimes and misdemeanors, both performing them and getting away with them. It was quite an education. He knew he ought to *tsk* and cluck, showing his disapproval, but these boys had no other means of survival. They were too smart and too independent for a workhouse, but, being homeless, not eligible for school. They had no parents; indeed, there seemed to be few adults who cared about them one way or another. That explained their loyalty to Gabriel Sandy.

Moriarty couldn't alter their circumstances, though he would like to find a way to teach them to read and write. Then perhaps when they got older, they could find their way out of the criminal underworld. Then he imagined Angelina's response to that idea, delivered between bursts of bubbling laughter.

"Professor Moriarty's School for Young Thieves? Wouldn't Sherlock Holmes have a field day with that one!"

* * *

They took a four-wheeler across town to Clerkenwell Road. Dipper and Scooch clung to the handholds, gawking out the windows, while Rolly sat back with his arms crossed, observing them with a superior air. They spotted Constable Norton at the corner of Saffron Hill from a long block away.

"Big bloke, you said, Perfessor?" Scooch asked as both boys sank beneath the windows.

Gus Norton was indeed a substantial individual, being both tall and broad. He'd been a fireman when Moriarty first met him in the course of an investigation. Moriarty had saved the young man's fiancée from hanging, earning the couple's eternal gratitude. Norton later joined the Metropolitan Police force, which offered greater chances for advancement. If his family kept growing at its current rate, he'd need that extra pay.

Moriarty Lifts the Veil

Moriarty instructed the driver to turn on Saffron Hill. The boys identified the house where Brant had gone in to change clothes. They stopped at the end of the block to let Dipper and Scooch out. Moriarty shook each small hand with great solemnity, thanking them for their service. Then he told the driver to circle back up to Clerkenwell before letting him and Rolly down.

Moriarty and Constable Norton greeted each other warmly. Moriarty introduced Rolly as his assistant, causing the boy to stand up straight and puff out his narrow chest. Inspector Forbes had explained the investigation to Norton, so Moriarty was spared another recitation.

"I want to get inside Brant's room," Moriarty said. "But I want to do it legally so no one can complain about my methods later in court."

They walked down to the house. Gus pounded on the door with his fist — a most constabulary sound. They heard a reedy voice calling, "I'm coming! I'm coming!" some time before the door opened to reveal a man past the midpoint of life, with strands of graying hair straggling out from under a knitted purple cap. He wore carpet slippers and a shabby dressing gown over his shirt and trousers.

"What do you want?" He eyed the constable's blue uniform with suspicion.

"We have reason to believe you're harboring a criminal," Norton said.

"I most certainly am not!"

"I believe you are," Moriarty said. "We've been watching him. He entered this house earlier this afternoon and left again a few minutes later. He might have taken the room under the name 'Brant.'"

"Sergeant Brant?" The landlord tucked his badly shaven chin in surprise. "Why, he's no criminal!" Then his mouth fell open as a new thought arrived. He shook his finger at them. "I can see why you might think it, though, come to remember. I saw him once, going out with his sleeve pinned up empty. Looked a mite fishy to me. But he explained it, right as rain. Said it was his job to make sure old soldiers are being treated right, paid up proper when they get their pensions at the post office. He tests 'em, see, by pretending to be a different soldier every time."

Moriarty and Norton exchanged knowing looks. "That's as may be," Norton said. "I still want to have a look in that room."

"All right, all right. Who's stopping you?" The landlord opened the door wide, then turned and went into a room on the right. He came right back out with a ring of keys and led them up the steep stairs to the second floor. He unlocked a door at the front of the house and stood back to let the others precede him.

The room was just large enough for a narrow bed, a wardrobe, a small table, and one wooden chair. The bed looked unused, covered with a small collection of military hats. The wardrobe held a variety of uniform jackets along with a few civilian ones in styles commonly worn by working men. A couple of canes and a pair of crutches leaned against the wall by the clouded window. A box on the dressing table held false whiskers, some tubes of face paint, and a small bottle of glue. Moriarty noted the cosmetics came from the same supplier Angelina used.

He pointed at the bed. "Doesn't he sleep here?"

The landlord shrugged his thin shoulders. "How would I know? I don't watch 'em day and night."

Moriarty remembered the two-Brants problem. "Does anyone else visit this room, with or without Sergeant Brant?"

"Only his old mum. Lovely woman, she is, with the nicest manners. Always a kind word. A widow, you know. Wears black with one of them black veils they put down over their faces. Never understood why. I wouldn't mind getting chummy with a widow, if you take my meaning, but I'd want a peep at her face first. Wouldn't want to waste me time on an old cow."

"Did she tell you her name?"

The man gaped at him as if were simple-minded. "Well, it's Mrs. Brant, ain't it? Gave her a cup of tea once. Had a nice bit of chat. She has a touch of Bristol in her voice, like me own old mum, God rest her soul."

Bristol? Angelina had mentioned that accent in her description of Mrs. Oxwich. He hadn't heard it himself, but he'd grown up in Gloucestershire, also in the West Country, and wasn't much good at accents anyway. Bristol had been the center of the slave trade a

Moriarty Lifts the Veil

century ago. Perhaps she'd learned her business at her grandfather's knee.

Norton and Rolly had been examining the uniforms, checking the pockets. Rolly said, "Wot's this? 'Ere, Perfessor. You'd best 'ave a look." He held out the sleeve of a red jacket with sergeant's stripes on the upper arm.

Moriarty and Norton moved together to peer at the item, which bore a crusty dark stain near the cuff.

"That's blood," Norton said. He took a penknife from his pocket and scraped up a morsel. "Yes, sir. Add a bit of water and you'd see the red. We'd better take this with us."

Moriarty agreed. "It's odd that Brant wouldn't have inspected the clothes he wore that day. His embezzlement scheme depends on a keen eye for detail."

"I thought he had an alibi," Norton said.

"He does." Moriarty gazed down on the box of false hair and thought about those distinctive whiskers and the round spectacles, so easy to spot in a crowd of men in uniform. A person of similar height, who knew how to manage that glue, could impersonate Brant whenever he — or she — liked.

Outside on the pavement, the three investigators traded views on this discovery. Rolly said, "Our man did it, plain as day. Both the thievin' and the murder. Dunno 'ow he faked a day at work, but the blood on his sleeve says 'e's guilty."

"He could have cut himself shaving," Norton says. "There's no way of knowing where that blood came from."

Moriarty agreed. "It's suggestive, but not conclusive. At least we know how he obtained the money he's been stealing from the soldiers. As for the murder, I believe that even if Brant didn't do it himself, he very likely knows who did."

Norton nodded. "We've got the goods on him for theft, thanks to you, Professor. And I'll bet you a week's pay he sings like a canary once Inspector Forbes starts squeezing him."

TWENTY-THREE

Gabriel Sandy chuckled at the contradictions in the two letters Digby had brought him that morning. It had taken a full day for the missives to wend their way across the metropolis, passing from hand to hand. Not exactly the Royal Mail, but then he had no fixed location.

He'd spent the last two nights at Lusby's Theatre of Varieties on Mile End Road, stretching out on a makeshift cot in the rope room high above the stage. The theater manager was an old friend of Angelina's, but that wouldn't help the police. Every music hall manager in the East End was an old friend of Lina Lovington's — or would claim to be. As an avid aficionado of music halls and their performers, Sandy had made many friends of his own inside that circle. Several had offered him shelter, not caring what charges the police had concocted against him.

He lay on his cot now, re-reading his letters by the light of a Davy lamp. Moriarty advised him to turn himself in. Sandy had been the first to discover Oxwich's body, after all, arriving minutes after the deed had been done. He might have seen the murderer on the street or noticed some other detail that would assist Inspector Forbes in his inquiries. He had a duty to offer his testimony. He couldn't hide forever. Did he truly want Colonel Oxwich, by the manner of his death, to cast him out of another good life?

No, he did not. Sandy wanted that life back. Driving a hansom cab in all weather was hard work, but he liked it. He felt free up there on his perch, traversing the streets of the city he loved. This skulking about and hiding in dark corners ran contrary to his nature. He preferred to meet trouble head-on. He'd run away out of instinct on Monday, not wanting to be caught in the barracks by men he knew. Then the running had taken on a life of its own.

Time for it to end. He would turn himself in today, if he could arrange for Moriarty to meet him at Scotland Yard. Things would go better with a friend at his side.

Angelina, unsurprisingly, advised the opposite. She thought he should hang on to his freedom until her husband caught the real murderer. She assumed, with wifely confidence, that he would achieve that goal in a matter of days. Sandy shared her high opinion of Moriarty's talents, but it had been four full days now with no better suspect in view. This killer was a crafty one. He wouldn't be easy to catch.

Angelina's letter had one stunning bit of news: she'd found Zuri. His true love was living at Chetwood House, the home of Viscount and Lady Chetwood. She was a servant there and not free to leave, but she had looked well and seemed to have gained a position of trust. Even so, Angelina had grave doubts about the goings-on in that circle of cavalry officers. She meant to put a stop to the buying and selling of young women, if she could, but they ought to get Zuri out before that. She would need Sandy's help to achieve that goal.

The thought lit a fire in Sandy's heart. He burned with the desire to rescue his damsel in distress and carry her off into the night. But where would they go? He'd be taking her out of one prison into another. Her exotic beauty would make it difficult for them to disappear into any English town. They'd have to move abroad and start from scratch, assuming they could cross the Channel without being caught.

He must be patient and do things the right way. The honorable way. He must turn himself in and take the consequences. Angelina was a fountain of ingenuity. She could rescue Zuri without his help.

A sharp knock sounded on the door. "Mr. Sandy? The beak is at the front door. You'd better scarper, and quick!"

Sandy jumped up and slung on his overcoat, stuffing the letters into a pocket. He clapped on his battered top hat and took two seconds to look around. Nothing important left behind, though it would be obvious that someone had been camping up here.

He closed the door behind him and went toward the back of the theater. When he reached the catwalk spanning the stage, he crouched low to peer down into the hall. No coppers yet. He jogged across the walk and down the winding stairs on the other side. He'd planned this route yesterday with help from the stage manager. He entered the headliner's dressing room, knowing it would be empty, and climbed out the window.

It was a ten-foot drop to the alley below, shortened to four by hanging at arm's length from the sill. He rolled sideways to break his fall as his feet struck the cobblestones, adding a layer of dirt to his coat. At least the filthy stones were dry. He jogged down the alley, trying to ignore the stink of stale piss that surrounded every theater, and slipped through the back door of a tavern called the Holly Bush. They had no love for the police in this establishment.

Sandy changed his hat and coat for ones he'd left hanging on the rack in the back hall. He saluted the publican as he strode through the bar and out the front door. There he thrust his hands in his pockets and willed himself to a stroll, whistling as he went. He passed one of his boys on the corner and gave him a short nod.

He headed east toward Limehouse, aiming for the Strangers' Home on West India Dock Road. He could darken his face and hands with a little charcoal, wrap his head in a turban, and spend the day among the lascars and Oriental sailors waiting for an outgoing ship. He spoke Hindi and a smattering of Burmese, enough to fool the average copper.

Sherlock Holmes was another matter.

Moriarty's letter warned him that Scotland Yard had put the famed detective on his trail. Sandy had read the stories John Watson wrote for *The Strand*. They described Holmes as the master of disguises who loved to wander the East End dressed as a trash-picker or a street vendor. Worse, Sandy was used to the bird's-eye view from the back of his cab. Mindful of his horse, he never entered the narrowest alleys and avoided lanes with pitted cobbles or lines of hanging laundry. Now those were the safest routes.

He reached an intersection and paused to glance each way before crossing. Down one side street he saw four boys squared off, snarling at one another with raised fists. Two of them were his. The other two must be Baker Street Boys, the rival gang Holmes had formed to run errands and keep watch on suspects. He must have set them after the fugitive as well. They were virtually invisible and knew these streets like foxes knew their woods.

Moriarty Lifts the Veil

Sandy turned around and took another path. He felt exposed out here on his feet, disoriented without his cab. He eyed an old man wrapped in a blanket, sitting on the pavement crooning to himself. He couldn't see the nose or judge the height. Could that be Holmes?

What about that woman pushing a cart of weather-beaten vegetables? She looked taller than average and had a scarf wrapped around the lower half of her face.

Sandy picked up his pace. His body ached to run fast, but that would only attract attention. He needed to get inside the Strangers' Home and transform himself into a lascar. But first he had to find a post office to send a note to Moriarty. The professor was probably out, but he'd go home for tea. They could meet at Scotland Yard at four thirty and get it over with.

Post offices were fewer and farther between in this district of breweries and almshouses. The major streets with their constant traffic and throngs of pedestrians were safer than the mazes of alleys that branched off on either side. Worse predators than the police hunted through these crowded slums.

He finally found a post office on Commercial Road. He went inside, striving to hide his face without looking furtive. He used the paper and pens provided at the counter to scribble a note, giving the Strangers' Home as a return address, then bought a stamped envelope and posted it.

He went back out onto on Commercial Road, matching his pace to the working men trudging along the pavement. He didn't spot any likely lads idling about the corner of West India Dock, but a tramway ran down the middle of the road, making it difficult to scan the other side of the street. He didn't dare risk an open approach. His sense of peril rose as he neared his haven. He decided to walk down the west side of the road to scout the front of the building before coming back up the east.

That turned out to be a wise precaution. He passed the Strangers' Home, crossed the street, and was walking slowly back when a tall man in a top hat and black coat emerged from the building. He stood on the stoop, surveying the road as if waiting for a cab. Two boys broke out of the passing throng and met him on the steps in front of the arched doors.

Holmes!

Sandy shrank against the wall, then backed up and dove into a dim passageway behind the Salvation Army Shelter. He crouched behind a row of rubbish bins, waiting for his heart to stop pounding so he could think. The passage ran on a few yards and then turned sharply. With luck, it would lead him out the other side to West India Dock. He could lose himself in the crowds and find some way to hop on a tram to carry him out of danger.

Someone opened a window over his head and threw down a load of dirty water. Sandy stood up and started moving. It wouldn't do to be drenched. That would make him memorable. He rounded the curve in the dim passageway, aiming for the arched brick opening at the end. He emerged, blinking at the brighter light. He turned to the left and nearly walked into a tall man in a top hat and a long coat who was leaning against the brick wall with a crooked smile on his angular face.

"Ah, Mr. Sandy," Holmes said. "You've led me a merry chase. But now it's time to face the music."

TWENTY-FOUR

On Friday afternoon, Moriarty conducted his own search of his house, looking for his wife. He was going out and expected to be gone past teatime if all went well. But they should talk before he went. Things might not go well; worse, he could be wrong from start to finish.

He finally found her closeted in her dressing room with Peg. They'd strewn gauzy fabrics everywhere; in fact, he had trouble distinguishing his wife from the general chaos because she was draped in the filmy stuff from head to toe.

Peg nodded a greeting at him from her seat by the window, where she sat sewing circles of gold metal to a piece of scarlet silk.

"What on earth is going on in here?" he asked.

"We're working on costumes for the charade tomorrow night," Angelina answered. She pulled the length of fabric off her head, leaving her amber hair entrancingly mussed.

He smiled at the sight. "One thing to look forward to this weekend at least." He tossed an armful of gauze on the bed so he could sit in the chair.

"You look ready to go out," she said. "Are you off to Scotland Yard?"

"Later, I hope. But I wanted to discuss a theory with you before I meet Inspector Forbes again. You wanted a night free of grisly topics, so I didn't tell you about my chief discovery yesterday."

"One evening of peace," she said. "I thought we could both use it."

He nodded. "Yes. Now it's time to make my final move — unless I'm way off track."

Angelina sat on the edge of the bed. "Tell me."

"Rolly found dried blood on a jacket in Brant's secret lodging. It could be his, of course. There's no way of knowing without asking him. But he is involved in the colonel's murder somehow. Someone signed his name at the gate. And the murderer left blood on a pair of gloves and an overcoat. It's possible the sergeant's jacket was stained at the same time."

"Likely, I would say," Angelina said. "Otherwise, it would be another one of those fishy coincidences. The more there are, the less convincing they are, don't you think? But doesn't Brant have an unshakeable alibi?"

"Unfortunately. But he also appears to have a confederate, whom I believe is your Mrs. Oxwich."

"Not *mine*, darling, I beg you." Angelina made a sour face. "What sort of confederate?"

"I'm not sure. The landlord told us Brant had a regular visitor — a widow in a black veil with a Bristol accent."

"Hm." Angelina pursed her lips. "That's a bit vague. And yet another coincidence. That's too many for me."

"Me too. And I must say she makes a better candidate for the organizer than the colonel. That man was practically an idiot."

"Whereas she is most distinctly not one. She operates an international slave-trading ring, after all. That must take considerable coordination at both ends. And she rules her small community with an iron fist, by all accounts. Yes, I can believe it." Angelina cocked her head, peering at him with bright eyes, as if searching inside his mind. "You've connected the embezzlement and the bloody jacket, haven't you?"

Shrewd woman. "It's purely speculation at this point. As you say, there are too many coincidences. Brant's room had everything one might need to transform oneself into an army sergeant, from the uniform to the brushy whiskers."

"Whiskers take practice," Peg said. "That glue is tricky. And devilishly sticky."

"But she could practice all day long, couldn't she?" Angelina said. "At home, with her captive staff. Add a pair of round spectacles and you fit the description of your Sergeant Brant."

"Not mine, I beg you." Moriarty smiled. "She could have done the murder, in terms of time and place, though the method seems ruthless for a woman."

Both Angelina and Peg snorted at that.

Moriarty Lifts the Veil

Moriarty held up a pacifying palm. "I won't argue the point. What I can't see is a motive. Why not let her husband face the authorities? They could throw all the blame on Brant. They've played that trick before as well, with our friend Sandy."

Angelina arched her graceful eyebrows. "I believe I can help you with that motive. Oxwich wasn't a well-behaved helpmate, as it turns out. Not when he was at home." She proceeded to relate a story as sad as it was familiar, of a master oppressing his female servants in the vilest possible way.

"Despicable," Moriarty said, "but I don't follow your logic. According to your observations, Mrs. Oxwich is a heartless tyrant. Why would she care if her husband abused the servants? They have no one to complain to and no families to defend them."

Angelina gave him an exasperated look. "Because, my darling man, those poor women lose more than their innocence. Once they become pregnant, which has now happened twice that we know of, they also lose their market value. The colonel's inability to keep his hands off them threatened her whole trade, costing her hundreds of pounds a year. Add the loss of Brant's payments, however much they were, and she would find herself reduced to living on her legitimate income. Which, evidently, was not enough."

* * *

The motive made sense. It fit the crime and the character of the killer. But none of them could come up with a way to bring the colonel's murder home to his wife. They agreed to let it simmer, hoping one of them would have a flash of inspiration. Meanwhile, Moriarty had work to do. He warned Angelina not to expect him home for tea and went off to the East End to meet the three discharged soldiers. They were just the men he needed to wrap up Sergeant Brant and deliver him to the authorities.

He found them a few blocks away from Sandy's flat, with directions from Zeke. With Moriarty's letters of reference, clean uniforms, and a spot of barbering, they'd been able to secure additional employment mucking out a couple of nearby stables.

"We're back on our feet," Fowler told him. "Thanks to you and Captain Sandy. Small steps, but sure ones."

Moriarty smiled, glad to see the improvement. "I need a favor, if you have the time."

"For you, anything," Fowler said. The others nodded their assent.

Moriarty told them what he'd learned about their cases. They were good listeners, but when he uttered the name "Jeremy Brant," they let loose a volley of groans and curses.

"That sniveling toady?" Sergeant Fowler sneered. "Who'd guess he had the courage for it?"

"Did you know him?" Moriarty asked.

The sergeant shrugged. "Not well. He was an office boy. Always angling for a softer berth. Kissing Mrs. Colonel's rosy arse, running errands for her instead of doing a soldier's proper job."

"That's interesting," Moriarty said. "So their relationship goes back to India."

"If that's what you call it." Fowler gave him a shrewd look. "I'll bet I could make a guess about that favor you're wanting."

Moriarty met his gaze. "I mean to bring Brant to Scotland Yard today, and I thought you lads might like to help me."

That brought a broad grin to each homely face. "We'd like nothing better," Fowler said.

Private Webb smacked a fist into his palm. "Where do we find the miserable cur?"

That was the easy part. They waited outside the War Office at four o'clock and followed Brant as he walked home. They knew where he was going; they just had to be sure he didn't alter his pattern on that particular day.

He didn't. They closed in behind him when they reached the theater district.

Moriarty trotted toward him. "I say, Sergeant! I believe you forgot something!"

Brant turned around, recognized him, and adopted a haughty sneer. "I have nothing to say to you, Mr. Moriarty."

"Not me." Moriarty grinned and pointed at the three soldiers behind him. "These fellows. Former colleagues, I believe."

Brant recognized them. His eyes widened and his jaw dropped. He turned and tried to run, but Webb had come up on that side to block his route. The three angry men surrounded him and hustled him into the nearest alley.

Sergeant Fowler snarled, "You owe me thirty pounds, Brant. I'll take it now."

"You're mad! I owe you nothing."

"Not mad," Private Webb said. His jaw tightened, his fist curled, and he punched the sneaky thief square in the belly. "Just incorrigible."

Brant cried out to Moriarty, who had become distracted by something on the bottom of his shoe.

"What's this?" he asked himself, louder than necessary. He turned his back on the soldiers to scrape his foot on the stoop of a service door. He let a minute pass, giving the men time to express their frustrations, then called, "That's enough, my friends. We want him to be presentable."

He hailed a passing growler, and they all piled in. When they reached Scotland Yard, the men yanked Brant out of the carriage and handed him over to Moriarty. "We'll leave him to you now, Professor," Fowler said. "Let us know how it turns out."

The soldiers melted into the passing throng. Moriarty gripped Brant by the arm and marched him up the steps under the watchful eyes of two constables. All resistance had been knocked right out of him.

"Delivery for Inspector Forbes," Moriarty said to the officer at the desk inside.

A constable was dispatched with the message. He returned in a matter of minutes with the inspector.

"Ah, Mr. Brant," he said. "I'm glad you've decided to do the right thing by turning yourself in. You'll find it's better than waiting for the axe to fall." To Moriarty he added, "I won't ask how you persuaded him. Now we take him up to Bow Street to have him arraigned by the magistrate."

They went back out to climb into a police van, which the inspector whistled up. A constable sat next to Brant, one strong hand wrapped around the smaller man's arm. Moriarty sat opposite him. As the van jerked into motion, he said, "Sergeant Fowler is one of the men you ruined. An honest man, proud of his years of service in

Her Majesty's Army. He was at the Battle of Maiwand." He paused to nod at the constable, who shot a scowl at his prisoner.

"Must be a damned sight braver than the rest of us," Forbes said.

"He's a hero in my book," Moriarty said. "But thanks to Sergeant Brant here, his dream of entering the carter's trade was shattered. Discharged with a fraction of what he was owed, he's been forced to live on the street, begging for his daily bread."

Both policemen turned dark scowls toward Brant. The sergeant said nothing. He kept his gaze focused on the leather seat showing between Moriarty and Forbes.

They arrived at a handsome building recently constructed in the new style, with layers of red brick and white stone. The courtroom inside was liberally fitted with oak screens and benches. The judge sat atop a high dais, wearing his red robes with wide ermine cuffs. A tightly curled gray wig adorned his head, and a pair of narrow gold spectacles perched near the end of his long nose.

A hum of conversation filled the room. Lawyers in black suits came and went from the tables on opposite sides of the aisle. Behind the bar on long benches sat the full variety of central London: members of the gentry in fine clothes, men and women of the working classes, a few prostitutes in gaudy dresses, and a couple of surly ruffians. Most of them must have been waiting their turns before the judge, but others appeared to be mere observers. One woman sat with a black reticule filled with yarn, knitting away with the air of a person enjoying a public show.

The judge spoke a few words to the small group clustered before him, then pounded his gavel. That group left and another began to approach. But the judge spotted Forbes hovering at the top of the aisle and beckoned him forward.

"What do you have for me today, Inspector?" he called in a voice that carried as clearly as his gavel.

"A nasty one, Your Honor." Forbes ushered Moriarty, Brant, and the constable to stand before the bench. He provided a neat summary of Brant's crimes, noting that they had an abundance of proof and witnesses to boot. "I recommend jail for this one, Your Honor. He has little attachment to the community and is known to be clever at disguises. Furthermore, he withdrew a large amount of cash money two days ago."

Moriarty Lifts the Veil

Moriarty pulled at Forbes's sleeve to turn him away from the bench. "There's more." He spoke in a low voice. "I haven't had a chance to tell you, but I strongly believe this man has been colluding with the person who murdered Colonel Oxwich."

Forbes glared at him. "One moment, Your Honor, if you please. We may have a further charge." He put a hand on Moriarty's shoulder to turn him full around. "Who is this person?"

"The wife. Mrs. Oxwich. Please bear with me. I know it sounds mad. But that woman is up to her neck in foul deeds." He described the slave-trading operation as succinctly as he could, explaining the threat the colonel posed to her profitable venture. "She may be the one who invented the discharge scheme as well. Brant was collaborating with her, I'm certain of it. He may have abetted her impersonation of him in the barracks that morning."

The judge interrupted them. "You should have sorted this out before you came. Do we have another charge to add to embezzlement of government funds?"

"We do, Your Honor." Forbes shrugged at Moriarty. "In for a penny, eh? We believe this man was an accessory to the murder of Colonel Samuel Oxwich. I assume you've heard of that case."

"Everyone in England has heard of it," the judge said. "Accessory, eh?" He peered at Sergeant Brant over his spectacles. "Have you anything to say for yourself, young man?"

"I wish to speak with counsel first, Your Honor. I fear anything I say will be misconstrued."

The judge grunted. "You can do that in jail. Inspector Forbes has a good record in this court. I'm inclined to accept his assessment." He banged his gavel once and began to call out his judgment when a great disturbance arose at the front door.

"Your Honor! We must approach at once!" Inspector Lestrade trotted up the aisle with an air of great importance, followed at a more stately pace by long-legged Sherlock Holmes. The detective gripped the arm of Gabriel Sandy, whose weary face and slumping shoulders conveyed his resignation.

Holmes elbowed Lestrade aside as they passed the bar. "I'm Sherlock Holmes, Your Honor, consulting detective. I've brought you the Oxwich murderer!" His voice rose across those last words, which he aimed partly at the clot of journalists lounging on the front bench.

They sat up and scrambled for their notebooks.

"Another one?" the judge asked with an impish grin. "I know who you are, Mr. Holmes. You're in the nick of time. I've just been handed an accessory to that same crime. Funny, though . . ." His sharp eyes turned from Brant to Sandy, then back to Holmes. "They don't seem to know each other, do they?"

The two prisoners eyed one another with wary interest. Then Sandy said, "I've seen you before. You're the chap who passed me on Officer's Row Monday morning. You're a bit taller today, though."

"I've never seen you before in my life," Brant said. "I had nothing to do with that murder, Your Honor. Nor any other."

"Now he speaks," the judge said with a note of wry amusement.

"Who is that man?" Holmes demanded, regarding Brant down the length of his nose.

"The embezzler," Moriarty said. "The one with a real motive for murder."

"I never murdered anyone!" Brant nearly shouted the words, but no one paid him any mind.

Holmes stepped back and pointed a long finger at Moriarty. "Do not trust this man, Your Honor. He undoubtedly brought this red herring in to obscure the trail."

The judge's lips crooked at the choice of words, which were especially apt, given the color of Brant's jacket. "How's that, Mr. Holmes?"

"You may not have heard of Professor Moriarty yet, Your Honor, but you will as time goes by. His goal here is to protect his henchman Mr. Sandy."

Moriarty expelled a noisy sigh. "For the last time, Holmes, I don't have henchmen. Mr. Sandy is a friend. You can't have failed to notice, Your Honor, that we got here first. How could we have known the infamous Sherlock Holmes would arrive at this precise moment?"

Holmes's eyes narrowed. "Mark my words, Your Honor. The professor has been constructing a network of criminals. For all we know, he wants you to send this Brant to jail as a punishment for standing up to him."

"Oh, I say, Holmes!" Moriarty snapped. "That really is going too far! Leave me out of your drug-addled fantasies, I beg you. And let Watson check you into a nice rest home while you're at it."

Red spots flared under the edge of Holmes's ridiculous fake beard. He drew in a breath, and began to deliver the case against Sandy, which did indeed sound very damning in his decisive tone. Moriarty refused to let it stand, however, countering every point with an argument for Brant as murderer.

Their voices rose as they pressed their cases, until they were silenced by the pounding of the judge's gavel.

"Enough!" His Honor bellowed. "I can't put two men behind bars for the same crime, and I very much doubt that total strangers — as these two clearly are — aided and abetted one another. Inspectors, get your stories straight. Gentlemen, settle your differences elsewhere. I've already determined that this one" — he pointed the gavel at Brant — "will be committed to Newgate until his trial on the charge of embezzlement. I'll take the accessory charge under advisement."

"Thank you, Your Honor," Forbes said. "I'll present evidence for the second charge on Monday." He frowned at Moriarty, who nodded, hoping he could come through by then with something stronger than a Bristol accent.

"As you for you, Mr. Sandy," the judge said, "Mr. Holmes has been right more often than not. Although he does have the most infuriating tendency to turn my courtroom into a theater. I know the police have been after you all week. So I am charging you with the murder of Colonel Oxwich and committing you to Newgate as well."

"What about bail, Your Honor?" Moriarty interjected. "Mr. Sandy may not look it at the moment, but he is a gentleman. His father is Viscount Draycott of Devonshire."

"A viscount?" The judge frowned and gave Sandy a longer look. "That changes things. Very well, I'll release him on bail in the amount of one hundred pounds." He pounded the gavel to underscore the finality of his ruling.

"One hundred pounds." Moriarty patted his pockets, knowing he had less than ten in bills and coins on him. His watch wasn't worth more than five. He wondered if they'd take an IOU.

Another disturbance arose at the front door. "Stop, Your Honor, I beg you!" John Watson came running up the aisle, waving his hat. "Do not arrest this man!"

"Too late for that," the judge observed. "He was arrested before he got here. I've just arraigned him."

"He's going to prison, where he belongs," Holmes said. "What are you doing here, Watson?" He practically bared his teeth as his only friend.

"I can't allow you to do this, Holmes. I simply can't. You've gone too far this time." Watson faced the judge. "I'm Dr. John Watson, Your Honor, and I'm here to vouch for Mr. Sandy."

"How did you know?" Holmes asked. "I haven't been home all day."

The judge's eyebrows rose at that. "Home?"

They ignored him. "One of your boys came to tell me you'd caught Mr. Sandy and meant to bring him here."

"One of *my* boys?" Holmes shook his head. "I don't believe it."

"Must have been one of mine," Sandy said, smiling for the first time. "Zeke, probably. He has the cheek to come to you on his own initiative."

"I'm grateful that he did," Watson said. "Your Honor, this man is incapable of murder, especially one of such a cowardly nature. Captain Sandy, as he was then, fought at the Battle of Maiwand. He was cited for bravery in that action. More, he saved my life and who knows how many others. Whatever happened to that colonel, this honorable man had nothing to do with it."

"Maiwand, eh?" The judge looked impressed. He gazed at Sandy with his lips pursed. "Well, my ruling stands. Let the lawyers fight it out. I'm afraid he's on his way to Newgate, Doctor, unless you happen to have a hundred pounds in your pocket for bail."

"I have, Your Honor. I feared it would come to this." Watson put his hat back on his head and dug out his notecase. He extracted a sheaf of bills and counted them out on the bench, there and then.

"A clerk will take that." The judge chuckled. "Why do they always think *I* want their money?" He pounded his gavel twice more.

Moriarty Lifts the Veil

"Mr. Sandy, you are hereby released on bail. Don't leave the county and be sure to keep the authorities apprised of your address."

Moriarty clapped Sandy's shoulder, grinning like a loon. Watson clapped him on the other shoulder.

"I can't begin to thank you," Sandy told him.

"My debt is not half-paid." Watson glanced at Holmes, who was turning an unhealthy shade of red. "But I fear I must say good night. A patient is in need of my attention."

He took Holmes in charge, turning him bodily around and walking him down the aisle. Then he paused to pull out a flask of something and made him take a swallow before guiding him out.

"Let's go home," Moriarty said. Sandy readily agreed.

They sank into the leather upholstery of a hansom cab with sighs of relief. In mutual accord, they made the trip from Bow Street to Bellenden Crescent in restful silence. That was shattered by Angelina's squeals of delight when she greeted them in the entry hall.

"You're not leaving this house tonight," she scolded Sandy. "We'll send Zeke a telegram to let him know you're safely under our roof."

"I won't argue with you," Sandy said. "Frankly, I'm done in."

"Of course you are." She rattled off a list of tasks to Rolly, from lighting the fire in the guest room to scouting out a pair of Moriarty's pajamas. Then she moved on to Sandy. "You'll want a nice hot bath and then a good hot meal."

"Whiskey first, I think, my dear." Moriarty smiled at her eagerness to erase the stress and struggle of Sandy's harrowing week.

They repaired to the drawing room and settled in soft chairs with stiff drinks. Moriarty and Sandy took turns filling Angelina in on the events of the day.

"I'm glad Sergeant Brant is behind bars," she said. "I hope they keep him there for a long, long time. You've wrapped your case up beautifully, James. But you know, darlings, we're only halfway home. We still have to bring that vicious Mrs. Oxwich to justice."

TWENTY-FIVE

Angelina guided the conversation onto gentler paths for the rest of the evening. The men were too tired for more strategizing. She played the piano for them after dinner, and they all went to bed early.

Saturday morning brought renewed energies and a shared sense of purpose. James had resolved his case; she meant to do the same, though hers had expanded far beyond its original bounds. She would do her level best to wring a confession out of Mrs. Oxwich, force those army officers and wives to reckon with their slave-trading, and rescue Zuri. She felt fairly confident about that last one. The other two . . . well, she could at least stir things up.

They gathered around the dining table for breakfast. Sandy looked so much younger without his beard; more like the cavalry officer he once had been. A week driving his cab would even out the color of his cheeks and chin, especially if this lovely stretch of weather held.

James peered over the top of his newspaper. "Here's an item of interest — a notice from yesterday's police court. 'Mr. Gabriel Sandy was apprehended by Mr. Sherlock Holmes after a week-long manhunt and charged with the murder of Colonel Samuel Oxwich. Mr. Sandy was subsequently released on bail.'"

Sandy frowned. "People won't like that. They'll wonder how I got off so easily."

James smiled. "Fortunately, the people have no say in this matter."

"Typical of Holmes to make sure his name is mentioned," Angelina said. "Was there anything about Brant?"

"There is, but his apprehension is credited to Inspector Forbes."

"That is so unfair!" Angelina shook her half-eaten slice of toast at her husband.

James laughed it off. "I'm glad, to be honest. Holmes loves the publicity, but I'm happier in the shadows. I have a wife in the limelight. That's plenty for me."

Angelina gave him a forbearing look. He really would hate being the subject of gushing accolades in the *Illustrated Police News*, or heaven forfend, the hero of a series of popular stories in *The Strand*. Leave that kind of notoriety to Mr. Showboat Holmes.

A sobering thought crossed her mind. "I wonder if Mrs. Oxwich has seen those notices."

"She might have." James folded his paper and set it aside. "If I were her, I'd be scouring the papers for anything relating to the murder investigation. She must be on tenterhooks."

Sandy nodded. "I know I was. She may be relieved to see that I've been charged. It lets her off those hooks."

"Not if you're loose, darling," Angelina said. "She'll be wondering what you'll do. Will you come after her? What do you know?"

"She must be worried about Brant." James reached for a second soft-boiled egg and deftly removed the top. "He'll sing like a canary, to use Constable Norton's apt phrase. Anything to reduce his own sentence."

"But what does he know, really?" Angelina asked.

James shrugged. "He certainly knows that Mrs. Oxwich knew about the discharge scheme. She abetted it and profited from it, if my theory is correct. He may know that she borrowed one of his costumes."

"I'm not so sure about that," Sandy said. "All you have is a spot of blood on a red jacket." He frowned at the last piece of toast. Angelina slid the rack toward him and rang for more.

"There's the Bristol accent," James said. "Don't forget that. Although a good barrister would demolish both of our so-called clues in a minute."

Angelina laid her fork and knife on her empty plate and poured more tea for everyone. When Rolly came up with a rack of fresh toast, she sent him straight down for another pot. "Let's see if we can work out what she must have done to borrow that costume and murder her husband. If we follow her step by step, we might discover more clues."

"Good idea." James drank some tea. "Well, when Forbes and I interviewed her on Wednesday, she said the colonel had told her about our confrontation with him. We saw him Friday afternoon. He told her about it Friday evening. She must have written to Brant on Saturday to get that note back from him in time to leave it on the desk Monday morning."

"Who else could have done that?" Angelina asked. "Leave that note."

The two men frowned at each other, shaking their heads.

"Corporal Turner," James said. "But why would he involve her?" He tapped his hand on the table. "Besides, I've ruled him out. He showed me his bank book, for heaven's sake! And he has no access to the books in the War Office."

"By all means, let's close that door," Angelina said. "We have our man. Now when did Mrs. Oxwich pick up that costume? It couldn't have been Monday, could it? She would have had to leave Staines at what — four o'clock in the morning?"

"She'd have been noticed at that hour," Sandy said. "I only got out there so early because I couldn't sleep."

"So not Monday." Angelina nodded, pleased to see some pieces coming together. "Not Sunday either, I think. For all she knew, Brant would be there packing things up." She cocked her head at her companions. "Why didn't he pack up and run? He must have the most extraordinary self-confidence."

James gave a short laugh. "He must indeed. How could he be certain none of the men he robbed had a connection with someone powerful? An officer, a cousin in the legal field . . ."

Sandy said, "I'd go on Friday, when I could be certain he was at work. Then I'd have the costume at home and have plenty of time for the journey to and from the city. I wouldn't be worried about providing an alibi either. Who would care?"

"That's right," Angelina said. "She could stop off at Oxford Street and buy something to justify her visit to town."

James wasn't having it. "You're saying she planned to kill her husband *before* she knew the embezzlement scheme had been exposed."

"That didn't matter to her," Angelina said. "Once the colonel was gone, the scheme would have to stop anyway. She'd be out in the open, so to speak, without him to hide behind. She meant to throw Brant to the wolves from the start if things went wrong. That note from him was just icing on the cake."

"Cake for the wolves, eh?" James quirked a smile at her mixed metaphor. "Then we're supposing your motive was sufficient in itself."

"What motive is this?" Sandy asked.

Angelina gasped. She'd forgotten that he didn't know all about the captive princess. She filled him in on that dramatic tale, pleased with his eye-popping response.

"I'd murder the brute myself!" Sandy declared.

"Get in line," James growled.

Angelina scowled at them. Were they deaf to their own words? "Of course neither of you would do any such thing. That's the whole point of this discussion, isn't it? You'd give the brute a sound thrashing, throw him into the street, and then pursue him with the full force of the law. I'm saying that Mrs. Oxwich had an excellent motive to eliminate that horrible man. He was spoiling her merchandise and putting her operation at risk of exposure."

"We understand that," James said, a trifle tartly.

"We were merely expressing our disgust," Sandy added.

Angelina accepted that with a cluck of her tongue. She took a sip of tea and then said, "Ha! Harini will testify, I'll bet. She's fully recovered her natural hauteur. She'll be a spectacle too, with that black kohl around her eyes and her gleaming silks and glittering jewels."

"I'd like to see that." Sandy grinned.

James returned to the main topic. "The landlord on Saffron Hill might have seen Mrs. Oxwich on Friday. She rather overplayed her role with him. He's got a bit of a crush. He'll testify too, I suspect. He'll be miffed at being used and fearful of getting in trouble himself."

"Wonderful!" Angelina cried. "The more witnesses, the better. Can she really have come through the gate at the barracks without the guard noticing something amiss? Her disguise can't have been that perfect."

Sandy shook his head. "I doubt he pays much attention to officers, even non-commissioned ones. When I came through that morning, he was busy chaffing a group of his chums. He barely glanced at me, though he did make me sign in."

"Hmm." Angelina tried to imagine Mrs. Oxwich's morning. "I suppose she had that manservant of hers — Rajesh — drive her to the barracks. He must have waited for her somewhere nearby."

"There are so many coaches and wagons buzzing around that barracks," James said. "Horses, pedestrians, traffic of all kinds. Who would you ask? Although it might be worth putting a notice in the local paper. Did anyone see an Indian man in a turban loitering in a coach near Odstone Barracks last Monday morning?"

Sandy rejected that idea with a short laugh. "All he'd have to do is trade the turban for a top hat and he would disappear into the throng."

"Speaking of her servants," Angelina said, "someone must have helped her with those whiskers. Her personal maid could testify against her — if we can get to her."

"The authorities could compel her testimony," James said. "Threaten her with expulsion, for example."

Angelina frowned. She didn't want the servants to be punished. She wanted them to be rescued. Given paid-up passage home if that was what they wanted, or better positions as proper servants if they wanted to stay in England.

James's face grew somber. "Mrs. Oxwich must be aware that her servants are her greatest vulnerability, especially the one who helped her with her costume. That woman could be in grave danger."

"I don't think so," Sandy said, "though I could be wrong. I have the sense that Mrs. Oxwich assumes her servants are completely under her control. She doesn't think of them as people, not really. I remember that about her and some of the other wives. They see the servants as some sort of automatons. They have no wills of their own."

"I hope that's true," Angelina said. "I mean, that she doesn't see them as a threat. Because I can't think of a way to protect them until we get her locked up."

"And here we are, full circle," James said. "All we have is a visit to a flat full of uniforms and a tale told by a frightened girl. The flat connects her to Brant, but not to the murder."

Angelina glowered at him, though none of this was his fault. "Then we'll just have to get a confession out of her, won't we?"

* * *

After breakfast, the men went off to hire a roomy four-wheeler to carry them out to Chetwood Park. They paid extra so Sandy could drive. Then they went to Sandy's flat to collect Zeke and some clothes. The boy might be needed to run messages or mind the horses. And he hated the idea of being left out of this great adventure.

Angelina supervised the packing. They didn't need much, just enough for one day. They could wear their travel clothes that afternoon. Angelina and Moriarty must have dinner clothes, of course, and then her costume for the charades. Thinking about a long drive in flimsy harem garb, she had a few extra blankets stored in the coach. If all went according to her half-baked plans, they'd be home again sometime in the wee hours.

* * *

Lord and Lady Chetwood greeted them on the wide steps leading up to their palatial home. Her Ladyship gave James a head-to-toe inspection with a predatory gleam in her pale blue eyes and a coy smile on her thin lips. She took his arm going into the house, giving his biceps a blatant squeeze.

James's face took on that bland expression that told you absolutely nothing. Lady Chetwood batted her lashes and babbled gaily, to no avail. Angelina almost laughed. James could wear that face for days — months — if necessary.

Lord Chetwood made the usual welcoming remarks, promising some excellent shooting on Sunday afternoon. Happily, they'd be gone before poor James was subjected to that hated pastime.

He did manage to make one conventional request that would also further their plans. "I'd like nothing better than a tour of the grounds this afternoon, if that could be arranged. Give my wife and me a chance to stretch our legs after the long drive."

Lady Chetwood didn't like that idea, but she could hardly object. "Feel free to explore. We've a lovely Greek folly and a yew maze some people find amusing."

"Delightful," James said without a hint of feeling.

The housekeeper — an Englishwoman — showed them to their rooms. Their meagre baggage was delivered soon after by two Indian men. Peg and Rolly came upstairs for a consultation. Their job was to map out the house as best they could and get as much downstairs gossip as possible. Who else was here among the officer clan? Which wife was likely to wander off with which husband after the charades? What did the Indian servants think about it all?

Angelina didn't expect much on that last question. They had their own language. They probably kept their gossip inside their own ranks.

The grounds were beautiful, and they really did need to stretch their legs. "I'm glad that dreadful woman didn't come with us," James said. "Will I have to fight her tonight too?"

"I expect so." Angelina didn't know whether to be outraged or amused. "You can be fairly direct if she refuses to take your hints. We'll be leaving soon after, and you won't see her again. You can shake her off and even push her into a chair if you must. I suspect she'll be well boiled by that time. Pick a nice deep sofa and she won't be able to get up."

They circled the house, noting the exits. There would be too many people around the front doors and the kitchen steps for their purposes. The greenhouse attached to the side looked promising. One could duck down behind a towering palm or rubber plant if anyone should happen to pass through at the critical moment. And there were doors at each end of the two long wings.

They chose a likely path leading out from the garden behind the greenhouse and soon found themselves in a shady wood. Dappled sunlight danced on emerald grass, and the light breeze smelled of flowers and fresh earth. James sighed with pleasure. "I wouldn't mind having a place like this to retreat to on the weekends."

"You mean on Mondays," Angelina said. "Weekends are the busiest times for us theater folk."

He let it drop. Now was not the time for that never-ending debate.

They spotted a small white structure up ahead. As they approached, they saw that it was a circular building, open on two sides and ringed with columns.

"This must be the Greek folly," Angelina said.

"And there's Sandy." James pointed past the folly to a dense thicket, behind which she could make out the lines of the coach. A soft whinny confirmed the guess.

They hurried forward and found Sandy and Zeke stretched out on blankets, enjoying a picnic lunch. They all agreed that the location would suit their purposes admirably. The folly was too far from the house for straying couples, especially after dark. Sandy had reconnoitered the roads in and out of the estate and assured them they could escape without going past the main house.

"Zuri will know where the folly is, don't you think?" Sandy asked. His gaze kept turning in the direction of the house, his eyes filled with longing. The building wasn't visible from here, but it seemed to tug at him like a rope.

"Of course she does," Angelina said. "Don't worry. She'll find you. And Sandy — if things get out of hand, don't wait for us. They can't hold *us* prisoner. We'll simply weather whatever storm there might be and hire another coach in the morning."

TWENTY-SIX

Moriarty straightened his tie in the mirror and smoothed the fringe of hair around the back of his head with his hand. Angelina had gone off to locate Sandy's dancer, a crucial player in tonight's plan. Then she meant to have a reckoning with Mrs. Reynolds. The cooperation of the major's wife was equally crucial for the second half of the plan.

He considered the Zuri-escape plan more elaborate than necessary, but Angelina had been so keen on its cleverness, he hadn't had the heart to intervene. And he could appreciate the poetic justice in absconding with the star performer in the middle of a show. Everything depended on the relative incapacity of the audience, but from what he'd heard, their state of inebriation could be safely assumed.

The Oxwich plan was another matter. Angelina believed she could persuade Mrs. Reynolds to lure Mrs. Oxwich to this house tonight by threatening blackmail. The threat would be based on fictitious gossip among the Indian servants, which had reached Mrs. Reynolds's ears. True, servants did gossip about their masters and mistresses. One supposed they had little else to talk about, especially when living in rural isolation, as these people did. And lady's maids often passed juicy tidbits on to their mistresses, according to Angelina.

The specific gossip underlying the threat concerned false whiskers and a pair of round spectacles. The servants at Balmer Park had whispered about their memsahib leaving the house last Monday morning dressed as a man. These whispers had traveled from one house to another the way such things do among country neighbors. If Mrs. Reynolds could add two and two to get four, surely Mrs. Oxwich could also calculate the value of her own freedom.

It might work. The colonel's wife must be desperate for news, fearing discovery at any moment. She might even be relieved that the blow came from her inner circle. She saw herself as the commander of the wives, a leader among women. She would be confident that she could control Mrs. Reynolds and negotiate a favorable outcome.

Moriarty strongly preferred the women meet here, in this house full of weekend guests, than at Balmer Park. He couldn't follow his wife there without being observed; besides, his mere presence would queer the pitch. Here, with a dozen tipsy couples giggling off to private dens, he could easily hide himself behind a drapery or a potted plant and listen to the whole thing. The plan depended on a couple of good witnesses secreted about the scene. And he wanted to be on hand in case things turned ugly.

Angelina would induce a confession from Mrs. Oxwich using a combination of threats and taunts. The hidden witnesses would later bear witness in court to what they had overheard.

The plan was quintessential Angelina, though Moriarty could spot a dozen holes. Success depended on her manipulative abilities — the skills of a confidence trickster. But Mrs. Oxwich had shown herself to be capable of sustained deception. She might not crumble so easily.

They had to have a confession. Their skimpy evidence was not enough. Moriarty couldn't think of a better way to elicit one. He only hoped his wife wasn't underestimating the Oxwich woman's capacity for violence. She'd killed twice, that they knew of, to protect her illicit business.

But all of that was hours away yet. In the meantime, he had the afternoon to kill. He'd like to find a group of men engaged in some leisure activity and try to get a sense of their qualities before everyone got too drunk.

He prowled around the ground floor, finding no signs of the other guests. He strolled through a well-stocked library, a billiards room, and a gun room that let out onto the service yard between the wings. The women were presumably napping or fiddling with their clothes, but where the dickens were the men?

He went out the gun-room door and walked toward a wide yard backed by a long, two-story brick building. That must be the stables, with housing for male servants upstairs. He heard some shouts coming from the other side and strode toward them. A group of men had gathered around a paddock to watch two stable hands put a stunning black horse through its paces.

"My, that's a magnificent animal," Moriarty said as he approached the group.

Lord Chetwood shot a grin over his tweed-covered shoulder. "Funny. That's what my wife said about you."

Coarse barks of laughter shook the group. Moriarty managed to produce a grunting chuckle, though he was shocked to the core. What kind of a man would make such a joke about his own wife? He turned his face toward the horse, which trotted prettily around the field. Moriarty nodded as if satisfied with what he saw while his mind recovered from the affront.

The glossy animal made a focal point for the overlapping layers of green grass and nodding trees that stretched into the distance, merging into the clear blue sky. A classic English view. Moriarty had seen paintings of India composed entirely of shades of brown, from sandy flatlands to rust-red hills. Perhaps the shock of shifting between those starkly contrasting landscapes and social milieus had damaged these men's moral compasses. They'd come adrift from their foundations.

His musings were interrupted by a clap on the back hard enough to jolt him forward half a step.

"Buck up, old chap." A man with freckles underneath a fading tan gave him a leering grin. "Lady C always takes first turn with the newcomers. *Noblesse oblige* and all that, you know. But you'll enjoy yourself, never fear. Her Ladyship is very" — he licked his lips, all the way around — "pliable, shall we say."

More guffaws followed that description. From the looks on their faces, Moriarty deduced that every one of these men had shared that experience.

He let himself show some confusion. "To be honest, I'm not entirely sure I understand how all this works."

That elicited another round of coarse laughs, accompanied by some graphic gestures. The freckled man said, "You'll pick it up quick enough. You're Lina Lovington's bedmate, after all. You must have *very* flexible tastes. Eh? Eh?" He laughed right in Moriarty's face.

Moriarty Lifts the Veil

It was all he could do not to punch the sneering idiot squarely on his freckled nose. But Major Reynolds cut off the laughter with one stroke of his hands.

"Have pity, lads. We were all new once upon a time." He laid a hand on Moriarty's shoulder. "The women choose, you see, usually during their dance. We call it charades because that's how it started, but now it's always just them on the stage in their tantalizing costumes, doing their Hindu dance. Very erotic, I don't mind telling you. You'll know when you've been chosen. Letting them lead was Lord Chetwood's inspired idea. Ensures their cooperation, don't you see?"

"And playing potluck adds to the thrill," another man commented. "Some ladies have their favorites, but others like to mix it up. So you never know what kind of a ride you'll have." His eyes shone with a lecherous gleam. His licked his lips too, in eager anticipation.

"After you've done your duty by the wives," Lord Chetwood said, "you might — just might — graduate to the inner sanctum." He winked at Major Freckles.

"What's that?" Moriarty tried to sound intrigued, though his stomach churned with disgust. He had no desire for any woman other than Angelina and couldn't bear the thought of her with another man. The intimacy of the bedroom sustained the beating heart of a marriage, in his view. It should be regarded as sacred.

Lord Chetwood bit his lower lip as he gave Moriarty a narrow look. Then he nodded as if he'd answered a silent question. "How about a little tour? Whet your appetite for tonight's games."

He beckoned Moriarty to follow as he walked back to the sprawling mansion. He opened a door at the rear of the west wing and allowed his guest to precede him up a plain staircase. The landing on the first floor was bare, apart from a wooden bench. Two doors confronted them — one of polished oak, the other brightly painted in the delicate scrollwork of an Arabian painting. They offered the visitor a choice between the mundane and the magical.

Lord Chetwood chose the magic. He turned the handle and thrust the door wide, revealing a chamber to rival that of an Ottoman pasha. Colored silks draped both walls and ceiling, embellished with gold stars and silver crescent moons. The furnishings consisted of low couches and tufted cushions scattered about an enormous

Turkey carpet. A trio of young Indian women clad in their nightclothes rose from a low bed, cooing welcomes at the viscount. They flicked their dark eyes toward Moriarty with candid curiosity.

Lord Chetwood kissed each of them, then shooed them into another room with firm pats on their bottoms. "Better rest up, my dears. You won't get any sleep tonight!" He turned to Moriarty with a broad grin. "Like what you see?"

Moriarty cleared his throat. "It seems very authentic."

Lord Chetwood's smile held a touch of sadness. "Colonel Oxwich and I designed this together. We combined elements from Arabian tales and Indian paintings. He was a most imaginative man when it came to the masculine pleasures. I miss him."

Moriarty hummed a solemn note. He would have chosen something quite different for Oxwich's epitaph. The words "venal" and "soulless" would feature prominently.

Lord Chetwood shook himself and sighed. "You might think it's too soon after his death for such frivolity. But these weekends take some planning. And I truly believe he would want us to carry on. He'd have been the first through that door tonight if he were still among us."

"Does everyone come up here after the charades?"

"Oh no. Only the select few. It's no fun if there are more men than women, don't you see. You want a certain ratio there. And the wives must be satisfied, or the whole jolly enterprise falls apart."

"Ah. I can see that." Moriarty laughed weakly. He wanted nothing more than to throw this monster out the window. "Had to buy a theater for mine. Not that I don't enjoy it myself." He tried a few winks but feared it looked more like a nervous tic.

Lord Chetwood was too pleased with himself to notice. "We knew you'd fit right in, both of you. Actors and all that. Creative, what?" He winked back. "Always glad to have fresh blood. Perks us up, if you understand me."

Moriarty threw a glance at the padded door through which the half-naked women had disappeared. "Are all the uh" — he coughed to avoid naming their function — "recruited from the servants?"

"Most of them. We managed to sneak in a couple of pros from Jaipur, but Mrs. Oxwich put her foot down. They make poor servants, I'm afraid. Useless on the passage home. Mrs. Oxwich does a fine job with that end of things. Best not to interfere. So the old hands train the new, with my help, of course. They're all skilled in the ancient Indian arts of love." He gazed toward the rumpled bed with heavy lidded eyes and licked his fleshy lips. "Something for you to look forward to, old chap. Keep you coming back, eh?" He dug an elbow into Moriarty's side.

"I'm surprised Mrs. Oxwich approves of these monthly weekends of yours. From what my wife tells me, she's quite the termagant. Runs a very tight ship, as I understand it."

Lord Chetwood's oily smile hardened. "She knows which side her bread is buttered on. One word from me and the shipments stop and she's forced to live on a colonel's pay. I could train English girls for my games if it comes to that. Plenty of pretty ones living on the street in the rougher parts of town. Clean 'em up, dress 'em up, and there you are, as right as rain."

Moriarty lifted his upper lip, hoping this brute would interpret it as a smile. He let his gaze travel around the room, counting up the laws being broken. Slavery, prostitution, importing persons of known ill character, corruption of the young . . .

He promised himself he would be here when the police broke open that painted door.

TWENTY-SEVEN

"It must be this way," Angelina told Peg. "We took a wrong turn at the very start. But if we go down these stairs, we should end up somewhere near the hall."

"Why anybody'd want to live in such a bloomin' great monstrosity of a house is beyond me." Peg shifted her cosmetic case to the other hand to grip the mahogany bannister. She took each carpeted step as if descending into a pit of hell. She'd been bristly and out of sorts from the moment they entered the countryside.

"Did you learn anything downstairs?" Angelina asked.

"Nothin' useful. They're all business, this lot. Here's the laundry room, here's the schedule for the toffs. It's like I figured — whites talk to whites, and blacks talk to blacks. Rolly might have better luck, being a right little charmer when he wants to be. I'll tell you one thing. Those Indians might not speak English, but they understand it well enough."

"That's worth knowing."

They reached the bottom of the winding stair and found themselves at the back of a wide corridor. Angelina gestured with her armload of gauze. "Great hall is that way, I'll bet."

They found it at last. The front of the vast oak-paneled room was empty, apart from the portraits and heads of animals hanging on the walls. But a row of enormous rugs hung across the center, as if they'd been strung up to dry. Angelina and Peg pressed through a narrow gap into an Oriental theater surrounded by the brilliant tapestries. A stage at the back stood a foot off the floor. Low sofas and big tufted cushions had been placed at irregular intervals throughout the space for the audience.

Peg scoffed at the arrangements. "Do they think ladies can sit on those things in evening clothes?"

"The wives change into loose robes." Zuri Padmani came out from behind a silk drapery hanging behind the low stage. She placed her palms together and bowed. "Mrs. Lovington, I hoped you would come, but I did not believe it. The games they play in this house are not nice." She spoke in a low voice — not whispering, but softly enough not to be overheard should anyone enter the hall.

"We're here for you, Miss Padmani." Angelina matched her tone. "And for one other thing. We won't be here long enough to play their games. What do you mean by loose robes?" She hadn't brought anything like that. "I thought the women wore harem costumes and danced."

"Not all. Some sit and watch. Some like to watch the men watching. That is how they choose."

"I see," Angelina said, though she didn't. "Is there a place we can talk for a few minutes?"

"In the wardrobe. No one is there who speaks English."

She led them behind the stage and into a chamber the size of two dressing rooms at the Galaxy. There were several racks of costumes, both male and female, and three dressing tables stocked with cosmetics. Rainbows of scarves and veils draped from the backs of mirrors and the ends of the long racks.

Peg went over to hang up Angelina's pieces. Then she examined the other garments in detail, clucking her tongue and shaking her head. Angelina and Zuri sat on stools facing one another.

Angelina noticed a tall man in a turban standing mutely by the wall. "Who is he?"

"He is my guard. He will stop me if I try to leave." Zuri frowned at him and spoke a few tart words in their language. He made an adjustment to his turban, pressed his palms together, and gave her a small bow. She returned her attention to Angelina. "He is new. He will learn."

Angelina met the dancer's eyes. "Forgive me if this is too personal, but you seem so intelligent and so capable. How did you get into this terrible situation?"

Zuri smiled. "You wish to hear my story."

"I do."

She lowered her luscious eyelashes in a slow blink and began to tell it. Her lilting accent gave the tale a romantic flavor. She kept her gaze somewhere past Angelina's shoulder and her hands folded in her lap as she spoke.

The story began seven years ago, when she learned that Gabriel Sandy had left his regiment in disgrace. She determined to come to England to find him and then make her way onto the stage. Sandy had told her about the marvellous variety theaters of London. She longed to be a part of that world and to become a great star with her dancing. She knew Mrs. Oxwich brought women to England to work as servants. She made a bargain with the colonel's wife to work as a chambermaid while she learned English and saved some money. Such servants earned sixteen pounds a year, she was told. That sounded like a fantastic sum to her.

But she received no money, nor any help learning English. She taught herself by practicing with the English servants in the kitchen or the laundry room, when she could. The Indians weren't allowed to speak it. They would be whipped if they were caught.

Then came her turn to work a weekend at Chetwood House. She danced in the charade with the others and caught the eye of Lord Chetwood. He fell in love with her, or so he said. Really, he wanted to own her, like a horse or a house. He made Mrs. Oxwich transfer her to his household.

Zuri thought of the story of Scheherazade holding her master at bay with her stories and tried to remember every tale she'd ever heard. She told His Lordship that he must give her time to fall in love with him as well. He enjoyed treating her like a prize to be won. He kept her in a well-appointed private room in the same wing as his harem. She had good food and little work, apart from the charades. He liked for her to speak English and sometimes taught her himself, so sometimes she could go out to translate for the other Indians. But she was more a prisoner than ever, and she had to endure Lord Chetwood's attentions.

Angelina sympathized with the woman's ordeal. She could imagine striking that original bargain in order to escape an unwanted husband and a life of wifely drudgery. Zuri had been betrayed by Mrs. Oxwich — another crime to lay at that woman's feet. She patted Zuri's hand. "Has His Lordship, ah . . . has he forced himself on you?"

"Not yet. Tell Gabriel I am still whole. But for how long, I do not know. At first, he said he would give me one thousand and one nights, like Scheherazade, if I would dance a different story for him every night."

"My stars! That must be challenging."

Zuri lifted one graceful shoulder. "It would be if he were not so stupid. But he is more impatient since we saw Gabriel that day in London. It is the first time I left this place. We went to the city to look at silks from India. I should not have said Gabriel's name. Now His Lordship is angry with me. He says I must surrender soon, willing or not."

Angelina grimaced at that dire fate. "Then you'll be happy to know that Gabriel is here, now, in a carriage hidden behind the Greek folly."

Zuri's eyes lit up. "I knew he would come!" Then the lights went out. "But he must go away. You must all go. It is not safe for you. His Lordship is the leader. The other men will obey him. And I cannot go even to my own room without a guard following."

Angelina gripped her hand. "I suspected it would be like that. That's why I cooked up my little plan."

"Plan?"

"You'll escape during the charades — the dance. We'll dress all the women — wives and servants — as much alike as possible. We'll cover everyone's hair with veils. We'll use lots of kohl around the eyes and paint to stain our faces brown. Hands and bellies too, I suppose." That sounded messy, but it must be done. "You must teach me what you can of that dance you do, that storytelling dance of the hands. You'll go out first with me and Mrs. Reynolds close behind. We'll shift positions constantly, some moving forward, others moving back. Make it as confusing as possible."

"They will confuse." Zuri nodded, her dark eyes shining. "They drink a lot. And also smoke the *ganja*."

"The more befuddled they are, the better. After a few rounds of shifting front to back, you'll end up in back. Just leave. Walk straight out. Don't stop for anything. Ignore your guard. Let him follow you — Sandy can deal with him. Get outside and run for the Greek folly. Do you know where it is?"

Zuri nodded. "Gabriel will be there?"

"Yes. There are blankets in the coach. You won't be cold. Our servants should be there too, with our things. My husband and I will be right behind you. But if we're not, don't wait for us."

"We will wait." The dancer's tone brooked no argument.

Angelina let that go. Sandy understood. "We three must look as much alike as possible. Mrs. Reynolds will play you right up to the end."

"She will not agree." Zuri shook her head. "She is one of them."

"Not entirely. She's angry about what happened to her ayah."

"Ganesa." Zuri's eyes flashed. "I am angry too. We all are. She was kind to everyone and much loved. That colonel forced her one weekend. Then his wife took her away. No one has seen her in any house. We fear she is dead."

"I'm afraid she is. Mrs. Oxwich and her servant killed her." An idea sparked in Angelina's mind. She might have more allies in this house than she had thought. "Tell everyone — the Indian servants, I mean. It's not a rumor. It's the truth. Make sure everyone knows. Let them be angry about it. Because with a little help from Mrs. Reynolds tonight, I'm going to send that evil woman to prison."

"I do not think Reynolds Memsahib will help us. She is too afraid."

"Oh, she'll help," Angelina said. "Or else she'll be sharing Mrs. Oxwich's jail cell."

* * *

They spent half an hour on the stage practicing that entrancing dance of the hands. Zuri had a supernatural grace which Angelina could not hope to emulate. But she could perform well enough to fool a group of men whose wits were addled by lust and alcohol.

Now she must go reckon with Mrs. Julia Reynolds. Zuri asked a servant to guide Angelina to a bedroom on the second floor of the east wing. The Reynoldses had been granted one of the better guest rooms. Half again as large as the Moriartys', it faced the front, so they could see people coming and going.

Angelina swept in behind the servant, not waiting for an invitation. "We need to talk." Fortunately, the major appeared to be out.

Mrs. Reynolds sat up on her bed with a cry of outrage. A novel with a lurid cover fell to the floor. "How dare you barge into my room!"

"I have no shame." Angelina gave her an impudent smile, then switched to a serious demeanor. "We really must talk. I mean to bring Mrs. Oxwich down tonight, and I need your help."

"Down? What do you mean?"

Angelina pulled the stool from the dressing table beside the bed and sat. "You never asked how Ganesa died."

"Ganesa? Why bring that up now?" Mrs. Reynolds glared at her. More outrage, which was to be expected, but also a flicker of fear. Why? She hadn't done it.

"She was strangled." Angelina had grown heartily sick of that word. "Harini — remember her?"

"The one who wouldn't work. I heard you bought her. More fool you."

"I did it to rescue her. It turns out she's a princess in her own country, a rajah's daughter who was taken against her will."

"Good lord." Mrs. Reynolds let out a groan, her whole body going limp in surrender.

That was easy. But Angelina couldn't give herself credit. The woman must have been tossing and turning with guilt ever since that afternoon at the mortuary.

Mrs. Reynolds gave Angelina a bleak look. "They're only supposed to take ones who want to come."

"After being promised wages and English lessons to start a little business when they return. I know. But those things never actually happen, do they?"

Mrs. Reynolds shook her head. "Who did it?" she asked in a small voice.

"Mrs. Oxwich and her servant Rajesh. They drove her to Limehouse, strangled her, and threw her into the river."

"Oxwich!" Mrs. Reynolds sounded happy all of a sudden. The gloom vanished from her pretty face. "Are you sure?"

Angelina stared at her for a moment, wondering at the transformation. Then she understood. The poor woman had blamed her husband for murdering her favorite maid. Great Scott! No wonder she'd been so defensive at the mortuary.

"I knew you had a hidden reason," Angelina said. "What a nightmare, to live with a man you believe capable of such an act. That's why you came to me in the first place, isn't it? You wanted me to find out if your suspicions had merit. Then you wanted me to be the one to accuse him."

"I didn't know who else to ask," Mrs. Reynolds said. "But I had to know. Was she . . . was she carrying . . . ?"

"Yes, she was. I don't know whose child. One of the men here this weekend, I imagine. You sent her here. You must have known what would happen."

"Not at first. I thought it was just us, trading husbands and wives. Younger officers turned up too sometimes. That's how I met my lieutenant. It wasn't until Ganesa went missing that I learned some of the men were taking the servants too."

Angelina's stomach turned. How long had this wickedness been going on? These people lived out here in utter isolation, with no neighbors, gossipy tradesmen, or village constables to hold them accountable. They might be princes in their own private fiefdoms, with total control over their households.

"You're sick of the whole thing, aren't you?" she asked. "The slavery ring, the abuses. You wanted someone to put a stop to that too."

Mrs. Reynolds sniffed, running a finger under her nose like a little girl. "At first, it seemed so natural. Of course we would bring our household staff home from India with us. We'd gotten used to one another. But things are so different here, aren't they? English servants have families. They have ambitions. They save their wages and go off in ten or fifteen years to buy a pub or a boardinghouse in Bristol."

"It can be terribly frustrating," Angelina said, thinking about the mouse maids and their dairy farm.

"One thing led to another," Mrs. Reynolds went on. "We didn't plan to keep them captive. They just had nowhere to go. And they can't complain, can they? You can treat them however you like."

"We can end it, you and me," Angelina said. "I mean to bring charges for slave-trading against Mrs. Oxwich. Once the police start to investigate, they'll charge the others too, I have no doubt."

"Including me?" Mrs. Reynolds swung her feet off the bed and got to her feet. She pulled a shawl around her shoulders, as if for protection, and went to stand near the window.

"If you help me, it will count in your favor. You're the one blowing the lid off, aren't you?"

Mrs. Reynolds hugged herself tightly. Her brown eyes held a calculating look. "The police won't care about one dead foreigner. You saw how easily intimidated they were when I dropped a few titles. A viscount, an honorable colonel's wife . . . They'll ask a few polite questions and let it go."

"But it isn't just one dead foreigner. Mrs. Oxwich killed her husband."

"What!" Mrs. Reynolds gripped the back of a slipper chair for support. "You've gone mad!"

"I have proof. Not very good proof, but her servants can fill in the rest."

"They never would."

"Oh yes, they will. They're angry, all of them, about Ganesa. I've told Zuri to spread the word about how she died. But we don't have to persuade them ourselves. We just have to get Mrs. Oxwich to admit to it."

Mrs. Reynolds's porcelain brow creased. "Impossible. You're stupid as well as mad."

"Neither, thank you." Angelina got up to lean on the bedpost. "I can bring this whole filthy house of cards tumbling to the ground. And I think you know it."

A long silence followed while Mrs. Reynolds fiddled with the fringe of her shawl. Angelina waited, listening to a clock tick somewhere in this overdecorated room. The bed had a tester and was draped in brocade curtains, as if they'd inherited it from some Jacobean ancestor. But the house couldn't be more than fifty years old.

At last, Mrs. Reynolds spoke. She seemed to have gathered strength during her inward debate. "What do you want me to do?"

"Two things." Angelina told her about the plan for the charades. "You must help persuade the other wives that it will be fun to dress alike to tease the men."

"They'll love it. Things have been feeling a little routine the past couple of months."

"Tonight will be far from routine." Angelina drew in a big breath and let it out with a sigh of relief. One "yes" always made the second

241

one easier to win. "Then I want you to write a letter to Mrs. Oxwich. Right now, before I go. Tell her you've heard an intriguing story from one of your Indian servants. You must have someone else in your house who speaks both languages."

"My Hindi is fairly good, actually. I pretend otherwise because it isn't *pukka*. My children learned it in the nursery and often use it with each other, so I had to learn it for self-defense. What's the gossip?"

"Mrs. Oxwich disguised herself as a sergeant in order to enter the barracks unrecognized."

Mrs. Reynolds's mouth gaped open. "Is that possible?"

"Of course. Actors and actresses do it all the time. She must have had help with the costume, gluing on the whiskers and probably dusting her cheeks with a little dark powder. Men tend to be browner than women since they don't make as much effort to shield their faces. So her maid knows how she was dressed on Monday morning when she left the house. The whole staff probably knows it, as well as what time she left. They're her alibi. Without them, she has nothing, apart from a great big motive. The colonel was tampering with her stock in trade."

Mrs. Reynolds winced at the term. "You want me to threaten her with blackmail. I will promise to keep my servants quiet if she — what? Gives me money?"

Angelina shrugged. "Unless you can think of something better. She took two hundred quid off me. Ask her for that."

Mrs. Reynolds smiled. "She's the greediest witch I've ever known. She'll fight like a badger to keep from paying."

"She'd rather pay than hang. Tell her to come here tonight. Say you want people around for safety. Tell her to come after the charades." Angelina frowned. "When does that start?"

"About an hour after dinner. It's the last event of the evening. Everyone scatters afterward."

"That's what I'm hoping," Angelina said. "As for where . . . You know this place better than I do. Someplace private but convenient to the hall. I'll arrange for some witnesses. I'm not sure who or how yet. It won't be just our word against hers."

"How about the library? It has enormous drapes and a high-backed sofa. And the windows open onto the front lawn." Mrs.

Reynolds bit her lip. "But you know, she can be rather terrifying. I doubt I can get a confession out of her."

Angelina gave her a saucy smile. "Just get her into the house. I'll do the rest."

TWENTY-EIGHT

Moriarty picked out a piece of beef and managed to gulp it down with little chewing. The menu card named the dish "Beef Vindaloo." He'd expected something like Antoine's savory curries, not this fiery concoction. His tongue felt like he'd licked a burning coal. But Major Freckles, seated across from him at the long table, had raised a challenging eyebrow at him as the course was served. He'd be damned twice over before he pushed the dish aside and asked for something milder.

Most of the men and women at the table were old India hands, accustomed to overspiced food. Still, he'd bet a hundred pounds they insisted on roast salmon with Dutch sauce when they were in India. These were restless, jaded people, at home nowhere; he'd learned that much in one afternoon.

Each course required its own wine, and the glasses were kept filled. That beverage did nothing to soothe the fire in his mouth, so Moriarty drank more water than the others. Just as well. He would need his wits about him that night if they were to effect their escape without attracting attention.

Lady Chetwood, seated on his right, leaned across him to reach a small bowl filled with a white sauce flecked with green. She made sure he got a good look at her breasts, which were exposed by the deep décolletage of her pink satin gown. The youthful color brought out the shadows beneath her eyes and the blotchy patches on her chest. Moriarty found her thoroughly unappealing. But according to the rules of the game, he was her chosen prey that night, and he was expected to comply.

He pushed out a small laugh and let her spoon the white sauce onto his plate. It did help soothe his burning tongue. He heard Angelina's musical laugh and allowed himself one glance down the long table to where she was sitting. Major Reynolds, curse him,

Moriarty Lifts the Veil

leaned right up against her, performing the same service. She tasted the cool sauce and granted the officer a grateful smile. She batted her lashes at him the way she did when she was playing the coquette.

Moriarty clenched a fist under the table. Their plan depended on stealth, but he wouldn't mind finding an opportunity to land one good blow on that major's ruddy nose.

* * *

The men lingered over the port and cigars after dinner, even though everyone was eager to get on to the main event. "We have to give the women time to change," Lord Chetwood explained. They talked about horses, a subject about which Moriarty knew next to nothing. But the port was good, and the tobacco erased the last lingering effects of that turbulent meal.

A manservant entered and murmured something in his master's ear. His Lordship winked at the men and pushed back his chair. "They're ready for us, gentlemen." He led the way into the great hall, which had been transformed into a grander version of the harem in the west wing.

Huge rugs had been suspended from the high ceiling to carve out a more intimate space. Tall candelabras provided the only light. Most of them stood around the stage, but a few had been placed in back to create an ambient glow. Chaise longues big enough for two sat in a semicircle around the low stage, along with several round cushions large enough to lie on. Small tables stood near each chaise. Most of them bore figured brass pots, clearly of Indian origin, which emitted a pungent smoke.

Moriarty's lip curled; he hated incense. One could never get the smell out of a wool jacket, and it always gave him a headache.

He chose a sofa near a gap in the hanging carpets that led to a side door. He'd taken his time circling the enclosed area, orienting himself and marking his avenues of egress. Lord Chetwood sprawled on a chaise directly in front of the stage. Major Reynolds took the next one over and signaled for a bottle of wine. The other men scattered themselves about. Several women — officers' wives, not servants — dressed in silk saris came in and found sofas or cushions.

Men and women alike seemed to love the tarry smoke, some of them pointing their noses directly at the brass burners.

A gong sounded. Everyone fell silent. Another rumbling boom shimmered over them, then a third. An Indian man with a long-necked guitar-like instrument emerged, followed by a man with a drum and an Indian woman. They seated themselves below the rear of the stage and began to play. The woman sang in a trilling, high-pitched voice — a song with words Moriarty didn't understand.

Then many hands thrust aside the silk curtains concealing the back of the stage, and three women dressed in filmy skirts and low-cut bodices with exposed bellies danced onto the stage. Three more followed them, then another three. They all wore veils held by bands of patterned silk. The veils floated out as they whirled in unison, creating a billowing sea of colored silk. Their arms, loosely covered in nearly transparent gauze, rose and fell with the rhythm of the twanging strings and rolling drum.

The room filled with the pungent smoke, which seemed to be carried along by the plaintive music. Moriarty watched the dancing women stepping forward, stepping back, whirling as they changed positions, their arms rising and falling, their hands reaching and beckoning. Their torsos writhed from side to side in an erotic movement that wholly captured a man's attention.

He felt like a pigeon caught in the gaze of a serpent. He struggled to focus on the dancers' faces, searching for Angelina. How could he fail to recognize his own wife? But they all looked the same, their skin the same bronze from forehead to navel, their hair concealed by many-colored veils. Even their eyes had been transformed into the same seductive almond shape by thick outlines of black paint.

Moriarty lolled against the back of his chaise, head spinning. The music seemed to enter his very sinews and flow through his veins. The floating draperies of the dancers melded with the flickering candlelight and the pungent smoke. Everything seemed both more intense and farther removed. The dancers filled his vision while the other people in the room fell away. He could no longer tell how many women were on the stage. Had Zuri left? Where was Angelina?

The thought that he should get up and go out crossed his mind but failed to take hold of his body. Then he saw a servant in a plain sari enter and stand next to the stage. One of the dancers left the formation to bend down and listen to her. The dancer nodded and uttered some reply, then rejoined the dance. She twirled and writhed toward another dancer, matching her rhythm long enough to exchange a few words. Then they both melted into the group.

Could this be the news that Mrs. Oxwich had arrived? Moriarty was serving as one of the witnesses. He must move, get up and find his way out of this hypnotic chamber. His feet were already on the floor; that helped. He doubted he could have lifted his legs off the deep sofa. He centered his weight, set his hands on his thighs, and looked again at the stage.

A dancer separated from the group. She twirled once, causing her veil to float across the lower half of her face. Her hips rotated seductively as she danced toward him, reaching for him with writhing arms and beckoning fingers. Her eyes gleamed with promise. She wanted him. She drew him forward on invisible threads, pulling him to his feet.

It must be Angelina. Moriarty stumbled up to the stage, taking the offered hand. Her other hand slid up his shoulder to his neck, pulling him closer to her ripe body. He breathed in a heady perfume of rose and musk as her breasts pressed against him. He reached up and twitched her veil aside, leaning in to plant a kiss on his wife's lips.

Then he stopped, gaping at the painted face of Lady Chetwood. He tried to pull away, but she twined both arms around him. One of her legs wrapped around his calf. She was stronger than he would have guessed.

"No, my lady, I beg you." His voice sounded husky. He got his hands on her shoulders and pushed, his own torso writhing in an attempt to evade her grasping hands. Out of the corner of his eye, he saw the two whispering dancers step down from the stage and slip through the gap in the hanging carpets. Major Reynolds followed them.

Other men were climbing up to the stage now, following beckoning fingers. Lusty laughter rose as they recognized their summoners. Moriarty grabbed Lady Chetwood by the hand and pulled her off the stage. She giggled as he guided her to a low cushion and pressed her down.

"Wait right there," he told her. "I'll get some wine."

She sprawled on her back, arms over her head, displaying her bosom in a pose that would have attracted some other man, at some other time. But Moriarty had work to do, and besides, he loved his wife.

He staggered after Angelina and the other dancer, obstructed by pairs of lovers stumbling onto cushions and couches. Once past the hanging carpets, he gulped in a lungful of fresher air. He made it across to the small side door and leaned against the jamb for a moment to recover his wits.

A tall Indian servant in a turban materialized at his side, gripping his arm to help him through the door.

"Really, Moriarty," the man said, in the unmistakable crisp tones of Sherlock Holmes. "You must develop a tolerance for narcotics. You're far too easily disabled."

"What narcotics?" Moriarty was less surprised at his adversary turning up in Indian garb than he might have been on an ordinary day. But he'd been drawn into a weird, prolonged hallucination; naturally, Holmes would play a part.

The detective smiled smugly. "The hashish they're burning in there is laced with opium. Couldn't you smell it? I, of course, am practically immune to the stuff unless it's injected."

Moriarty shook off Holmes's hand, balancing on his own two feet. He took a deep breath and expelled it. "My head's clearing now. What a murk! And a dashed unpleasant sensation. I don't know how you can stand it." He patted himself on both cheeks, then eyed the great detective. "How do you happen to be here, Holmes?"

"I set a couple of my Baker Street Irregulars on your tail when you left the police court. They overheard you in the carriage hire the next morning, planning an overnight drive to a place called Chetwood House. I took the train and beat you here by a good hour. They have no security of any kind in this house. Really very careless. I wandered about at will until I found that costume room and borrowed these clothes. They suit me, don't you think?"

They did. He looked splendid in the loose cotton trousers and high-collared jacket. He'd removed his false beard and darkened his face. The turban made him seem even taller. The hawk-like nose only added to the authenticity of his appearance.

Moriarty Lifts the Veil

"Why did you come?" Moriarty asked. "You can't have found out about Zuri. We've never spoken of her outside the house."

"I didn't know about her until this afternoon. I thought you were planning to hide Gabriel Sandy beyond my reach until you could spirit him out of the country. Now that I know about Miss Padmani, your plan makes more sense. Nasty bunch out here, aren't they? Bears out what I've always said about the countryside. Most people look at these well-tended estates and are impressed by their beauty. When I look at them, I think of their isolation and of the impunity with which all manner of crime may be committed behind their gates."

Moriarty was inclined to agree. He couldn't host opium-fueled orgies on Bellenden Crescent without his neighbors calling the police. He regarded Holmes with a cool eye, his vision now only slightly fuzzy. A sly smile curved on the detective's lips as he allowed the inspection.

"You know about Mrs. Oxwich," Moriarty said.

Holmes nodded. "Lestrade told me everything you told Forbes. I expect your wife has gone to elicit a confession. Let's hurry, shall we? We don't want to miss it."

"Generous of you to come all this way to serve as a second witness." Moriarty paused for a response. When none came, he said, "If you knew Mrs. Oxwich killed her husband, then you knew we weren't planning to help Sandy escape. There would be no need. You wouldn't come out here just to watch bored country gentry misbehave. So what do you really want?"

The sly smile widened to a grin. "Why, credit, of course. I can't have you besting me in the biggest murder case of the year."

His candor startled a laugh from Moriarty. "Credit? Is that all? You're welcome to it. The last thing we want is this kind of notoriety." They shook hands on it.

"If that's settled," Moriarty said, "we'd best move along. Do you know which way they went?"

"I believe they're meeting in the library."

"Then take me to the library, damn you, and stop blathering."

Holmes led him unfalteringly through a short maze of corridors. They found the door they wanted barred by Rajesh. As tall as Holmes, with broad shoulders and muscular arms, the Indian constituted an impassable barrier. They'd have to make a commotion to budge him, which would alert the women inside.

Moriarty could hear the music of Angelina's voice, though he couldn't distinguish the words. He longed to see her, but even more, he feared to miss the crucial exchange. He pulled Holmes away from his attempt to persuade Rajesh in Hindi to let them pass. When they were far enough not to be overheard, he murmured, "Let's try the windows. How do we get outside?"

Holmes navigated surefootedly outside and around to the library windows. Cool, night air blew the last dregs of hashish from Moriarty's head. The windows were open several inches with the drapes pulled back. Moriarty and Holmes crawled over and pushed through some shrubs to sit beneath the sill.

Moriarty glanced at his unexpected companion and smiled to himself. Holmes might be the most insufferable nuisance, but he was also one witness Scotland Yard would be sure to take seriously.

Chapter Twenty-Nine

Major Reynolds caught up with Angelina outside the library door. He clasped her by the waist. "I can think of more comfortable places, my sweet."

"Oh, stop. We don't have time for that." She pulled him inside the book-lined chamber. Mrs. Reynolds's servant had thoughtfully left the gas lamps burning for them.

"On the other hand, no one will disturb us in here tonight." Major Reynolds reached for her again.

"Give it a rest, I said. I'm not interested and never will be. Just get in here." She pushed him behind one of the floor-to-ceiling drapes. He spluttered a protest. She stopped it with an upraised finger. "Mrs. Oxwich killed her husband. There's next to no evidence, but it's true. I mean to make her confess, right here and now. You're my impartial witness. So stand still, be quiet, and listen."

He pressed his lips together in a frown but let her shake the drape over his feet.

Angelina peeked out the door, hoping to see James hurrying forward. He'd seemed awfully wobbly back there in that opium den. They'd been above the smoke on the stage. The veils and the dancing also helped avoid the worst of the effects. But James was so sensitive.

Mrs. Reynolds had gone out to meet their victim on the lawn to give Angelina time to get her witnesses in place. Now she came up the corridor with Mrs. Oxwich at her side. Rajesh, the tall manservant, paced behind them.

Blast! Well, James would just have to fend for himself when he managed to straggle along.

"We can talk in here," Mrs. Reynolds said. "No one uses the library on charade night."

"I should think not." Mrs. Oxwich followed her in, then stopped at the sight of Angelina. "What's she doing here?"

Her imperious sneer made Angelina acutely aware of the contrast in their clothing. Mrs. Oxwich presented the portrait of a grieving widow, wearing a somber black suit with a half veil on her small black hat. She'd lifted the veil over the brim to expose her face, but her dark features had been made for mourning.

Angelina and Mrs. Reynolds had stepped straight off the stage to come to this meeting. They hadn't thought about how awkward it would feel to face a properly dressed woman in their gaudy harem costumes. Not to mention the chill once they stopped dancing.

"She's here for moral support." Mrs. Reynolds folded her arms across her bare midriff. "She knows everything. I hired her weeks ago to find out what happened to my ayah."

"Hired?" Mrs. Oxwich's lip curled as if she'd been introduced to a streetwalker.

"My husband and I take small cases — problems of a personal nature, usually." Angelina's decades on the stage kept her hands at her sides. She would act as if she were dressed for a court appointment and hope that confounded veil would refrain from drifting across her face. "Sadly, this one turned out to be more complicated, didn't it?"

"I have no idea what you're talking about."

"Oh, I think you do." Angelina gestured at a group of chairs, but Mrs. Oxwich looked down her nose at them. No matter. This business was better done standing up. "I found her. Ganesa. The lost ayah."

"Where? In a brothel?"

Hot red patches flared in Mrs. Reynolds's cheeks. "How dare you! How *dare* you, after what you've done! I had to identify her, you know. I had to go to the mortuary in Whitechapel and look down on my dear servant's ruined face. It was *horrible*."

Mrs. Oxwich said nothing, though her eyes narrowed. This was one tough nut.

Angelina said, "The coroner told me she'd been strangled and put into the river near Limehouse. Her body was found at the West India Docks." She paused, got no response, and went on. "You strangled her."

"Nonsense." Mrs. Oxwich appeared utterly unruffled. What was she made of? "I'm not strong enough to assault a strapping, big girl like that."

"Not you personally," Angelina said. "You had your man do it — Rajesh."

Mrs. Oxwich's eyes darted to the door.

"He's outside, guarding the door, isn't he? He seems very loyal."

"He's devoted to me."

Angelina found that hard to believe. Nothing about this woman inspired devotion. She must have promised him something highly desirable. "Is he? How far does it go, that loyalty? Will he be willing to hang alone, without speaking a word in his own defense? Will he take full responsibility?"

Mrs. Oxwich leveled a black look at her, loaded with enough hostility to send a shiver up Angelina's spine. The witch might poison her servant — all her servants — before Angelina could convince the police to arrest her.

Then a flash of inspiration struck. "But wait!" She placed a coy finger on her cheek as she turned to Mrs. Reynolds. "Is it legal for the British government to execute a foreigner?"

Mrs. Reynolds had a spine after all. She played along without a hitch. "I don't believe it is, now that you mention it."

"No, I don't believe it either." Angelina cocked her head. "Wasn't that German fellow — oh, what was his name! — sent back to Germany to be tried by his own people?"

"Von Hausenberg?" Mrs. Reynolds gamely supplied.

"That's the one," Angelina said. "The same thing could happen to Rajesh, couldn't it? He'll be sent back to India to be tried there. After that months-long journey, of course."

"Oh dear," Mrs. Reynolds said. "Anything might happen then. One must pass through virtual thieves' dens, you know. And he would suffer worse than hanging once he gets home. Much worse. Indian prisons are —" She broke off with a shudder.

"He might prefer to be tried here," Angelina said, adopting a speculative tone. "If he's cooperative, he might only get life in an English prison. If he delivers his accomplice, or in this case, his mistress, he might only get a dozen years or so."

Mrs. Oxwich's face remained implacable, although she glanced again at the door — twice. Wondering if he could hear them, probably. *They understand more English than they speak.* "We'll have to wait and see, won't we?"

Almost there! Who would care, other than the guilty ones? But she needed something completely unambiguous.

"She was pregnant, you know," Angelina said. "The coroner determined that."

Mrs. Oxwich puffed that away. "I'm not surprised."

"Oh, you wicked woman!" Mrs. Reynolds shook her fists. "What a fool I was to trust you! I never should have let her come to this house."

Mrs. Oxwich pounced on that with a gleam in her black eyes. "Yes, it's your fault. You know full well what goes on around here. You're to blame for everything that happened to that girl."

"I didn't know, not back then." Tears welled in Mrs. Reynolds's eyes. "Your husband and Lord Chetwood were just getting started. They wanted easier access to the women in the other houses. When you brought in that dancer, that's what gave them the idea of changing the charades."

"What will Lord Chetwood say, I wonder?" Angelina said. "He sent her back for you to deal with once your husband had ruined her. He doesn't want mums in his little games, does he?"

"You seem to be well informed," Mrs. Oxwich said. "More gossip from the servants? You shouldn't listen to a word they say. They're like children; all Indians are. Silly, superstitious children. That's why they need us to manage their country for them."

"I find them to be quite intelligent and observant," Angelina said. "Harini, for example. The princess your confederate kidnapped in Jaipur."

"Pshaw. Surely you don't believe anything that stunted child has to say. She made up that absurd story to get out of doing her work."

"No, it's true. It's been confirmed by none other than Sherlock Holmes. You've heard of him. The great consulting detective?" Angelina heard a faint snort from beyond the window and had to repress a smile. James had found his way into position after all.

"Never heard of him." Mrs. Oxwich sniffed disdainfully.

Moriarty Lifts the Veil

Angelina pressed on. "He's been to India on government business. He brought back a portrait of Harini, given him by her father, Rajah Chand. She's living with my friend Lord Brockaway now at his home in Mayfair. He's in the Foreign Office, so it was nothing for him to exchange telegrams with his colleagues in India. The rajah is on his way here even as we speak. I suspect he'll believe his daughter's absurd story, don't you?"

"Arrant nonsense," Mrs. Oxwich said, but her stony facade was starting to crumble. She gazed at the door as if wondering how fast she could reach it.

"Don't leave yet," Mrs. Reynolds said. "We haven't discussed my terms."

"I won't pay you one single penny. Your claims are as offensive as they are false."

Angelina smiled. She could feel the tide turning. "Harini told me everything the servants in your house had to say about Ganesa's disappearance. They said you and Rajesh bundled the woman into your carriage one day, against her will. You were gone for several hours and then returned without her."

"She wanted to be left at Ayah House," Mrs. Oxwich said, making her first mistake. That could easily be checked. "I'm not responsible for what she might have done after that."

Angelina regarded her coldly. "You're not responsible for much, are you? Harini also told me the real reason you wanted her out of your house. It seems your husband was unable to keep his hands off her. She's only a child, for pity's sake! You were afraid you'd have another pregnant girl to dump in the river. Two was bad enough. You thought you'd gotten away with them. But with three, things get risky, don't they? Someone, somewhere, is bound to start asking questions. So you decided to nip that problem in the bud."

Mrs. Oxwich glowered at her, her upper teeth working her lower lip.

Angelina decided to make a leap. She shouted a little laugh. "I must say, I'm impressed, Mrs. O. It isn't easy to walk like a man, not after a lifetime in skirts. The guard at Odstone must have been half-blind."

"That corporal ought to be cited for dereliction," Mrs. Oxwich said. "He barely even looked —" She clapped her lips together.

"It had to be done, though, didn't it?" Angelina lowered her voice, falling into a soothing cadence. "You couldn't let your husband ruin all your hard work, could you? He should've respected you instead of thwarting you at every turn. It can't be easy, training those raw recruits, turning them into functional English servants."

"You have no idea," Mrs. Oxwich growled. "They're impossible, some of them. Born liars, like that Harini. And the men — these officers! Filthy, lecherous brutes! It's an affliction, I understand that, my father suffered the same thing, but if it can't be cured, it must be stamped out. No one wants a servant with a child in tow. That's time and money down the drain. I couldn't afford more losses or risk more bodies washing up where the police could find them. What was I supposed to do?" She shouted the last words.

Angelina nodded. "I think that's good enough, don't you, Major?"

"Quite enough." Major Reynolds flung aside his drape and strode forward to grip Mrs. Oxwich by the arm. "Could've knocked me over with a feather at first. Queer thing is, I'm not all that surprised. That trading scheme of yours — your school for ayahs, as you used to call it — had become an obsession. Even old Oxwich worried about it, and he wasn't the swiftest horse on the track."

Mrs. Oxwich turned her obsidian glare on him. But the battle-hardened officer merely shook his head.

Angelina took a deep breath. Mission accomplished! She went to raise the window so James could climb in. "Did you hear it all?"

"Enough." James stood up, brushing mulch from the seat of his trousers.

Then Sherlock Holmes unfolded his lanky frame and swung nimbly into the room.

"Mr. Holmes!" Angelina cried. "My stars!" He looked marvelous in that Indian costume — perfectly authentic. But really, must the man horn in on *everything* they did? As James climbed inside, she muttered, "How can he always be absolutely everywhere?"

Holmes laughed. "It's a gift." He touched his turban as if tipping a hat. "Well played, Mrs. Moriarty. That confession wasn't as explicit as one might wish, but it's enough to convince me. I'll convince the police. And once we get the servants talking, we'll have so many details, a full confession won't be necessary."

He gave the villainess a long look, from head to toe. "I'd hand you over to Rajah Chand if it were up to me." Then he moved toward the door. "I'd best take that servant in charge. I'll find a room where I can lock him in. Best lock this one up too until the police can get here." Then he walked out the door, closing it behind him.

Angelina rather enjoyed his praise, though she would never admit it.

"He'll make an excellent witness," James said.

"That's true." She brushed a twig from his shoulder. "Did you have much trouble with the hashish? I didn't know until it was too late to warn you."

James dismissed that with a wave of his hand. "I managed. I had more trouble fending off Lady Chetwood, to be honest."

"Where is she now?"

"In the arms of Morpheus, most likely. I shoved her onto a low couch right next to one of those pernicious incense burners."

Raised voices drew their attention toward the Reynoldses. The major still held Mrs. Oxwich by the arm, but his focus had shifted to his wife. "What I don't understand, Julia, is why you didn't come to me with your concerns about Ganesa? I cared about her too, you know. She practically raised our children."

Mrs. Reynolds bit her lip and cast her gaze to the floor.

He stared at her for a moment, then gave a bitter grunt as comprehension dawned. "You thought I did it. That I put her in that condition and then threw her in the river. How could you?"

She looked at him with a challenge in her eyes and shrugged.

He shook his head, more in disappointment than anger. "I never touched her. I swear it. I never touch any of them. I like my women willing, and a slave can't give consent." He took a few steps toward her, pulling Mrs. Oxwich along. She stood by him impassively, her gaze turned inward, as the Reynoldses embarked on a heated exchange.

Angelina took her husband by the hand. "Our work is done here, darling. Shall we gather the flock and go home? We can knock up the constabulary in Staines on the way."

"First we should scout out a lockable —"

A scream drowned out the rest of his words, a high-pitched, feminine scream that filled the night with fear and fury.

Angelina and James rushed to the windows, thrusting back the drapes. Bright moonlight lit the whole lawn, revealing a tableau straight out of a melodrama. Lord Chetwood stomped toward the house with Zuri slung over one shoulder. She kicked and pounded on him to no avail. Gabriel Sandy lurched after them, several yards behind, clutching his head in one hand.

Things had not gone as planned at the Greek folly.

"Sandy!" James shouted and leapt out the window. He ran toward his friend and tried to stop him, only to be pushed away.

Angelina clambered out the window and ran toward Zuri. She kicked at Lord Chetwood's calves as she tried to pull the Indian woman free. He thrust out one strong arm and sent her staggering.

Then James ran up and stood in front of the panting lord with his hands on his hips. "Put her down, Chetwood. It's over."

"Get off my land," His Lordship snarled. "She's my property, and I mean to keep her."

"You can't own people," Angelina cried.

Then Sandy caught up with them. He didn't bother to threaten or scold. He stepped up and drove his fist straight into His Lordship's midsection. Chetwood expelled a loud grunt and doubled over. James and Angelina caught Zuri as she slid down and helped her to her feet.

Sandy and Chetwood traded blow after blow, legs planted wide for balance. Sandy had the advantage of youth and many years driving a cab, but the injury to his head hindered him, making him reel from side to side.

James left Zuri in Angelina's care and shrugged off his dinner jacket. He watched the fight acutely, shifting around the combatants with his fists raised. He plainly wanted to jump in, but equally plainly didn't want to insult Sandy by interfering. It appeared he would rather let his best friend be beaten to a bloody pulp than impinge upon his honor. *Men!*

Now other people came spilling out of the house and around from the sides. Officers and wives wobbled, still unsteady on their feet, as they tucked in shirts or wrapped shawls around their shoulders. Servants, both men and women, followed after them, picking up their pace and passing them as they saw what was happening on the lawn.

Moriarty Lifts the Veil

One of the officers, quicker than the others, ran to the aid of Lord Chetwood. James pointed at him and shouted, "You're mine!" The officer answered, "Ha!" and swung a blow, which James handily avoided. That must be the freckled major who had offended him so badly that afternoon at the paddock.

Angelina spared a moment to admire her husband's fighting trim. Light on his toes, ready to dance in or out, he held his back straight, throwing his fists with the precision of steel pistons. No wasted movement, no bravado. He dropped his man in short order.

Sandy let out a mighty roar, swinging a long arm to land his fist square in the middle of Chetwood's face. The older man staggered backward and fell hard onto the grassy lawn. Zuri shook off Angelina's comforting arm and ran forward to kick him in the side. She lifted her foot to do it again, but Sandy caught her around the waist and pulled her back. He held her tightly as she strained forward, shaking her finger and cursing a blue streak — or so it sounded. She was using her native tongue.

A broad grin spread across Sandy's battered face, so she must have been hitting the mark.

Angelina surveyed the chaotic scene, made all the stranger by the silvery moonlight. Most of the onlookers had stopped a few yards away, clutching each other as they watched the unfolding events. One woman, however, walked steadily toward the front drive in short, quick steps with her face averted, like someone trying to pass unnoticed.

Mrs. Oxwich! Did she climb out the window? In *that* skirt?

Angelina cried, "Mrs. Oxwich!" and pointed at her.

Zuri's head whipped around. She twisted in Sandy's arms and shouted over his shoulder at the other Indian servants. It sounded like *"Ooh-say pahkado!"* Whatever it meant, it roused them to action, especially the women. They moved toward her, gliding swiftly across the grass. Several fanned out to prevent her from escaping into the grounds. The first to reach her grabbed her arms, jerking her to a stop. They held her fast while the others clustered around, surrounding her in a tight circle. And there they stood, watching her with stony faces.

Silence fell across the yard. Then all the English people began jabbering at once. They swarmed over to pepper Angelina with questions. She hadn't the slightest interest in answering them. She spotted Major Reynolds helping his wife out of the library window.

Finally! Their marital difficulties had certainly opened up a Pandora's box of crimes and scandals.

She tilted her head in their direction. "Ask them," she said and turned her back.

Lord Chetwood groaned and tried to stand up, but three young Indian women in skimpy costumes broke through the crowd. They pulled off their satin slippers and began beating him with them, whacking away with furious shrieks as he gathered himself into a tight ball.

One of the gentlemen stepped forward, saying, "Here, now!" But two of the wives pushed him back. One said, "They've earned it." The other nodded. "Let it end now. Enough is enough."

Angelina couldn't have put it better. She smiled as James's arm circled her waist and turned her toward their friends. Zuri stood with her back against her true love's strong chest, her hands resting on his encircling arms.

James asked, "Are you up to a little drive, Sandy? We needn't go farther than the nearest inn tonight. But I feel a powerful urge to put this place behind me."

Sandy kissed the top of Zuri's head. "I've never felt better in my life. But don't we have things to do yet?"

"Not us." James pointed toward the house, where a tall man in a turban strode toward the servants surrounding Mrs. Oxwich. He spoke to them in their language, judging by the comprehension on their faces. The whole group began to move inside, slowly, not breaking the circle.

James chuckled. "I believe we can leave the mopping up to Sherlock Holmes."

EPILOGUE

Moriarty learned the fates of the principal actors in the recent dramatic events chiefly from the newspapers, along with one brief visit to Inspector Forbes.

Mrs. Oxwich was remanded to Newgate Prison without the option of bail, her late father's title notwithstanding. Her husband's murder had grown too notorious for lesser measures. And in the end, everyone turned against her — not just the servants whom she'd brought to England under false pretenses and sold into slavery. Most of the officers' wives spoke up as well, eager to throw their former superior under the train to protect themselves.

The colonel's bloody murder quickly buried the slave-trading charges. The newspapers lavished page after page on Mrs. Oxwich's audacity, her craftiness, and her sheer, unwomanly ruthlessness. The gatehouse guard was interviewed repeatedly — as well as demoted. His description of her disguise grew more impressive with each repetition. Sandy was besieged by reporters. He and Zuri had to flee to Lord Brockaway's hunting box in Cornwall after their wedding — but more on that later.

Lord Chetwood managed to avoid criminal charges by the simple expedient of paying his harem girls enough money to buy a lodging house in Bristol in exchange for their silence. They transformed themselves into respectable landladies with a steady clientele of foreign merchants and Oriental college professors.

His Lordship avoided prison, but he was discharged from the army "with ignominy." He didn't need his discharge pay, but he and his wife were shunned thereafter. They had to sell the family estate and move to Northumberland. Their daughter's engagement was broken off and their son rejected from Sandhurst Academy. They were ruined, which Zuri allowed was good enough, considering.

Angelina supervised the disposition of the servants; or rather, she enlisted the directors at Ayah House to work it out. Those who wanted to go home were sent, at Lord Chetwood's expense. Each was given enough money to start a small business or pay a handsome dowry back in India. Those who wanted to stay in England were found better positions, with wages and Thursday afternoons free. All were paid in full for their months of service to date, from Mrs. Oxwich's hoard of ill-gotten gains. Ganesa was buried in the Reynolds family plot.

Moriarty made it his business to call upon the adjutant general every day to inquire about his progress in restoring the funds stolen from Sergeant Brant's victims. There was ample evidence to convict Brant and sentence him to twenty years in prison. Luckily, he'd been stockpiling the money, which added up to hundreds of pounds, in three different banks. The army retrieved it minutes after the gavel fell, but so far, the soldiers had not received a penny.

"Soon, soon," the AG said. After a couple of weeks enduring Moriarty's basilisk glare, he managed to release enough funds to restore Sergeant Fowler and his friends to their rightful status. They'd grown so close in their time of trouble that they all went in together on a goods transport venture. Private Appleton gave his money to the Salvation Army, for which he was promoted to sergeant and allowed to beat the drum when they went out to march around the town.

Dr. Watson finally persuaded Holmes to check into Holloway Sanitarium for a rest cure after finding him unconscious on the floor of their flat with a needle in his arm. Rajah Chand visited him there to present him with an emerald ring and his eternal gratitude. The staff were instructed to keep all newspapers away from the patient until his name disappeared from the front pages. Watson guessed that would be enough time for Holmes to recover his native vitality. No walls could hold the questing sleuthhound after that.

Sandy and Zuri were married in Shoreditch Church, two weeks after the fight on the lawn at Chetwood House. The pews were filled with a colorful assemblage of street urchins dressed in cast-off finery and Indians in bright saris or yellow turbans. The minister, having grown up in the East End himself, took it all in stride.

The groom glowed with pride. Moriarty thought he looked rather thunderstruck, a feeling he remembered well from his own wedding. The bride, radiant in white satin, shone with purest joy. Zeke, wearing the shiniest top hat ever created, paced behind them with the ring on a velvet pillow. Angelina wept copiously throughout the ceremony. Afterward, the happy couple sneaked out the back door to avoid the press. Moriarty treated them to a private car on the express train to Cornwall, where they spent a month in blissful solitude getting reacquainted.

The rains came back, and a new series of sensational murders in the East End pushed the Oxwich story out of the news. Things returned to normal at the house on Bellenden Crescent.

One thundery evening, Moriarty brought his wife a glass of sherry, grateful for the thick drapes that turned their drawing room into a cozy haven. Although they weren't expecting company and had no plans to go out, Angelina still wore the ruby necklace and matching earrings Harini had given her before sailing for India. She only took them off to go to bed, but they'd have to go into the safe one of these days. They were worth more than the house and everything in it.

They did look well on her, bringing out the coppery undertones in her hair. Moriarty chuckled as he took his seat. "The two hundred pounds you paid for your princess turned out to be a sound investment."

"James!" Angelina pretended to be shocked, but she caressed her treasure with possessive fingers. "Worth more than Holmes's ring, don't you think?"

"Only fair since you did all the hard work."

"He did supply the confirmation we needed at the critical moment. And he managed the chaos at Chetwood House after we left." She sipped her sherry while giving him the look that said she was about to probe his supposed feelings. "Do you really not mind Holmes getting all the credit? Your brilliant exposure of the embezzlement scheme never reached the front page."

"I imagine the army had more to do with that than Holmes. There are still some forces in Great Britain larger than his self-regard." He returned her probing look. "What about you, my dear?

Doesn't it rankle that you were reduced to a mere assistant in exposing Mrs. Oxwich?"

She trilled a laugh that sounded slightly false to a husband's ear. "I don't need *that* kind of notoriety. We don't want scandalmongerers stealing seats from legitimate theatergoers, now do we?"

"A sale's a sale," Moriarty said, drawing an unbelieving glare from his wife. "But you're right. Let Holmes have the front page. He has so little else."

"He has Watson and his new boy, Lestrade."

"Balanced by our Inspector Forbes. That's another positive result from this adventure."

Angelina hummed in the way that meant she was done with that topic. She took a slow sip of her sherry, her expression sobering. "I don't like the way Holmes kept bleating about you and your supposed network of criminals in public. It's funny when it's just among ourselves, but it's another thing altogether if it gets into the papers. Or if Scotland Yard begins to take it seriously. You don't want people thinking of you as a master criminal."

Moriarty dismissed that with a snort. "A pure Holmesian fever dream. He gets bored with the ordinary kind, so he conjures up an enemy worthy of his image of himself."

"Yes, but he's put your face on it."

Moriarty shrugged. "It will pass, my dear. Someday he'll stumble onto a real master criminal and drop me like a broken toy."

"If there is such a thing. But perhaps we should make an effort to stay out of his way in the future."

"Nonsense! I refuse to be limited by another man's delusions. Let him stay out of our way." Moriarty jutted out his chin to emphasize his resolve.

Angelina sighed. "Very well. No limits. Our clients need us, having no one else to help them. And we can't always predict where their troubles will lead." She emptied her glass and set it on the table with an air of finality. Then she gave Moriarty a sly look from under her thick lashes. "I did save one souvenir from our night in the country — my harem costume."

Moriarty felt a pleasant tingle rising through his body that had nothing to do with the sherry. "Oh?"

She clucked her tongue and tossed her head dismissively. "But you've had enough of that nonsense, haven't you? I could just pack it—"

"No, no." Moriarty held up a hand. "You put a lot of work into learning that dance, or so you said. Telling a story with the hands and the movements of the torso. . ." He faltered as his wife produced a throaty chuckle that turned the tingle into licks of flame.

"We might do a double act, Zuri and I, some day." She batted her lashes at him, all innocence. They both enjoyed that game. "I really ought to practice, and it's no fun without an audience. Are you sure you wouldn't mind?"

Moriarty met her dancing eyes. Kidnapped princesses, clashes with the irascible Sherlock Holmes, and the occasional exposure to narcotics — worth it, all worth it, for this wife whose value was far above rubies. He smiled. "I am, as always, at your service, my dear."

HISTORICAL NOTES

I fashioned everyone in this book out of whole cloth, except for Sir Arthur Conan Doyle's immortals: Sherlock Holmes and James Moriarty. I reshaped them for my own narrative purposes. This is one of the risks of fame — that your works will outlive you and become the playthings of lesser minds.

I didn't have the courage to slander a real British Army barracks, so I made one up: Odstone Barracks, home of the equally fictional Middlesex Regiment. Odstone is based on Brock Barracks, which has some lovely Victorian buildings. I don't know of any irregularities at Brock or any other army regiment at that time, though there might have been some. Embezzling and pilfering goods is a long-standing tradition in military services, or at least, that's what everyone seems to think. But it is dashed difficult to find articles about fraud in the armed forces! If you know of any, please write to me at castle@annacastle.com. I strongly prefer to base my stories on crimes that existed.

I spent an inordinate amount of time trying to make sense of regiments, battalions, companies, and so forth. Hopeless! The second half of the nineteenth century saw a series of reformations of the British military in which every unit seemed to change its name at least twice. I did try to get the right units in the Maiwand Pass at the right time.

Slavery was abolished in Great Britain in 1833, but human trafficking persists to this day, especially of the low-profile domestic service variety. I felt safe enough with that bit of invention, although in my stories, everyone who is not a villain always gets a happy ending.

If you spot something missing, something wrong, or just want to lecture me about the British military services in the late Victorian period, please write to me at castle@annacastle.com .

ABOUT THE AUTHOR

Anna Castle holds an eclectic set of degrees: BA in the Classics, MS in Computer Science, and a Ph.D. in Linguistics. She has had a correspondingly eclectic series of careers: waitressing, software engineering, grammar-writing, a short stint as an associate professor, and managing a digital archive. Historical fiction combines her lifelong love of stories and learning. She physically resides in Austin, Texas, but mentally counts herself a queen of infinite space.

BOOKS BY ANNA CASTLE

Keep up with all my books and short stories with my newsletter: www.annacastle.com

The Francis Bacon Series

Book 1, Murder by Misrule.

Francis Bacon must catch a killer to regain the queen's favor. He recruits Thomas Clarady to chase witnesses from Whitehall to the London streets. Everyone has something up his pinked and padded sleeve. Even Bacon is at a loss — and in danger — until he sees through the disguises of the season of Misrule.

Book 2, Death by Disputation.

Thomas Clarady is recruited to spy on the increasingly rebellious Puritans at Cambridge University. Francis Bacon is his spymaster; his tutor in both tradecraft and religious politics. Their commission gets off to a deadly start when Tom finds his chief informant hanging from the roof beams. Now he must catch a murderer as well as a seditioner. His first suspect is volatile poet Christopher Marlowe, who keeps turning up in the wrong places.

Dogged by unreliable assistants, chased by three lusty women, and harangued daily by the exacting Bacon, Tom risks his very soul to catch the villains and win his reward.

Book 3, The Widow's Guild.

London, 1588: Someone is turning Catholics into widows, taking advantage of armada fever to mask the crimes. Francis Bacon is charged with identifying the murderer by the Andromache Society, a widows' guild led by his formidable aunt. He must free his friends from the Tower, track an exotic poison, and untangle multiple crimes to determine if the motive is patriotism, greed, lunacy — or all three.

Book 4, Publish and Perish.

It's 1589 and England is embroiled in a furious pamphlet war between an impudent Puritan and London's wittiest poets. When two writers are murdered, Francis Bacon is tasked with ending the tumult once and for all. But can he and his assistants stop the strangler without stepping on any very important toes?

Book 5, Let Slip the Dogs

It's 1591, Midsummer at Richmond Palace, and love is in the air — along with the usual political courtships and covert alliances. Secret trysts, daring dalliances, and a pair of pedigreed hounds keep Francis Bacon and his gallant team busy while trying to catch one devilishly daring murderer.

Book 6, The Spymaster's Brother

Anthony Bacon is home from France. An invalid, his gouty legs never hinder his agile mind. He's built the most valuable intelligence service in Europe. Now the Bacon brothers are ready to offer it to the wealthiest patron.

Then Francis finds the body of a man who's been spreading dangerous rumors about Anthony. Clues point to his private secretary. Can they sort through the lies before disaster strikes?

The Professor & Mrs. Moriarty Series

Book 1, Moriarty Meets His Match

Professor James Moriarty has one desire left in his shattered life: to stop the man who ruined him from harming anyone else. Then he meets amber-eyed Angelina and his world turns upside down. Stalked by the implacable Sherlock Holmes, he's tangled in a web of murder and deceit. He'll have to lose himself to save his life and win the woman he loves.

Book 2, *Moriarty Takes His Medicine*

Professor and Mrs. Moriarty help Sherlock Holmes investigate a case he can't pursue alone: a doctor who may be committing murders for hire, ridding husbands and sons of their fussy, wealthy wives and mothers. When Angelina defies James to enter the lion's den, he must abandon his scruples and race the clock to save her — and himself.

Book 3, *Moriarty Brings Down the House*

An old friend brings a strange problem to Professor and Mrs. Moriarty: either his theater is haunted or someone's trying to ruin him. The pranks grow deadlier, claiming the first victim; then someone sets Sherlock Holmes on their trail. The Moriartys must stop the deadly pranks threatening a West End Christmas play before someone they love is killed.

Book 4, *Moriarty Lifts the Veil*

Professor and Mrs. Moriarty each take on a small case to fill the time before their next play opens. They place a bet on who will finish first. James will find out if three old soldiers have been cheated of their discharge pay. Angelina must find a missing servant, presumed to have been poached. But as they start asking questions, things take a dark turn. They uncover corruption at the heart of a circle of Army officers. A man is murdered, a friend is blamed, and Sherlock Holmes is sent to catch him. The Moriartys must use all their courage and ingenuity to save their friend, stop the loathsome crimes, and put the killer behind bars.

Printed in Dunstable, United Kingdom